Learn Grafana 7.0

A beginner's guide to getting well versed in analytics, interactive dashboards, and monitoring

Eric Salituro

BIRMINGHAM - MUMBAI

Packt>

Learn Grafana 7.0

Copyright © 2020 Packt Publishing

Commissioning Editor: Mrinmayee Kawalkar
Acquisition Editor: Devika Battike
Content Development Editor: Sean Lobo
Senior Editor: David Sugarman
Technical Editor: Utkarsha S. Kadam
Copy Editor: Safis Editing
Project Coordinator: Aishwarya Mohan
Proofreader: Safis Editing
Indexer: Priyanka Dhadke
Production Designer: Joshua Misquitta

First published: June 2020

Production reference: 1240620

Published by Packt Publishing Ltd.
Livery Place
35 Livery Street
Birmingham
B3 2PB, UK.

ISBN 978-1-83882-658-1

www.packt.com

About the author

Eric Salituro is currently a senior software engineer with the enterprise data and analytics platform team at Zendesk. He has an IT career that spans more than 30 years, over 20 of which were spent in the motion picture industry working as a pipeline technical director and software developer for innovative and creative studios such as DreamWorks, Digital Domain, and Pixar. Before moving to Zendesk, he worked at Pixar, helping to manage and maintain their production render farm as a senior software developer. Among his accomplishments is the development of a Python API toolkit for Grafana aimed at streamlining the creation of rendering metrics dashboards.

About the reviewers

Šimon Podlipský is a software development engineer with a master's degree in management and software quality management from the University of Economics in Prague. His passion is contributing to open source software, including Grafana. He also maintains and develops the Grafana JSON data source, which you can try out yourself after finishing the book.

Hugh O'Brien is a 15-year veteran of cloud infrastructure and performance monitoring. He is Head of Infrastructure at Thrive Global and has previously worked at Zendesk, Jet.com and Intel. His presentation at Kafka Summit 2018 "ZFS: Better Living Through Filesystems" (viewable online) is basically just a sequence of Grafana screenshots. He has, for no discernible reason, used Grafana/Prometheus to instrument his home router (Wi-Fi RSSI as radar), android phone (XYZ accelerometery for activity detection), and soon his car's CAN bus (emissions, maybe?). He holds a degree in Computer Engineering from his hometown of Limerick, Ireland, and is the only living person who knows the origins of the 2.4GHz ISM band.

Packt is searching for authors like you

If you're interested in becoming an author for Packt, please visit authors.packtpub.com and apply today. We have worked with thousands of developers and tech professionals, just like you, to help them share their insight with the global tech community. You can make a general application, apply for a specific hot topic that we are recruiting an author for, or submit your own idea.

Table of Contents

Preface

Grafana is an open source analytics platform used to analyze and monitor time-series data. This beginner's guide will help you get to grips with Grafana's new features for querying, visualizing, and exploring metrics and logs, regardless of where they are stored.

This book begins by showing you how to install and set up the Grafana server. You'll explore the workings of various components of the Grafana interface, along with its security features, and you will learn how to visualize and monitor data using InfluxDB, Prometheus, Logstash, and Elasticsearch. This Grafana book covers the advanced features of the **Graph** panel and shows you how **Stat**, **Table**, **Bar**, **Gauge**, and **Text** are used. You'll build dynamic dashboards to perform end-to-end analytics and label and organize dashboards into folders to make them easier to find. As you progress through it, this book delves into the administrative aspects of Grafana by creating alerts, setting permissions for teams, and implementing user authentication. Along with exploring Grafana's multi-cloud monitoring support, you'll also learn about Grafana's Loki system, which is a backend logger for users running Prometheus and Kubernetes.

By the end of this book, you'll have gained all the knowledge you need to start building interactive dashboards.

Who this book is for

This book is for business intelligence developers, business analysts, data analysts, and anyone interested in performing time-series data analysis and monitoring using Grafana. Those looking to create and share interactive dashboards or looking to get up to speed with the latest features of Grafana will also find this book useful. Although no prior knowledge of Grafana is required, basic knowledge of data visualization and some experience with Python programming will help you understand the concepts covered in this book.

What this book covers

Chapter 1, *Introduction to Data Visualization with Grafana*, provides a brief introduction to the use of data visualization in general and specifically in Grafana. We will then move on to installing a Grafana server onto your machine, using either a native installer or a Docker container. Launching the server and connecting to it with a web browser will also be covered.

Chapter 2, *A Tour of the Grafana Interface,* explores the workings of the major interface components once you have loaded the Grafana web app.

Chapter 3, *An Introduction to the Graph Panel,* dives into the Graph panel for a closer look at how to work with the major components of the panel after creating a test data source. We will also identify common panel elements in preparation for looking at other panels.

Chapter 4, *Connecting Grafana to a Data Source,* shows you how to install a supported data source (such as Prometheus, InfluxDB, OpenTSDB, or Elasticsearch) as a Docker container, load an actual time-series dataset, and visualize the data.

Chapter 5, *Visualizing Data in the Graph Panel,* is where we will show some of the more advanced features of the Graph panel.

Chapter 6, *Visualization Panels in Grafana,* takes a quick tour of the other major panels (Singlestat, Table, Heatmap, and Text) and how they're used. We will hold back on looking at the Dashboard and Alert List panels for later chapters.

Chapter 7, *Creating Your First Dashboard,* shows how to build a simple dashboard and some panels. We will explore the major components of a dashboard. Finally, we will become familiar with the dashboard interface by moving and resizing panels.

Chapter 8, *Working with Advanced Dashboard Features,* explores the powerful advanced features of the dashboard, including annotations, templating with variables, and dashboard linking, as well as techniques for sharing dashboards.

Chapter 9, *Grafana Alerting,* shows you how to create threshold alerts in the graph and connect them to notification channels.

Chapter 10, *Exploring Logs with Grafana Loki,* uses Loki and Explore to answer questions about a log dataset.

Chapter 11, *Organizing Dashboards,* shows you how to label dashboards and organize them into folders to make them easier to find.

Chapter 12, *Managing Permissions for Users and Teams,* shows you how to manage user permissions using teams.

Chapter 13, *Authentication with External Services,* shows you how managers can connect user authentication to a variety of external services.

Chapter 14, *Cloud Monitoring,* shows you how Grafana can provide monitoring support for cloud service infrastructure.

To get the most out of this book

In order to complete the majority of the exercises in this book, you will need to download and install Docker with Docker Compose. For the examples in the book, we will be downloading and installing other software and datasets, along with Grafana and Loki, so you will need an internet connection. You could download and install each software package independently, but besides Grafana itself, our tutorial instructions are designed to work with Docker. We do that so that all software dependencies and network management can be encapsulated within Docker Compose.

We will run a fair amount of software from the command line, so you should be comfortable with typing commands into a shell like Bash or Windows Command Prompt:

Software/hardware covered in this book	OS requirements
Grafana	Mac OS X, Windows 10 Pro, Linux, Docker
Docker	Mac OS X, Windows 10 Pro, or Linux
Loki/Promtail	Runs in Docker
Prometheus	Runs in Docker
InfluxDB	Runs in Docker
Logstash	Runs in Docker
Elasticsearch	Runs in Docker
OpenLDAP	Runs in Docker

In order to follow along with the exercises in Chapter 13, *Authentication with External Services*, you will need accounts with GitHub, Google, and Okta. To follow the exercises in Chapter 14, *Cloud Monitoring*, you will need to create an account with Amazon Web Services, Google Cloud, and Microsoft Azure.

The examples and software in this book have not been validated for security. They require an external internet connection and leverage open source software under a variety of licenses, so if you intend to use any of this software within a security-conscious computing environment (such as in an education or corporate environment), it is highly recommended that you consult your local IT professionals in advance.

If you are using the digital version of this book, we advise you to type the code in yourself or access the code via the GitHub repository (link available in the next section). Doing so will help you avoid any potential errors related to the copying and pasting of code. Each chapter folder includes dashboards, docker-compose.yml **files, and a** Makefile **to help out when running some of the command-line tools.**

Having an interest in science in general and data science, in particular, will go a long way toward making this book interesting and useful. It would also be helpful to have some programming experience with a scripting language such as Python, but since all the code is included, you can run it directly from a clone of the book's GitHub repository. Some familiarity with relational databases will help you understand some of the terminology and concepts behind time-series databases.

I hope to show, with the examples in this book, how easy it is to build simple data visualization pipelines with Grafana and today's open source tools. I also hope this book will inspire and empower you to seek out your own datasets to acquire, analyze, and visualize. Best of luck!

Download the example code files

You can download the example code files for this book from your account at `www.packt.com`. If you purchased this book elsewhere, you can visit `www.packtpub.com/support` and register to have the files emailed directly to you.

You can download the code files by following these steps:

1. Log in or register at `www.packt.com`.
2. Select the **Support** tab.
3. Click on **Code Downloads**.
4. Enter the name of the book in the **Search** box and follow the onscreen instructions.

Once the file is downloaded, please make sure that you unzip or extract the folder using the latest version of:

- WinRAR/7-Zip for Windows
- Zipeg/iZip/UnRarX for Mac
- 7-Zip/PeaZip for Linux

The code bundle for the book is also hosted on GitHub at `https://github.com/PacktPublishing/Learn-Grafana-7.0`. In case there's an update to the code, it will be updated on the existing GitHub repository.

We also have other code bundles from our rich catalog of books and videos available at `https://github.com/PacktPublishing/`. Check them out!

Download the color images

We also provide a PDF file that has color images of the screenshots/diagrams used in this book. You can download it here: https://static.packt-cdn.com/downloads/9781838826581_ColorImages.pdf.

Conventions used

There are a number of text conventions used throughout this book.

CodeInText: Indicates code words in text, database table names, folder names, filenames, file extensions, pathnames, dummy URLs, user input, and Twitter handles. Here is an example: "The first line of our main() function sets up the logging level."

A block of code is set as follows:

```
def main():
    logging.basicConfig(level=logging.INFO)
```

Any command-line input or output is written as follows:

```
% docker-compose down
```

Bold: Indicates a new term, an important word, or words that you see onscreen. For example, words in menus or dialog boxes appear in the text like this. Here is an example: "Click on **Create | Dashboard**; you should see a panel with three buttons."

Warnings or important notes appear like this.

Tips and tricks appear like this.

Get in touch

Feedback from our readers is always welcome.

General feedback: If you have questions about any aspect of this book, mention the book title in the subject of your message and email us at customercare@packtpub.com.

Errata: Although we have taken every care to ensure the accuracy of our content, mistakes do happen. If you have found a mistake in this book, we would be grateful if you would report this to us. Please visit www.packtpub.com/support/errata, selecting your book, clicking on the Errata Submission Form link, and entering the details.

Piracy: If you come across any illegal copies of our works in any form on the Internet, we would be grateful if you would provide us with the location address or website name. Please contact us at copyright@packt.com with a link to the material.

If you are interested in becoming an author: If there is a topic that you have expertise in and you are interested in either writing or contributing to a book, please visit authors.packtpub.com.

Reviews

Please leave a review. Once you have read and used this book, why not leave a review on the site that you purchased it from? Potential readers can then see and use your unbiased opinion to make purchase decisions, we at Packt can understand what you think about our products, and our authors can see your feedback on their book. Thank you!

For more information about Packt, please visit packt.com.

Getting Started with Grafana 1

In this section, you will learn how to install a Grafana server and create a dashboard with a single panel.

This section is comprised of the following chapters:

1
Introduction to Data Visualization with Grafana

Welcome to *Learn Grafana 7.0*! Together, we will explore **Grafana**, an exciting, multi-faceted visualization tool for data exploration, analysis, and alerting. We will learn how to install Grafana, become familiar with some of its many features, and even use it to investigate publicly available real-world datasets.

Whether you are an engineer watching terabytes of metrics for a critical system fault, an administrator sifting through a haystack of log output looking for the needle of an application error, or just a curious citizen eager to know how your city works, Grafana can help you monitor, explore, and analyze data. The key to getting a handle on *big data* is the ability to visualize it.

But before we find out how Grafana gives you that ability, let's briefly review a few basic concepts behind data visualization.

The following topics will be covered in this chapter:

- Data and visualization – an overview of the data landscape and how visualization is a useful solution
- Why Grafana? What makes Grafana an attractive solution?
- Installing Grafana – getting the Grafana application installed and running
- Connecting to the Grafana server – launching the application from a web browser

Technical requirements

Grafana is relatively easy to set up, but since it is a web server application, you will need to run a few commands to get it running. For the purposes of this book, we will assume that you will access Grafana from the same computer that you installed it on. The following are the technical requirements for installing and running Grafana:

- Familiarity with the command shell
- A terminal application or an SSH to the machine where you plan to install Grafana
- Docker (in order to run Grafana from a Docker container)
- Optionally, you will have the Administrator access to install and run Grafana from the command line, rather than in a Docker container

Tutorial code, dashboards, and other helpful files for this chapter can be found in the book's GitHub repository at `https://github.com/PacktPublishing/Learn-Grafana-7.0/tree/master/Chapter01`.

Data and visualization

In the not-too-distant past, most of us consumed data pretty much solely via a daily newspaper—on the financial pages, the sports section, and the weather forecast. However, in recent years, the ubiquity of computing power has immersed every part of our lives in a sea of data.

Around the clock, our built environment and devices collect innumerable data, which we consume. Our morning routine starts with a review of emails, social media posts, and news feeds on a smartphone or tablet, and whereas we once put down the daily newspaper when we left for work, our phones come with us everywhere.

We walk around or exercise and our phones capture our activity and location data via the GPS, while our smartwatches capture our vitals. When we browse the web, every single interaction down to a mouse click is logged and stored for analysis. The servers that deliver these experiences are monitored and maintained by engineers on a round-the-clock basis. Marketers and salesforces continually analyze this data in order to make business-critical decisions.

On the way to work, our cars, buses, and trains contain increasingly sophisticated computers that silently log tens of thousands of real-time metrics, using them to calculate efficiency, profitability, engine performance, and environmental impact. Technicians evaluating these physical systems' health or troubleshooting problems often sift through an enormous stream of data to tease out the signs of a faulty sensor or a failed part. The importance of this data is globally recognized. This is precisely why data recorders are the most valuable forensic artifact after any transportation accident, and why their recovery generates such widespread media coverage.

Meanwhile, in the modern home, a smart thermostat dutifully logs the settings on a **Heating, Ventilation, and Air Conditioning (HVAC)** system, as well as the current temperature both inside and outside the house. These devices continually gather real-time weather information in order to make decisions about how and when to run most efficiently.

Similar to the systems at home, but on a much larger scale, nearly every building we pass through during the day collects and monitors the health of a number of key infrastructure systems, from air conditioning to plumbing to security. No amount of paper could possibly record the thousands of channels of data flowing through these physical plants, and yet the building management system aggregates this data to make the same kinds of simple decisions as the homeowner does.

Moreover, these examples represent only a drop in the ocean of data. Around the world, governments, scientists, NGOs, and everyday citizens collect, store, and analyze their own datasets. They are all confronted with the same issue: how to aggregate, collate, or distill the mass of data into a form that a human can perceive and act on in a few seconds or less. The response to this issue is effective data storage and visualization.

Storing, retrieving, and visualizing data

For years, the basic language of data visualization was well-defined: using a chart, graph, histogram, and so on. What has been missing is the ability to rapidly create these charts and graphs not in hours or days but in seconds or even milliseconds. This requires processing power that draws representations of thousands and thousands of data points in the time it takes to refresh a computer display.

For decades, only the most powerful computers could manage the processing power required to visualize data on this scale, and the software they ran was specialized and expensive. However, a number of trends in computing have converged to produce a renaissance in data acquisition and visualization, making it accessible not only to domain practitioners but also to technically proficient members of the general public. They are as follows:

- Cheap general-purpose CPUs and graphics GPUs
- Inexpensive high-capacity storage, optimized for physical size and maximum throughput
- Web standards and technologies, including JavaScript and CSS
- Open source software frameworks and toolkits
- Scalable cloud computation at affordable prices
- Broadband networking to the enterprise, the home, and the mobile device

A common feature of virtually all of this data is that for each sample from a sensor or line in a log file is the snapshot from an invisible ticking clock: a **timestamp**. A dataset gathered from these data points across a period of time is referred to as a **time series**. A stored object containing one or more time series is a **time-series dataset**. An application that can provide optimized access to one or more of these datasets is called, naturally, a **time-series database**. While a whole class of NoSQL time-series databases, such as `InfluxDB`, `OpenTSDB`, and `Prometheus`, have sprung up, venerable SQL relational databases, such as `PostgreSQL` and `MySQL`, have added their own support for time-series datasets.

That's fine for storing and retrieving data, but what about visualizing data? Enter Grafana.

Why Grafana?

While there are many solutions in the data visualization space, Grafana is proving to be one of the most exciting, exhibiting rapid growth in scope and features, broad options for deployment and support, and an enthusiastic community contributing to its future growth. Before going into the specific features that make Grafana an attractive solution, let's take a look at the criteria we might use to characterize a useful data visualization application:

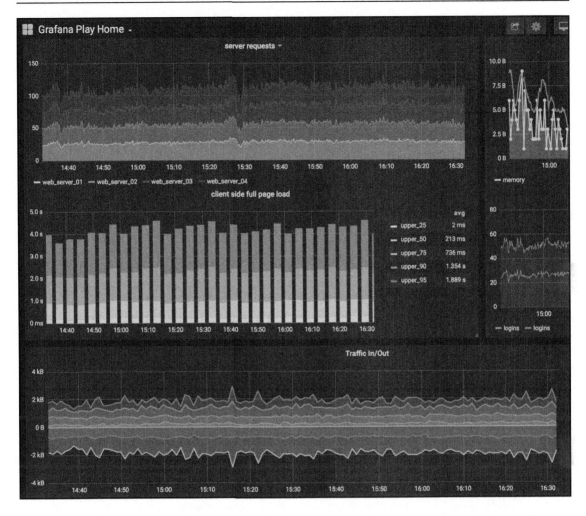

For the purposes of this book, we will be looking at particular software applications that fulfill four major functions: **exploration**, **analysis**, **presentation**, and **notification**.

Quickly loading and displaying a dataset with the idea of identifying the particularly interesting features for deeper analysis, sometimes referred to as *drilling-down*, is an example of *data exploration*.

After we have examined our data, we may want to analyze it next. That is, we may want to quantify the data statistically or correlate it with other data. For example, we may want to see what the maximum value or average value of the data is for a specific time range. We may also want to look at multiple datasets over the same time period to look for events that might be time-correlated.

Once we have identified the data we are interested in, we will want to *present* it in an aesthetically pleasing manner that also gives the viewer clarity about what the data represents, in effect helping to tell a story about the data, which would be otherwise difficult to do without specific domain knowledge.

Finally, we may need to observe the data over time, or even in real-time as it may represent critical data. If the data crosses into a realm of concern, we may need to be notified immediately.

While there are a number of powerful data analytics tools on the market that fulfill these functions, Grafana has a number of features that make it an attractive choice:

- **Fast**: The Grafana backend is written in Google's exciting new Go language, making it extremely performant when querying data sources or feeding thousands of data points to multiple dashboard panels.

- **Open**: Grafana supports a plugin model for its dashboard panels and data sources. The number of plugins is constantly growing as the Grafana community enthusiastically contributes to the project.

- **Beautiful**: Grafana leverages the attractive and powerful D3 library. Many of the popular dashboard tools, such as **DataDog** and **Zabbix**, can quickly generate beautiful graphs from thousands of data channels, but they only offer some limited control over the display elements. Grafana provides fine-grained control over most graph elements including axes, lines, points, fills, annotations, and legends. It even offers the much sought-after dark mode.

- **Versatile**: Grafana is not tied to particular database technology. For example, **Kibana** is a powerful, well-known member of **ElasticSearch**'s **ElasticSearch, Logstash, Kibana (ELK)** stack; it is only capable of visualizing ElasticSearch data sources. This gives it the advantage over Grafana of a better ability to integrate ElasticSearch's analysis tools in its graphing panels. However, due to its plugin architecture, Grafana can support a variety of ever-growing databases (at last count, over 30) from traditional RDBMs, such as MySQL and PostgresQL, to modern TSDBs, such as InfluxDB and Prometheus. Not only can each graph display data from a variety of data sources, but a single graph can also combine data from multiple data sources.

- **Free**: While they are very powerful tools indeed, **DataDog** and **Splunk** are commercial packages and, as such, charge fees to manage all but the smallest datasets. If you want to get your feet wet, Grafana is freely available under the Apache open source license, and if you do plan to run it in your enterprise, you can purchase tiered support.

These are just some of the criteria you might use to evaluate Grafana against similar products. Your mileage may vary, but now is a great time to be in the market for visualization tools. Grafana and its competitors each have their own strengths and weaknesses, but they are all very capable applications. Here's a short list of the few we covered:

- Kibana (www.elastic.co)
- Splunk (www.splunk.com)
- Datadog (www.datadoghq.com)
- Zabbix (www.zabbix.com)

With this in mind, let's install Grafana.

Installing Grafana

At its core, Grafana runs as a web server, and as such, it is not a typical double-click application. You will need to be comfortable with the command line and have administrator privileges on the computer you plan to install Grafana on. To download the latest versions of Grafana, check out https://grafana.com/grafana/download.

The Grafana application server runs on ***nix operating systems (Linux, OS X**, and **Windows**), and it can be installed locally on a laptop or workstation or on a remote server. It is even available as a hosted application if you'd rather not deal with setting up or managing a server application on your own.

In this section, we'll walk through the most typical installation options:

- Docker
- OS X
- Linux
- Windows
- Hosted Grafana on the cloud

Once you've completed the installation of your choice, proceed to the *Connecting to the Grafana server* section for instructions on how to access Grafana from a web browser.

Grafana in a Docker container

The easiest and least complex installation method is to run Grafana from within a Docker container. Docker is available for all major platforms and can be downloaded by visiting `https://www.docker.com/`.

After installing Docker, open a terminal window and type in the following command:

```
$ docker run -d --name=grafana -p 3000:3000 grafana/grafana
```

Docker will automatically download and run the latest version of Grafana for your computer's architecture. Bear in mind that since this basic container has no persistent storage, nothing will be retained if you delete the container. I suggest you run the container with a temporary volume so that Grafana's internal database will continue to exist, even if you destroy the container:

```
$ docker volume create grafana-storage
$ docker run -d --name=grafana -p 3000:3000  \
    -v grafana-storage:/var/lib/grafana \
    grafana/grafana
```

I recommend proceeding with Docker for the purposes of this book as it will allow an almost turnkey installation experience, as all the necessary dependencies will be automatically downloaded with the container. It will also install in its own sandbox, so you don't need to worry about installing a stack of software that will be difficult to delete later. Finally, in future chapters we will be setting up data sources using similar Docker containers, so managing the data pipeline as a combination of containers will be very consistent and straightforward.

Grafana for OS X

There are two options for installing and running Grafana for OS X:

- Homebrew
- The command line

Using **Homebrew** is the simplest option as it wraps all the installation chores in a single command. To get Homebrew, visit `https://brew.sh/`. If you want more control over where to install Grafana, the command line option is a better choice.

Homebrew

To install via Homebrew, use the following:

```
$ brew install grafana
```

If you want to keep Grafana running even after a reboot, use the `services` subcommand to launch the installed Grafana application as a service. You will first need to confirm services installation:

```
$ brew tap homebrew/services
$ brew services start grafana
```

The command line

To install via the command line, open a **Terminal shell window** and download an **OS X distribution tarball**, then untar it into the directory of your choice (replace `$GRAFANA_VERSION` with the current version):

```
$ wget
https://dl.grafana.com/oss/release/grafana-$GRAFANA_VERSION.darwin-amd64.tar.gz
$ tar -zxvf grafana-$GRAFANA_VERSION.darwin-amd64.tar.gz
```

Once you've untared the file, `cd` into the directory and launch the binary:

```
./bin/grafana-server web
```

Grafana for Linux

Linux comes in a number of flavors and each has a slightly different installation system. Typically, you download the binary and then run the installer on the package file. To get the latest Grafana binaries for Linux, visit `https://grafana.com/grafana/download? platform=linux`.

RedHat Linux

The installer for the **RedHat distributions** (**CentOS**, **RedHat**, and **Fedora**) is `yum`. To download and install (replacing `$GRAFANA_VERSION` with the current version), use the following:

```
$ wget
https://dl.grafana.com/oss/release/grafana-$GRAFANA_VERSION.x86_64.rpm
$ sudo yum install initscripts urw-fonts
$ sudo yum localinstall grafana-$GRAFANA_VERSION.x86_64.rpm
```

To start up Grafana, use `systemd`:

```
$ systemctl daemon-reload
$ systemctl start grafana-server
$ systemctl status grafana-server
```

To keep Grafana running even after a reboot, use the following:

```
$ sudo systemctl enable grafana-server.service
```

Debian Linux

The installer for the **Debian distributions** (**Debian** and **Ubuntu**) is `dpkg`. To download and install (replace `$GRAFANA_VERSION` with the current version), use the following:

```
$ wget
https://dl.grafana.com/oss/release/grafana_$GRAFANA_VERSION_amd64.deb
$ sudo apt-get install -y adduser libfontconfig1
$ sudo dpkg -i grafana_$GRAFANA_VERSION_amd64.deb
```

To start up Grafana, use the following:

```
$ systemctl daemon-reload
$ systemctl start grafana-server
$ systemctl status grafana-server
```

To keep Grafana running even after a reboot, use the following:

```
$ sudo systemctl enable grafana-server.service
```

Grafana for Windows

Installation for Windows is straightforward:

1. Go to `https://grafana.com/grafana/download?platform=windows`.
2. Download the latest *MSI installer* file from the download link.
3. Launch the `.msi` file to install.

Hosted Grafana on the cloud

If you would rather not install Grafana on your computer, or you don't have access to a computer that can run Grafana, there is another option—Grafana can host a free instance for you. There are restrictions—namely that in order to access a data source, you will need to upgrade a paid subscription—but if you want to follow this book up to the point where we use data sources, hosted Grafana might be a good solution. To sign up for the hosted version, go to `https://grafana.com/get` and select the link under **We Host It**.

Connecting to the Grafana server

Once you have installed and launched Grafana, open a browser page to access the Grafana application. It can be found at `http://localhost:3000`. If everything goes well, you should see a login page, as follows:

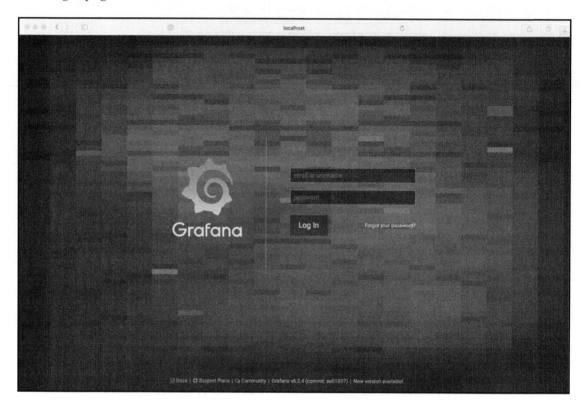

Log in with the `admin` username and the `admin` password. You will then be prompted to change it to something more secure. Once you have logged in, you should see the base Grafana interface:

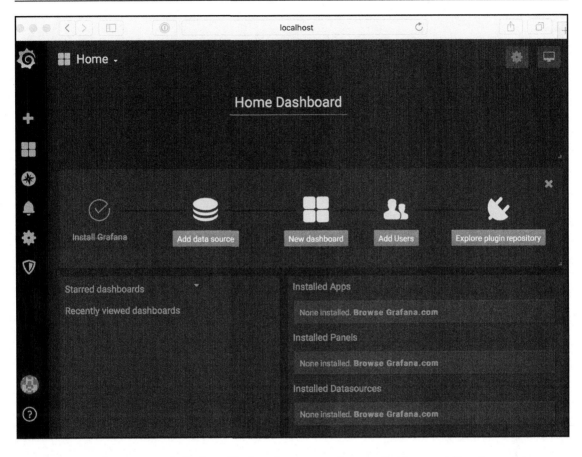

Great job! You've successfully installed and connected your Grafana application.

Summary

Congratulations! You now have a running Grafana server and are ready to take the next steps toward exploring the many powerful features of Grafana. In the upcoming chapters, we'll navigate the interface, analyze data sources, and learn about advanced management practices.

The official Grafana documentation can be found on their website at https://grafana.com/docs/.

A Tour of the Grafana Interface

2

By this point, you've successfully installed and run Grafana; so next, we're going to familiarize ourselves with the Grafana **User Interface** (**UI**). In this chapter, we will take a general tour of the default **Home** dashboard, mostly concentrating on the sidebar menu. While you will spend the majority of your time interacting directly with dashboards and panels, you will find the side menu is a helpful navigation hub, providing both quick access to simple creation pages and links to more complex functions, including data source creation, **Explore** mode, alert management, and server administration.

 This chapter is intended to provide a mostly high-level tour of these major functions; we will go into more detail about each function later in the book. I'll point out which chapters correspond to the topics covered. If you're already somewhat familiar with Grafana, this chapter should serve as a quick review and a point of reference.

Specifically, we'll cover the following topics in this chapter:

- Exploring Grafana-the **Home** dashboard
- Glancing at the sidebar menu
- Learning to use the icons on Grafana's left sidebar

Technical requirements

Tutorial code, dashboards, and other helpful files for this chapter can be found in the book's GitHub repository at https://github.com/PacktPublishing/Learn-Grafana-7.0/tree/master/Chapter02.

Exploring Grafana – the Home dashboard

After logging in to the Grafana application, you should end up on the **Home** dashboard, as shown. Here, I've annotated some of the key UI elements in the Grafana interface:

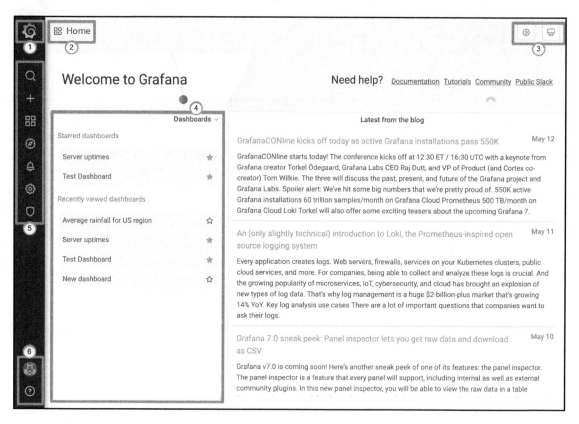

Here are the UI elements visible on the default **Home** dashboard:

1. The Grafana logo button: Returns the user to the **Home** dashboard
2. The dashboards button: Displays the current dashboard
3. The dashboard settings and view mode
4. The dashboard panel: Shows the favorite and recently viewed dashboards
5. The side menu bar: Provides navigation to common tasks and pages
6. The user and help buttons

Grafana is structured around two main interactive UI components that together constitute its core functionality: **dashboards** and **panels**. The page in the preceding screenshot is composed of a **side menu bar** to the left and a **dashboard** to the right—specifically, the **Home** dashboard. A dashboard is a kind of canvas upon which you can display one or more panels in a grid-style arrangement. It also serves as a web page, so you can bookmark or share it with a simple URL. The entire dashboard can even be imported and exported in JSON text file format, making it easy to share, save, or transfer to another version of Grafana.

The fundamental building blocks of the functionality of the dashboard are the panels. Panels fulfill a number of roles, from generating graphs, organizing data into tables, and displaying useful text to simply contain a menu list of dashboards—which happens to be the kind of panel you see on the **Home** dashboard in the preceding screenshot. Panels are implemented as a plugin to Grafana, so any capable developer can add to the variety of Grafana panels by creating new ones.

In Chapter 3, *An Introduction to the Graph Panel*, we'll be taking a much closer look at what might be considered the canonical Grafana panel—the **Graph** panel.

Glancing at the sidebar menu

Let's take a look at the more common sidebar menu buttons. Unless you are running Grafana in a special display mode, this menu bar will appear alongside your dashboard. Depending on the context, it may be accompanied by additional buttons, but we will look at the basic set.

The dashboards button

At the top of the dashboard is the dashboards button:

It displays the name of the current dashboard, and clicking on it takes you to the same dashboard search page as the search button described in the following section.

The dashboard panels

Below the dashboards button are the dashboard panels. Besides graphical data, panels can convey a wide variety of information, including textual and numerical data, spreadsheet-like tables, and lists of dashboards. The current **Home** dashboard serves as a landing page for the Grafana application by default, but you can always change the default to be any dashboard of your choosing.

The dashboard settings and view mode

At the upper right of the **Home** dashboard is a small gear icon that represents the dashboard settings button. Clicking on this button gives you access to a wide array of settings for the dashboard. Some of the main functions available from the settings page are as follows:

- General settings
- Annotations
- Variables
- Links
- JSON model

We will cover most of these settings in Chapter 8, *Working with Advanced Dashboard Features*.

To the right of the dashboard settings icon is the view mode icon. Clicking on this button cycles through three visual modes for the Grafana application, as follows:

- Dashboard and side menu
- Dashboard only—hides the side menu
- Kiosk mode

Learning to use the icons on Grafana's left sidebar

To the left of the dashboard itself is the left sidebar. These icons lead to some of the most powerful of Grafana's impressive features. For example, they enable you to do the following:

- Search for dashboards
- Create and import dashboards and folders
- Find dashboards
- Manage dashboards, dashboard playlists, and dashboard snapshots
- Explore data sources in a free-form fashion
- Manage alert rules and notification channels
- Configure data sources, users, and teams, download plugins, set preferences, and generate API keys
- Administer Grafana users and organizations and view the server settings and stats
- Return to the **Home** dashboard
- Set personal preferences
- Get help

Let's have a closer look at some of these features.

The Grafana logo

At the top-left corner of the sidebar, you'll find the Grafana logo:

The Grafana logo serves as the home button for the application. Clicking on the Grafana logo will take you to the **Home** dashboard, which can be set in the preferences.

Search

Selecting the search button has the same effect as the dashboard button mentioned earlier. It takes you to the dashboard search page. From here, you can do the following:

- Search for dashboards by name
- Filter the list of dashboards by tags

The display features a list of recent dashboards, as well as the content of the top-level (**General**) dashboard folder:

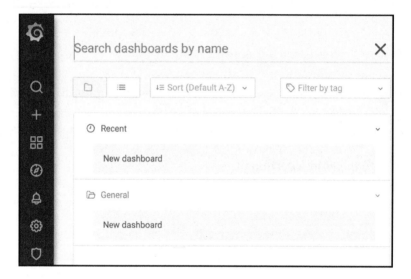

Create

The **Create** dropdown is indicated by the plus icon:

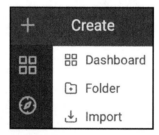

It functions as a link for quickly creating or importing dashboards and dashboard folders.

Dashboard

The **Dashboard** selection under the **Create** menu creates a brand new dashboard, containing a single panel to help get you started. While we're here, let's create a dashboard and see what happens! Click on **Create | Dashboard**; you should see a panel with two buttons:

The **Add new panel** button sets up a **Graph** panel and takes you directly to the **Query** pane, while **Convert to row** (obviously) converts the placeholder panel to a dashboard row. Rows are a powerful structure for dynamically building a dashboard page. Assign a special template variable to a row and Grafana will replicate appropriately configured panels on that row, each one reflecting the value of the template variable. We'll be taking a closer look at both rows and template variables in Chapter 8, *Working with Advanced Dashboard Features*.

Click on **Add new panel** to create a new graph panel. You'll be in **Edit** mode for the panel, so to get back to the dashboard, click on the big left arrow at the top left. You should now see a simple graph of some random data:

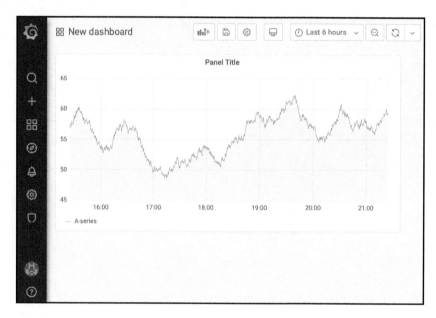

That was pretty easy, right?

You'll also notice some extra icons at the top right compared to the ones we saw earlier on the **Home** dashboard:

The following are the functions of these icons:

1. Adds new panels to the dashboard
2. Saves the dashboard
3. Dashboard settings
4. Cycles the view mode
5. Sets the time range for the graph
6. Zooms out the time range
7. Refreshes the dashboard and sets the dashboard refresh rate

You'll typically find the last three controls anytime you have a time series-based panel on your dashboard. We will go into more detail about the **Graph** panel in `Chapter 3`, *An Introduction to the Graph Panel*. Feel free to experiment with dashboard creation. Create a new dashboard and populate it with any number of panels. Until you hook up a data source, you'll be somewhat limited to what you'll be able to display. If you accidentally delete your panel or convert it into a row, you can always create a new one with the **Add Panel** button.

Folder

The **Create** | **Folder** selection of the dropdown is a handy way to quickly create a folder so that you can group dashboards and keep things manageable. You'll find that once you've created a handful of dashboards, keeping up with them on the **Dashboard** drop-down page can get pretty cumbersome.

Import

Finally, the **Create** | **Import** selection will launch the **Import** interface. From here, you can import a dashboard stored at `https://grafana.com/` or import a previously exported dashboard JSON file. This is one of the easiest ways to share a dashboard as JSON in a text file format, so you can even send it in an email message.

Dashboards

The **Dashboards** dropdown is indicated by the paneled square icon:

Each selection functions as a link to a tab in the **Dashboards** management page, while the **Dashboards** | **Home** selection leads to the **Home** dashboard.

Manage

Each selection in the **Dashboards** dropdown is simply a link to a tab on the **Dashboards** management page. The **Dashboards | Manage** selection leads to the **Manage** tab on the **Dashboards** page. The **Manage** tab is where dashboards can quickly be created and organized. Like the **Create** dropdown, the **Manage** tab provides the ability to create or import a dashboard or to create a dashboard folder. Similar to the dashboard dropdown, you can use the search box to find dashboards by name:

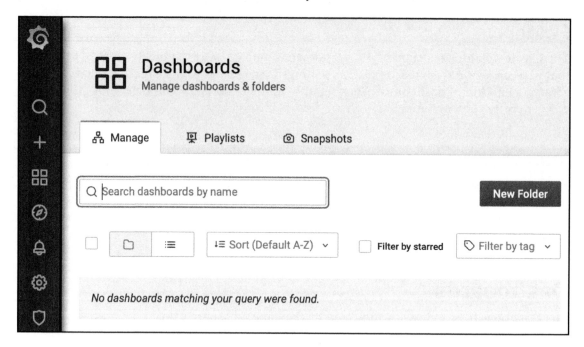

 The **New Dashboard**, **New Folder**, and **Import** buttons are virtually identical in function to their counterparts in the **Create** dropdown.

New Dashboard will create a new dashboard with a panel wizard, while **New Folder** and **Import**, like **Create | New Folder** and **Create | Import**, will execute their functions on the **Manage** tab.

Playlists

The **Dashboards | Playlists** selection takes us to the **Playlists** tab, where you can create groupings of dashboards orchestrated to run in a particular sequence and timing:

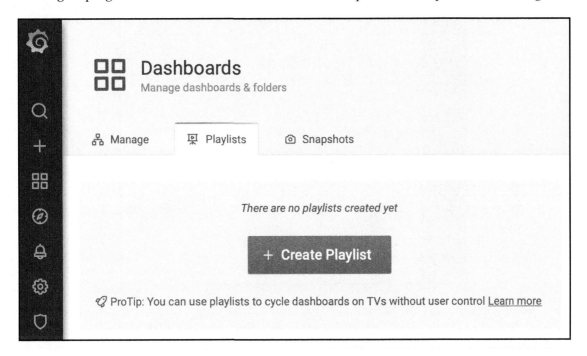

Typically, you use playlists when you want to set up an automated Grafana-driven kiosk-type display. Setting up a playlist such as this in Grafana is easy:

1. Click on **Create Playlist**.
2. Name your playlist.
3. Set the interval timing between playlists.
4. Add dashboards to the list.
5. Click **Create**.

Snapshots

The **Snapshots** tab, also accessed via the **Dashboards | Snapshots** selection, allows you to capture the state of a dashboard in what are called **snapshots**:

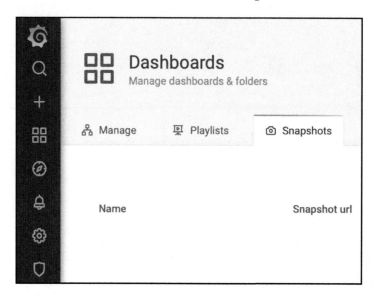

This displays your data sets, but without any way to access the original data sources and queries. Snapshots are a great way to share a *live* dashboard in scenarios where you need to demo your dashboards *offline* or can't share access to your data sources.

We'll be taking a closer look at the features of the **Management** page in Chapter 8, *Working with Advanced Dashboard Features*, and Chapter 11, *Organizing Dashboards*.

Explore

Explore is one of Grafana's most exciting features; it is a kind of data-driven scratchpad for exploring a data source prior to implementing it on a dashboard graph. It is integrated with Loki, Grafana's new system for ad hoc data exploration.

If you've ever worked with a dashboard-driven tool such as Grafana, you might have started with a dashboard, loaded up a graph panel, fed it the data, and then messaged queries or time frames looking for patterns. What if you could dispense with the overhead of building and configuring dashboard panels and go straight to the analysis? That is what **Explore** mode is for**:**

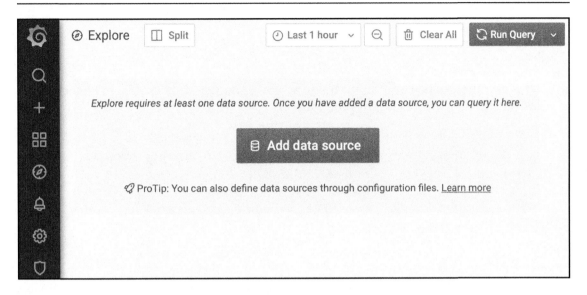

Explore gives you a fullscreen panel, so you can then immediately start exploring your data without concerning yourself with the panel or its appearance on a dashboard. With Loki, **Explore** takes things a step further. By integrating logging with your metrics, you can correlate metric indicators with significant logged events. If you've tried to troubleshoot a problem by repeatedly flipping back and forth between your graphs and logs, imagine working with them on the same interface!

We'll explore **Explore** and Loki in much more depth in Chapter 10, *Exploring Logs With Grafana's Loki.*

Alerting

A must-have for any time series-based data visualization application is **Alerting**:

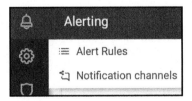

Like the **Dashboards** dropdown, the **Alerting** dropdown is a set of links to tabs on the **Alerting** page.

Alert Rules

Alerting rules are the data thresholds that activate an alert. From this tab, you can manage the alerts created in various dashboard panels. Once an alert is triggered, you'll need some form of notification so that you can be made aware of the alert. The process of connecting an alert rule to some form of notification is easy:

1. Establish one or more alerts on your dashboard panel.
2. Configure a notification channel to be activated on an appropriate alert state.
3. Set the alert to use one or more notification channels.

Notification channels

Notifications are stored in the next tab under the **Notification channels** tab. A notification channel can be as simple as an email address or as complex as an integration plugin, such as PagerDuty. Currently, there are nearly 20 notification integrations that support Grafana, and that number is constantly growing.

We'll look at how to set up alerting rules and to hook them up to notification channels in `Chapter 9`, *Grafana Alerting*.

Configuration

The **Configuration** page is Grafana's administrative command center. While you can certainly use Grafana as an application solely for yourself, it is also designed to work as a full-featured data visualization server that supports hundreds of users. From the **Configuration** page, you can do this and more. Similar to the previous dropdowns, each **Configuration** dropdown links to a corresponding tab on the **Configuration** page.

Data Sources

The primary tab on the **Configuration** page is **Data Sources**, and for good reason. Setting up the data sources that back your graphs will most likely be your primary administrative function within Grafana. From this tab, you can create any number of data sources from the available data source plugins:

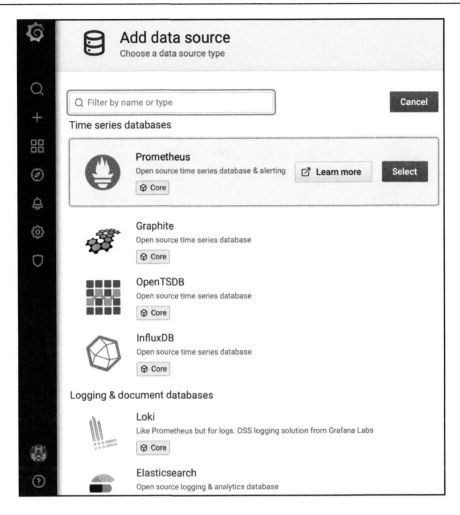

To set up a data source, typically, you will need to know a few things: the data source's server IP address and port, the correct authentication credentials to access it, and the name of the database on the server itself. There is one data source you can create that has no setup as it is an internal plugin to Grafana. The **Test DB** data source is a dummy data source that mimics the characteristics of a time-series database with random data. We will use the **Test DB** data source in the next chapter in order to get familiar with the Grafana panel before integrating it with a real data source.

We will take a detailed look at **Data Sources** in `Chapter 4`, *Connecting Grafana to a Data Source*.

Users

Selecting **Configuration** | **Users** takes you to the **Users** tab, where you can invite new users, set access levels for existing ones, or simply delete users entirely.

In the following example, clicking on the **Invite** button opens up a new user page where you can enter a new user's email address and an optional name. Click on the **Invite** button to add the new user with a role set in the dropdown. If the **Send Invite Email** toggle is enabled, an invitation will then go out to the user's email address:

Teams

Next to the **Users** tab is the **Teams** tab, accessed via **Configuration** | **Teams**. The **Teams** concept is relatively new to Grafana and is primarily used to establish UI settings for an entire group of users. Simply create a new team, then add users to the team. Default UI settings can then be established for all members of the team. A team can have its own **Home** dashboard, UI theme, or timezone setting. This feature is useful if you are managing Grafana for an organization of groups that each want their users to have a tailored Grafana experience.

More information on **Users** and **Teams** management will be covered in Chapter 12, *Managing Permissions for Users and Teams*.

Plugins

The **Plugins** page is an information page listing all the installed data sources and panel plugins. It also features a link to the plugins catalog on `https://grafana.com/` where you can download and install more plugins:

Preferences

Preferences sets the global interface parameters for an organization. Notably, here is where the home dashboard is set. In order to be eligible for designation as the home dashboard, a dashboard must be starred. Besides the home dashboard, here is where the UI style (light or dark mode) and timezone are also set:

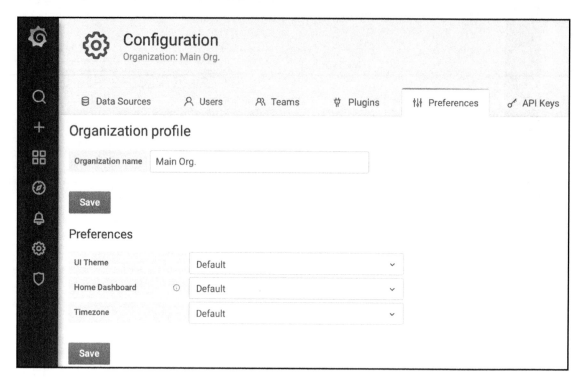

Organizations are Grafana's mechanism for supporting multiple independent Grafana sites from a single server. Each organization is completely independent of the others and has its own **Configuration**, **Data Sources**, **Users**, and **Teams** settings. While organizations are created and managed from the **Server Admin** page, the preferences for the current organization are set here. To set the preferences for another organization, you'll need to switch to that organization (see the following **User** button):

API Keys

Finally, **API Keys** is used by administrators on behalf of developers creating software applications that interact with Grafana using its REST API. An API key is a token used to authenticate an application bearing an issued key. An application bearing an API key will have access to all of Grafana, so you will need to be careful to create your API keys with the minimum necessary access and distribute them only to trusted developers.

Server Admin

The last of the middle set of sidebar icons is the **Server Admin** shield icon:

The **Server Admin** dropdown links to the **Server Admin** page and its tabs. The **Server Admin** pages are where you perform the more globally scoped administration tasks for your Grafana server. Here, you can add users and organizations and view the current server settings and statistics.

Users

The **Users** tab under **Server Admin** is similar to the **Users** tab under **Configuration**; however, in the **Server Admin** context, you have a great deal more control. Not only can you set up a new user, but you can also change the user's password, add them to various organizations, and even log them out of Grafana entirely. It's a pretty important page:

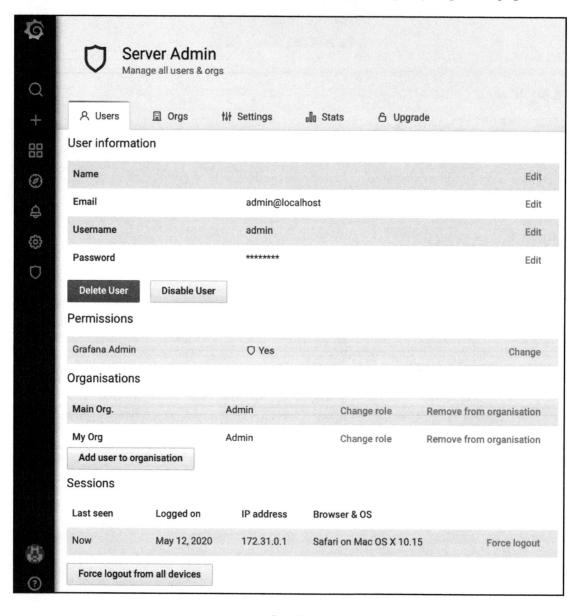

Here's a quick summary of the different sections under the **Users** tab:

- **Edit User**: Set a user's name, email, and username
- **Change Password**: Change a user's password
- **Permissions**: Enable admin permissions
- **Organizations**: Add users to organizations with specified roles
- **Sessions**: Review user logins and log out users
- **User Stats**: Enable/disable a user or delete a user

Orgs

As we discussed in the section on **Configuration** | **Preferences**, organizations are useful for creating entirely separate Grafana sites on one server. Go to the **Orgs** tab to add or delete an organization.

Creating or deleting an organization is simple (as shown):

1. Clicking on the **New org** button will take you to a page where you can set the name of a new organization.
2. Click on the red ✕ button to delete an organization:

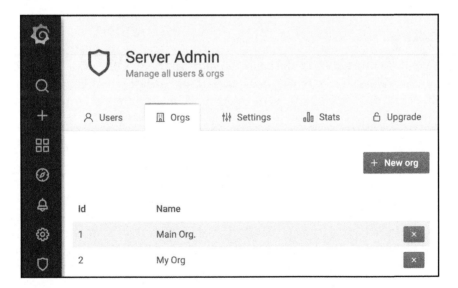

Once you create an organization, however, you will need to populate it with users before anyone can access it. For now, we will work solely within the default organization created for you when you installed Grafana; however, if you wish to find out more, Chapter 12, *Managing Permissions for Users and Teams*, will cover user and organization management in more detail.

Settings

Server Admin | **Settings** displays the current settings for the Grafana server configuration as stored in the `grafana.ini` file. It is beyond the scope of this book to discuss configuring the Grafana server via `grafana.ini`. If you want to learn more about how to configure the Grafana server, check out the documentation at `https://grafana.com/docs/installation/configuration`.

Stats

If you want to get an idea of how many resources from users to dashboards to alerts have been created on your server, select the **Stats** tab on the **Server Admin** page for a list of potentially interesting statistics.

Summary

There you have it—a quick tour of the basic Grafana interface. Of course, we have barely scratched the surface and we've hardly created a dashboard or panel! Before we start working with actual dashboard panels, now would be a good opportunity to explore the interface. Don't worry, you won't break anything! Here are some suggestions:

- When you are viewing a dashboard, click around and explore some of the basic dashboard controls.
- What happens when you click on a **Dashboard** title?
- What happens when you click on the gear icon on the dashboard?

In Chapter 3, *An Introduction to the Graph Panel*, we will cover a key feature of the Grafana interface—the **Graph** panel. If you plan to do any graphing, you're going to turn to the **Graph** panel. It's the most powerful and feature-rich of the panels available in Grafana, so we're going to spend the entire next chapter walking through its interface. After that, in Chapter 4, *Connecting Grafana to a Data Source*, we'll complete our introduction to Grafana's interface with a look at data sources and how they bring time-series data to Grafana.

An Introduction to the Graph
Panel

3

We've now come to the chapter you've been waiting for: using Grafana to actually graph something. In this chapter, we will examine the Grafana native plugin panel, known simply as the **graph** panel. While there are a number of different panels in Grafana to choose from, the graph panel is the go-to panel for producing beautifully styled metrics graphs. It is one of the most versatile panels, and on first viewing, it seems to have an intimidating set of features. Due to this, we will take a broader overview approach to the graph panel before diving further in later chapters.

Much like we did in Chapter 2, *A Tour of the Grafana Interface*, we're going to break down the major UI elements that comprise the graph panel. Since all panels are built from the same plugin architecture, you will find that many of the panels have a similar structure. Once you become familiar with the graph panel, that consistency across all data-driven panels will make it easy for you to pick up new panels, as well as to swap out panels, depending on your needs.

In this chapter, we'll cover the following topics:

- Touring the graph panel
- Generating data series in the Query tab
- Editing the graph in the Panel tab
- Monitoring with the Alert tab

Technical requirements

The tutorial code, dashboards, and other helpful files for this chapter can be found in this book's GitHub repository at https://github.com/PacktPublishing/Learn-Grafana-7.0/tree/master/Chapter03.

Touring the graph panel

Here is a typical graph panel in edit mode:

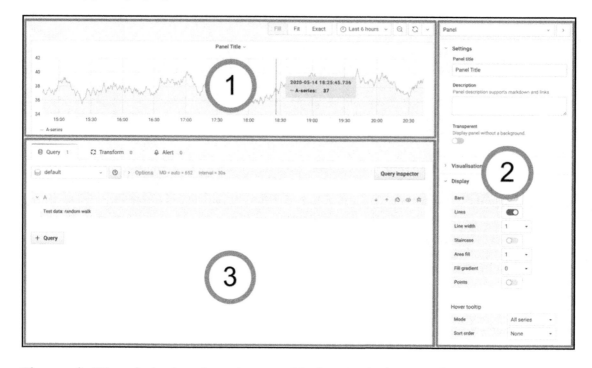

The panel's UI can be broken down into roughly three main functional areas:

1. **Panel display**: Preview display, and time picker
2. **Display settings**: Panel visualization type, styles, and links
3. **Data configuration**: Data query, data transformation, and alerting

Throughout this chapter, we will delve into each of these features. First, we will look at the **Query** tab in the context of how to use it to produce graphed data. Next, we will explore how the various display settings shape the look of the graph and how to set typical panel display features such as a title. Finally, we will see how the **Alert** tab can establish the monitoring rules for thresholds that, when exceeded, can trigger alerts. Of course, all of this is dependent on what we'll create next: a simple data source.

Creating a simple data source

A Grafana plugin that supplies panels with data is called a *data source*. Obviously, if you want to set up a graph panel, you will need such a source for data, but what happens when you create a graph panel without specifying a data source? Fortunately, Grafana has thought of this scenario, and even if you don't have even a single data source set up, the panel will still have something to graph: a built-in *fake* data source.

If you've already created a panel, you may have seen it graph a mysterious dataset that seems to come from nowhere. The data is coming from a built-in data source, simply called **Grafana**, which generates pseudodata in a pattern called a **random walk**. It's useful for producing a dataset that emulates some real-world metrics where each data point is a small, random increment from the previous one. It generates a smooth curve modulated with a bit of noise, and is the kind of pattern that exists in many physically based measurements.

Although it is useful, this dataset has some limitations; for instance, we can't use it to create multiple independent datasets. As I described in the previous chapter, let's start from the **Home** dashboard to set up a similar data source that can produce a richer variety of fake data for us to work with:

1. Return to the **Home** dashboard if you're not already there.
2. Select **Configuration | Data Sources**.
3. Click **+ Data Source**.
4. Scroll down to **Others** and select **TestData DB**.
5. Make sure **Default** is set to **On**.
6. Click **Save & Test** to confirm the data source is working.

If successful, you should get a green section that indicates the data source is working. The **Settings** tab should look like this:

Click on **Save & Test**, and then **Back** to get back to the **Configuration** page. You've successfully created your first data source!

Creating a graph panel

The first thing we need to do is create a graph panel. By now, you've probably already created a few panels, so this should be relatively easy. Let's start with a fresh dashboard so that we can keep things separate from the work we did previously:

1. Go back to the **Home** dashboard.
2. Select **Create | Dashboard.**
3. On the panel placeholder, click **+ new panel.**
4. By default, you will have created a graph panel.
5. Click the **Save Dashboard** icon at the top-right to save the dashboard for future reference. Get into the practice of regularly saving your dashboards.
6. Click **Apply** to save your panel changes.
7. To go back and edit a panel, click the **Panel Title** dropdown and select **Edit.**

After completing this little exercise, things should look something like this; not all that different from the first graph we created in Chapter 2, *A tour of the Grafana Interface*:

Now that you've designated the new **TestData DB** as the default data source, any newly created panel will use the default as its data source. Don't worry – you can always set it to use another data source with a quick menu selection.

Generating data series in the Query tab

If it isn't already selected, click on the **Query** tab to select it. The **Query** tab is where we will assign a data source to the panel's queries. With **TestData DB** set as the default data source, Grafana also sets up **Random Walk** to be the default query **Scenario**, so we are now ready to go with both a data source and a query that produces the displayed dataset series.

Before we go into the **Query** tab, we should probably talk a bit about its purpose. Rather than some similar applications that connect to a single database application, Grafana was designed to be agnostic about data. Grafana data source plugins are not only responsible for presenting a simplified query interface to the Grafana user but also for feeding the returned data into the Grafana 7 unified data model, which is used by many panels. Most Grafana users will find that, even with a simplified query UI, they can make relatively sophisticated queries.

In cases where a complex query is beyond the scope of the query UI, data sources such as MySQL and PostgreSQL will also support regular SQL queries. Other data sources such as Prometheus and InfluxDB support raw text queries as well. Bear in mind that the data source query interface will not provide protection against dangerous queries, so if you do plan to use native queries, consult with your database administrator about designating a user account with restricted permissions for your Grafana data sources.

What is a query?

Essentially, a query is a mechanism for extracting a data series for display by the panel. The **Query** tab allows multiple queries from the same data source or a mix of multiple data sources to be extracted. It can even reference a data source from other panels. Depending on the data source plugin, Grafana will convert the tab's queries into API calls to the data source server (similar to a SQL statement to an RDBMS), retrieve the data in an internal structure called a **data frame**, and then display some or all of it, depending on the current time range.

For now, we'll just use the current **TestData DB** as our data source so that we can concentrate on the different aspects of the graph panel interface. In the next chapter, we'll look more closely at how to query an actual third-party data source, rather than an internally generated one.

Query tab features

Let's have a look at the main features of the **Query** tab. Depending on the data source, individual queries will differ, but the overall interface will be the same, as shown in the following screenshot:

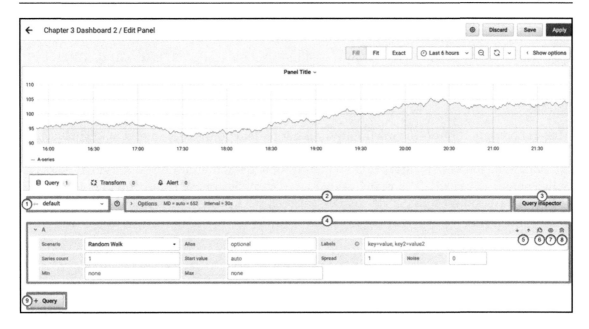

Here are the key features that have been identified in the preceding screenshot:

1. **Data source** menu
2. Query Options
3. **Query inspector** button
4. **Query**
5. Move Query Down and Up
6. Duplicate Query
7. Query visibility toggle
8. **Delete** Query
9. **+ Query** button

Let's have a look at each of these features and see how they work together to give you control over a data source query and the resulting data series.

The Data source menu

The **Data source** menu is where you will select the data source for the panel. In general, a panel will only contain queries from a single data source, so the pulldown will present all the available data sources. If you do want to combine multiple data sources into a single graph, select **Mixed**. You can then specify the data source as you add queries.

Query Options

Monitoring the value of a given point at a sample of time (called an **interval**) is critical to maintaining the proper visual representation of data. Next to the **Data source** menu is the **Query Options** section, which contains the various options for configuring how the panel handles how time series data is displayed.

Max data points controls the maximum number of data points that should be displayed, even if the time range is very wide. **Min interval** is used to give Grafana the sampling interval of the data in the **query** to help it determine the minimum time interval to display with a single data point. Setting the value to the frequency of each data point helps Grafana optimize the display of time series panels, especially when dealing with wide time ranges. For example, your data is written to a Prometheus database once every minute (the *sampling frequency*); here, you would set **Min Interval** to 1m.

In order to keep track of the interval of time represented by a single pixel, Grafana provides a helpful **Interval** display.

While the time range control at the top of the panel is used to set a global time range for all the panels on the dashboard, often, you want to override the time range for individual panels. Perhaps you want to see a 1-hour, 2-hour, and 4-hour range for your panel. You don't want to have to keep flipping the time range multiple times so that you can replicate the panel three times and set three different time ranges.

The **Relative time** setting is used to set the panel time range to one that's independent of the dashboard time range. The **Time shift** setting is useful for moving the panel's time range back some offset from the current time. Using both has the effect of altering the width of the window of time displayed and/or moving the endpoint of that window back in time relative to now.

To specify the time interval for **Min Interval**, **Relative time**, and **Time shift**, use the following time abbreviations:

Abbreviations	Time interval
y	Year
M	Month
w	Week
d	Day
h	Hour
m	Minute
s	Second
ms	Millisecond

Query inspector

The **Query inspector** button will open a text console revealing the contents of the query Grafana is submitting to the API. This is a very informative feature for a couple of reasons. If you are having trouble getting the results you want, **Query inspector** can give you an insight into how you might be making an incorrect query to the data source. Additionally, by viewing the actual generated query, you can determine how you might go about making it more efficient. A more efficient query can substantially improve the responsiveness of a Grafana dashboard, especially when it contains several panels.

Query

The query is, of course, the central interface element for deriving a dataset. It can contain a number of elements, depending on the data source. In the case of the **TestData DB** data source, it is simply a **Scenario** dropdown for selecting a number of different options for generating test data.

The **Alias** text field is for giving the dataset a name of your choosing. The data source will designate a name for each query, but that name is often not very descriptive, so adding an **Alias** is a good way to document the contents of the query. In later chapters, we'll look at some tips on how to use the **Alias** name to annotate the legend and to create display overrides.

Query controls

Clicking the query arrows moves the query up or down and has the effect of changing the order of the datasets as they are displayed. This has a direct impact, should you choose to stack multiple datasets (the **Display** section). Duplicating the query creates a copy of the current query directly below it. This saves some time if you want to use the same query but display different aggregations or change a single field (column). Clicking on the query trash can icon deletes the query.

Add Query

Add Query adds a new query below the current one.

Duplicating an existing query

With this in mind, let's go back to our query. Since we got a query for free when we created the panel, let's create another one, just to see how it affects the display:

1. Select the **TestData DB** data source from the dropdown.
2. Click on the **Duplicate Query** icon. You should now see two queries, both with the **Random Walk** scenario:

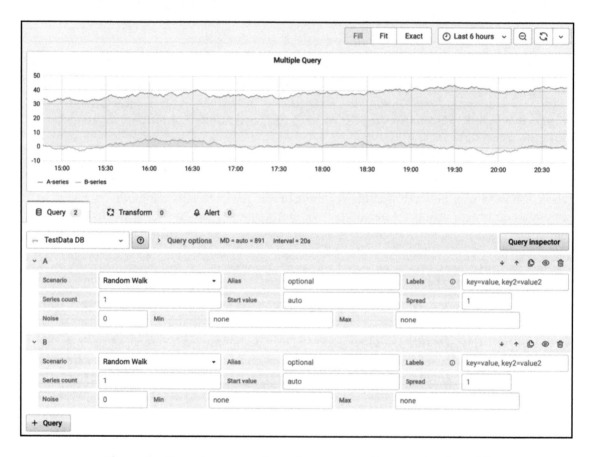

 If you don't see two separate series representing queries A and B, try setting the data source dropdown to the actual data source, **TestData DB**, rather than leaving it set to **default**.

Let's now move on to the **Panel** tab and see how we can use it to modify the look of our panel.

Editing the graph in the Panel tab

On the right-hand side of the graph display, you'll find the **Panel** tab, where you'll find a boatload of features for tailoring the look of your panel. The panel's myriad of options are available from one easily accessed column, with each one featuring a disclosure control so that you only need to see the options relevant to the task at hand.

The Settings section

Starting from the top of the **Panel** tab, the **Settings** section is used for general panel settings such as the title or description. As shown in the following screenshot, the **Settings** section contains three settings:

- **Panel title**: Sets the panel's title on the dashboard
- **Description**: Sets the content of the panel's information popup
- **Transparent:** Increases the panel's transparency:

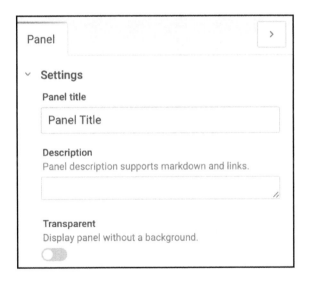

Setting the panel's **Title** is obviously a good practice if you want to make it clear what the panel represents. Titles support variable substitution, and in Chapter 8, *Working with Advanced Dashboard Features*, we will look at how to use variables to automatically set parts of the title. **Description** sets additional information about the panel. This can be displayed by hovering over the information icon (**i**) in the top-left corner of the panel. The **Description** setting supports markdown formatting for attractive text styling without the need for HTML editing.

Setting the panel title and description

Let's return to our panel and fill in these fields to give our panel a **Title** and **Description**. It's a good practice to set the title of your panels, as well as to provide a description, since it provides viewers with some context for the display:

1. Fill the **Title** text field with `My Awesome Panel` or some other text of your choice.
2. In the **Description** textbox, add the following text (or something similar with some markdown tags):

   ```
   ### My Awesome Panel
   This is where I'd like to make a description of my *awesome* panel.
   ```

Hover over the tiny **i** symbol in the top-left corner of the panel display to see your **Description** text in all its markdown-rendered HTML glory:

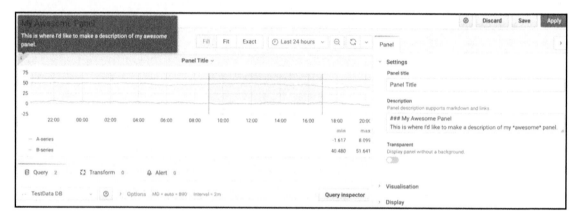

The Visualisation section

The **Visualisation** section serves as a quick mechanism for switching out the current panel for a different one. It has a **filter** field to help reduce the number of panels in the listing. Changing the panel will also alter the **Panel** tab and increase or decrease the number of options corresponding to the particular panel. The **Options** settings are cached so that they are not lost when switching between panels.

The Display section

The **Display** section is where you can make the most substantial changes to the appearance of the graph. Here, you can decide which combination of bars, points, or lines to activate when drawing the graph. It is here that you should take care when choosing the drawing objects that best represent your data. For instance, if your data represents a set of sampled quantities, you may not want to use lines that imply the data is continuous. Likewise, if the data doesn't represent a measurable quantity, a bar may not be appropriate.

Here's a look at the **Display** section:

Once you have determined what objects you want to represent your data, and depending on which objects you have enabled, additional options will reveal themselves. Most of the options in this group are fairly self-explanatory: **Area fill** determines the opacity of the fill color, along with a **Fill gradient** option, which gradually decreases the opacity. **Line width** sets the width of the lines. **Point Radius** sets the size of the points. Finally, the **Staircase** option forces the lines to be drawn in a perpendicular fashion, either horizontally or vertically.

The Hover tooltip

The **Hover tooltip** is designed to serve as a miniature legend that appears near any point that you hover over. The tooltip works in two modes: all series will draw the values of all dataset series on a single tooltip, while **Single** will only draw the value for the hover point. If you choose **All series** mode, **Sort order** will sort the series' point values in **Increasing** or **Decreasing** order; if **None** is selected, it will order them by how each data series is specified in the Query pane. If you choose to stack your series, you will also have a **Stack** value choice to display each point either as a **cumulative** value of the stacked points or each value as an individual one.

Stacking and Null value

Stacking displays multiple series, one on top of the other. Be mindful when stacking series where each series a) should use the same measurement units and b) be a portion of a larger whole. If you deviate from one of those rules, you may save some space by packing multiple series onto the same graph, but you may also create a misleading association between the series or otherwise confuse someone looking at your graphs. If you do choose to stack your series, you can make the part-to-whole relationship even more explicit by toggling the **Percent** setting on.

Setting **Null value** really depends on the specific nature of your data and how you want to display empty data points, called *nulls*. Setting it to **connected** effectively ignores nulls, so Grafana will interpolate the line graph between the points with values. Setting it to **null** will display the break in the graph where there is a null point, which may not be aesthetically pleasing, but may be necessary for making it clear if you have missing data. Finally, the **null as zero** setting treats null points as having a zero value, which will allow a cleaner graph but will still highlight the discontinuities. The proper choice is often a judgment call based on a balance between aesthetics and data visualization integrity.

The Series overrides section

Series overrides is a powerful tool for fine-grained control over some of the many settings Grafana typically provides by default, such as color, line or point size, stacking order, and so on, and is based on matching the name of the data series to a collection of settings overrides. We will cover **Series overrides** in `Chapter 5`, *Visualizing Data in the Graph Panel*.

The Axes section

Moving onto the **Axes** section, the graph panel will display up to two **Y-Axes** (the left- and right-hand sides of the graph), and the **X-axis**; you can turn each of the three axes on or off. Each axis is given its own settings grouping, as shown in the following screenshot:

Let's take a look at these now.

Left Y/Right Y

Since Grafana is data-agnostic, you can choose to display the **Y-axis** in almost any way you want. You can specify by **Unit**, set **Scale** as either **linear** or **logarithmic**, set the minimum (**Y-Min**) and maximum (**Y-Max**) values for Y, and set the number of **Decimals** in the axis values. You can also **Label** the axis.

X-axis

The **X**-axis can be set to display in three different modes: Time, which is a standard time-series axis; **Series**, which displays each data series as a bar graph based on the **Value** aggregation setting; and **Histogram**, which displays a histogram of all the Y values. The number of histogram buckets can be set manually with the **Buckets** option, and the **X-min** and **X-max** settings will truncate the left- or right-hand sides, respectively.

The Legend section

You've probably already seen the legend in action when you first set up the graph panel. The legend options are mostly designed to control the placement of the legend, or its contents. As shown in the following screenshot, it's covered by three groups:

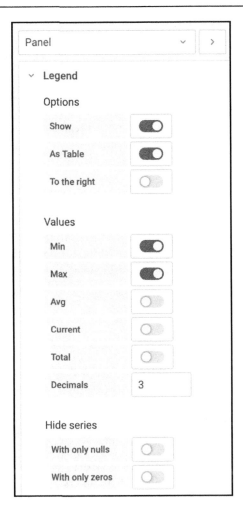

Let's take a look at these now.

Options

Options are used to control the overall placement and visibility of the legend. You can turn it on or off with **Show**. **As Table** arranges the entries in a tabular order, rather than linearly. It also has a nifty spreadsheet-like column sort feature when displaying **Values** (see the next subsection). **To the right** places the legend off to the right, rather than at the bottom of the graph. If you enable the right-hand side placement, a minimum width can also be guaranteed by setting **Width**.

Values

Normally, the legend is just used to map a color to a data series, but the **Values** group is great for displaying some simple series aggregation data. You can turn on **Min**, **Max**, **Avg** (Average), **Current**, and **Total**. Bear in mind that turning all of them on when the legend is on the right will dramatically reduce the display size for the graph itself. Set the maximum number of digits after the decimal with **Decimals**. If you don't see the values update, try toggling the visibility for one of them.

Hide series

If you need to conserve some space in the legend, especially if you have a lot of data series in your graph, you might be able to remove any series that contains no usable data. **With only nulls** will hide any series containing only nulls, while **With only zeros** does the same thing for series with only zeros. Note that this doesn't hide the series; it only hides the series entry in the legend.

The Thresholds section

While Grafana has an extensive alerting system, which we will look at shortly, perhaps you only want to see when your data crosses specific boundaries, but not necessarily get alerts. Perhaps you are preparing to establish alerts, but first need to determine what the typical boundary thresholds are. **Thresholds** graphically depict these boundaries as horizontal indicators set at specific values.

 Bear in mind that **Thresholds** and **Alerts** are mutually exclusive, that is, defining an **Alert** will disable **Thresholds**.

Specifying a threshold is easy: simply click the **+ Add Threshold** button. You will get an indicator on the graph that you can drag to set a threshold. Setting **value** in the field updates the indicator and vice versa. From there, you can set whether the threshold is crossed when the value is less than (**lt**) or greater than (**gt**) the threshold, the **Color** of the threshold area, whether to style the threshold area with a **Fill** and/or the indicator **Line**, and to which **Y-axis** the threshold applies.

Setting a threshold

Let's go ahead and set a threshold. This is also a good way to get familiar with the process of setting an alert:

1. **Select and add a threshold**: You'll now see a threshold entry. You can set multiple thresholds. The threshold can be set either by entering a value in the numerical value field or by dragging the threshold manipulator handle to the right of the graph display. **Note:** *The handle is only visible if there is no series when using the right-hand **Y**-axis.*

2. **Drag the indicator to a value somewhere around the halfway point on the graph**: Half the graph area will now be shaded. The region to be shaded indicates where the threshold lies. To set the threshold area above the line, set the threshold dropdown to **gt** (for *greater than*). To set the area so that it falls below the line, set the threshold dropdown to **lt** (for *less than*). For this exercise, leave the threshold set at **gt**.

3. **Set the color (or severity) of the threshold to warning**: The **Color** field is used to set the color of the threshold area. The color can be used as a visual cue to convey the severity of the threshold. We'll set the color to **warning**, which is an amber color (for caution).

Toggling the **Fill** setting to turn the region on and off while toggling the **Line** setting turns the threshold line on and off. The **Y-Axis** setting determines whether the threshold applies to the left or right Y-axis when the left and right Y-axes have independent ranges. You can delete the threshold by selecting the trash icon.

Your graph should look something like this:

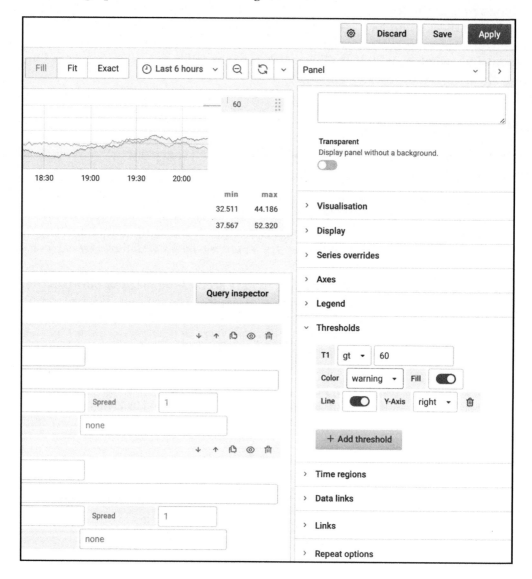

The Time Region section

Time regions are time periods during the day for one or more days of the week for which a corresponding threshold applies.

While similar to a threshold, specifying a time region is a little trickier in that you have to work in UTC time. Clicking on **+ Add Time Region** creates a new region. To specify the time, enter it in the text field, keeping in mind that all times need to be in UTC. You can also specify which day of the week begins the region and which ends it. **Color, Fill,** and **Line** work in the same fashion as they do in a threshold.

Setting a time region

Now, let's create a time region to go with our previously specified threshold (called *T1*). The time region narrows the time period for which a threshold is in effect:

1. Set the time range to **Last 24 Hours.**

2. Select **+ Add Time Region.**

    The 24-hour time range is to give you quick feedback as to whether you've correctly set the region. Unfortunately, there is no manipulator for setting time regions – you can only type in the start (**From**) and end (**To**) times.

3. Set the **From** time to `0900` local time, adjusted to UTC.

    Don't worry if you don't see the region yet. It takes both a **From** and **To** time to get a region. You'll need to convert 9:00 a.m. to UTC (*hh:mm* format) in order to determine the correct time for the field. We'll leave the **From** day dropdown set to **Any.** Normally, **Any** means the threshold is active every day at the **From** and **To** times, so the day setting can be used to extend the time region across multiple days (for example, a workweek of Monday to Friday).

4. Set the **To** time to `1700` local time, again adjusted to UTC.

    You'll need to convert 5:00 p.m. into UTC in order to determine the correct time for the field. We'll leave the **To** day set to **Any.**

5. Set **Color** to **Green** and enable **Line.**

This is roughly how the graph should look:

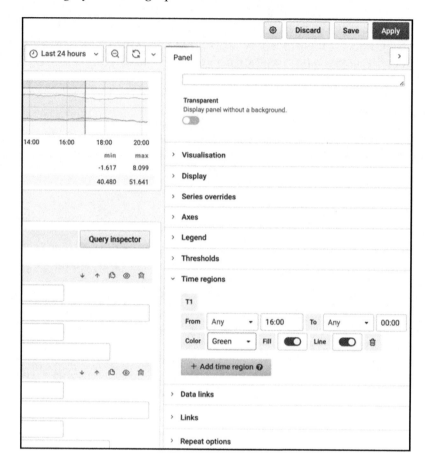

As we'll see later, the techniques for creating Alerts are very similar.

The Data links section

Data links connect graph data points to external resources. Data links can be as simple as a single static URL for a dynamic system that leverages template variables and links each data point in the graph with, for example, an external logging monitor. Metadata about each selected data point is available for constructing a specific URL corresponding to a log listing at the same time. To create a link from a point in this data series in another panel, use the **Data links** section.

Clicking **+ Add link** launches a dialog box with three settings:

- **Title**: Contains descriptive link text
- **URL**: Link to an external resource
- **Open in new tab**

Clicking on a graph data point will bring up a popup, which will display the data links below **Add annotation**. We will explore techniques for linking and annotating data and panels in Chapter 8, *Working with Advanced Dashboard Features*.

The Links section

If you would like to add links from the panel to other resources (other panels, dashboards, other websites, and so on), use the **Links** section.

Clicking **+ Add link** brings up a dialog box with three settings:

- **Title**: Contains the link text
- **URL**: Link to another resource
- **Open in new tab**

The link will appear at the bottom of the information (**i** icon) popup if the panel's **Description** contains text; otherwise, the corner will display a link icon and the link will appear when it's hovered over. This feature will be discussed in more detail in Chapter 8, *Working with Advanced Dashboard Features*.

The Repeat options section

The **Repeat options** section is used in combination with template variables to automatically generate additional panels. Select a template variable from the **Repeating** dropdown to select a parameter for creating the additional repeating panels.

We will look at template variables and how to use them to create panels in Chapter 8, *Working with Advanced Dashboard Features*.

Monitoring with the Alert tab

We have now come to the **Alert** tab, the last of the graph panel tabs. In this pane, you can configure the panel with an alert. While we are going to look at the Grafana alerting system in more detail in `Chapter 9`, *Grafana Alerting*, let's take a peek at the interface to get a feel for what it takes to create an alert (spoiler: not much!). Click on the **Create Alert** button to have a look inside an alert.

The following screenshot shows a newly created alert:

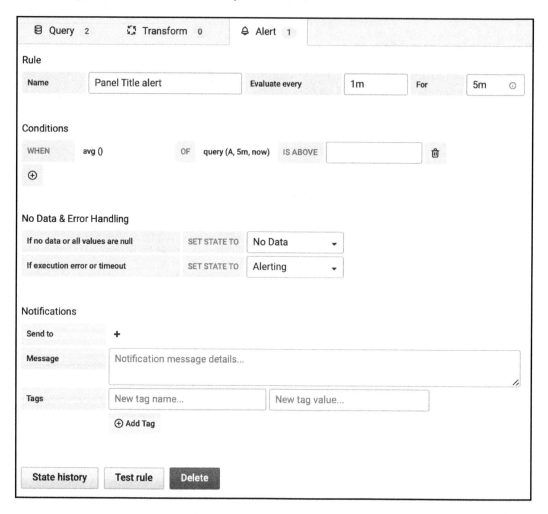

An alert is composed of four key components:

- **Rule**
- **Conditions**
- **No Data & Error Handling**
- **Notifications**

Let's take a look at them now.

Rule

An Alert rule can be broken down into two basic settings: the rule name and an evaluation period. The rule **Name** is used by Grafana to keep track of each rule so that it can continuously check each alert that's spread over every dashboard for a triggering event. As we found in the previous chapter, **Alerts** are managed in the **Alert Rules** tab, which can be found on the **Alerting** page. Once you have configured the Alerts, you'll find it much easier to manage them from this page, rather than clicking through many dashboards and panels.

Evaluate every is used to set the frequency at which Grafana should check for a threshold violation to trigger an Alert. Once the threshold has been crossed, the **For** field determines how long the threshold must be exceeded before actually triggering an Alert.

Conditions

Thresholds are set in the **Conditions** group. Simply put, the threshold condition is defined by an aggregation on a query that exceeds a certain value. If this sounds familiar, you will recall that it is similar to the definition of a threshold. Rather than simply triggering it on a single value, an aggregation is done over a time window, so an alert condition can represent a more qualitative measure than the simple quantitative measure of a threshold.

No Data & Error Handling

What happens if the query stops producing usable data or throws an error? That question is answered by the **No Data & Error Handling** settings. In this section, you'll be able to determine whether data loss or an error should trigger an alert or whether the system should wait it out. This is useful if you have a separate monitoring system for your data source servers that would otherwise trigger an alert, and you don't want to get two sets of alerts for essentially the same incident.

Notifications

Once the alert has been triggered, the **Notifications** group is where you determine what actions Grafana should take. Based on your configured notification channels, you can use **Send to** to send one or more channels the specified **Message**. Below the message are key/value pairs called **Tags**. Currently, those tags only feed Prometheus Alertmanager the additional information.

Try creating an Alert for yourself. You can use the **Test rule** button to check your rule conditions and see whether they fire. If you don't want to keep the Alert, go ahead and **Delete** it. We will cover Alerts in more detail in `Chapter 9`, *Grafana Alerting*.

Summary

That's it for the graph panel for now! I invite you to play around with the various settings, especially those in the **Visualization** panel. Here are some simple exercises for you to try out:

1. Create multiple data series in the **Query** tab. Try out the different **Scenarios** to see how they create different kinds of data. Rearrange the order to see what effect it has on the graph.
2. Play with different combinations of drawing objects in the **Display** section. Change the fill or size of points, lines, and bars.
3. Turn on the legend and test out its many options. Try clicking on various elements in the legend itself – you might find some surprises!

This chapter completes *Section 1: Getting Started With Grafana*. In this section, we installed the Grafana server, checked out the Grafana application interface, set up some simple dashboards, and graphed test data sources. In the next section, *Section 2: Real-World Grafana*, we'll start looking more deeply into these same features and learn how to use them in more realistic scenarios.

Real-World Grafana 2

The goal of this section is to present a more detailed look at working with Grafana by leveraging realistic example data.

The following chapters comprise this section:

Connecting Grafana to a Data Source

4

In previous chapters, we took a whirlwind tour of the Grafana UI. We looked at how graph panels query for datasets via data sources and how panels combine to form dashboard pages.

In this chapter, we will begin to apply our newly gained skills to more practical considerations. We will use real data, where possible, for analysis with a focus on solving real-world scenarios and create the kinds of comprehensive dashboards you would expect to see in a production environment.

Our first step in this journey begins (as always) with data. Here, we will configure a live database serving actual web service data (generated by Grafana itself!). We'll pull that data into Grafana as a data source, then we'll use the **Explore** tool to get a feel for what kinds of metrics are available. We'll also look at visualizing the data through a variety of queries. Finally, we'll learn how data is analyzed in the context of the aggregation.

The following topics will be covered in this chapter:

- Installing the Prometheus server
- Exploring Prometheus
- Querying the Prometheus data source
- Detecting trends with aggregations
- Data source limitations

Technical requirements

The tutorial code, dashboards, and other helpful files for this chapter can be found in the book's GitHub repository at https://github.com/PacktPublishing/Learn-Grafana-7.0/tree/master/Chapter04.

Installing the Prometheus server

Our first task is to get the Prometheus server up and running so that we can start serving real data. Prometheus is a powerful open source time-series database and monitoring system originally developed by SoundCloud. It followed Kubernetes to become the second Cloud Native Computing Foundation graduating incubation project. Grafana, having partnered with the Prometheus maintainers, includes the Prometheus data source as a first-class data source plugin.

 Tutorial code, dashboards, and other helpful files for this chapter can be found in this book's GitHub repository at `https://github.com/PacktPublishing/Learn-Grafana-7.0/tree/master/Chapter04`.

Installing Prometheus from Docker

We're going to start up Prometheus from Docker Compose and point it to a local configuration file. First, let's create the following configuration file and save it to our local `ch4/prometheus` **directory as** `prometheus.yml`:

```yaml
global:
  scrape_interval: 15s # By default, scrape targets every 15 seconds.

  # Attach these labels to any time series or alerts when communicating with
  # external systems (federation, remote storage, Alertmanager).
  external_labels:
  monitor: 'codelab-monitor'

# A scrape configuration containing exactly one endpoint to scrape:
# Here it's Prometheus itself.
scrape_configs:
  # The job name is added as a label `job=<job_name>` to any timeseries
scraped from this config.
  - job_name: 'prometheus'

  # Override the global default and scrape targets from this job every 5
seconds.
  scrape_interval: 5s

  static_configs:
  - targets: ['localhost:9090']
```

It is beyond the scope of this book to give fully detailed information on the Prometheus configuration file format. You can go to `https://prometheus.io/docs/prometheus/latest/configuration/configuration` to find out more. This is a relatively simple configuration file designed to do a couple of things. Now, follow these steps:

1. Establish a default scrape interval. This determines how often Prometheus will *scrape* or *pull* data from the metric's endpoint—in this case, every 15 seconds.

2. Set up the configuration for a job called `prometheus` that will scrape itself every 5 seconds. The target server is located at `localhost:9090`.

3. Next, create a `docker-compose.yml` file (this file can also be downloaded from this book's GitHub repository):

```
version: '3'
services:
  grafana:
    image: "grafana/grafana:${GRAF_TAG-latest}"
    ports:
      - "3000:3000"
    volumes:
      - "${PWD-.}/grafana:/var/lib/grafana"
  prometheus:
    image: "prom/prometheus:${PROM_TAG-latest}"
    ports:
      - "9090:9090"
    volumes:
      - "${PWD-.}/prometheus:/etc/prometheus"
```

The preceding Docker Compose file does the following:

- Starts up a Grafana container and exposes its default port at `3000`.
- Starts up a Prometheus container and exposes its default port at `9090`.
- Maps the `$PWD/prometheus` local directory to `/etc/prometheus` in the `prometheus` container. This is so that we can manage the Prometheus configuration file from outside the container. `$PWD` is a shell variable describing the working directory.

Start up both containers with the following command:

```
> docker-compose up -d
```

The `docker-compose` command will start up both containers in their own network so that both Grafana and Prometheus containers can contact each other. If you are successful, you should see something similar to the following output lines:

```
Starting ch4_prometheus_1 ... done
Starting ch4_grafana_1 ... done
```

To confirm Prometheus is running correctly, open a web browser page and enter `http://localhost:9090/targets`. You will see a screen as in the following screenshot:

Now that we have the Grafana and Prometheus servers running, let's move on to creating a Prometheus data source.

Configuring the Prometheus data source

From our `docker-compose.yml` file, we know that the Prometheus server host will be `localhost`, the port is `9090`, and our scrape interval is 5 seconds. So, let's configure a new Prometheus data source:

1. From the left sidebar, go to **Configuration | Data Sources**.
2. Add a new Prometheus data source and fill in the following information:

    - **Name**: `Prometheus`
    - **URL**: `http://localhost:9090`
    - **Access**: **Browser**

3. Click on **Save & Test**.

If everything worked correctly, you should now have a new data source, as in the following screenshot:

Now that we have a working data source, let's take a look at the data we're capturing in Prometheus.

Exploring Prometheus

Once we have the Prometheus data source properly configured, you might be wondering what kind of data we're likely to see. Turns out, since we configured Prometheus to scrape itself, we'll get a bunch of juicy internal server metrics delivered to the scraped endpoint and stored in the Prometheus database. So, let's dive in and get an idea of what's there.

Using Explore for investigation

Selecting **Explore** from the left-hand side menu activates the **Explore** tool. Basically, **Explore** includes special versions of both **Graph** and **Table** panel plugins, each looking at the same data source query. Make sure to select your Prometheus data source from the dropdown, then select a metric data series by selecting **up** from the **Metrics** menu. This is probably the simplest metric available: it shows 1 if the server is up and 0 otherwise. You can see, from the following screenshot, that (obviously) our Prometheus server is up and running:

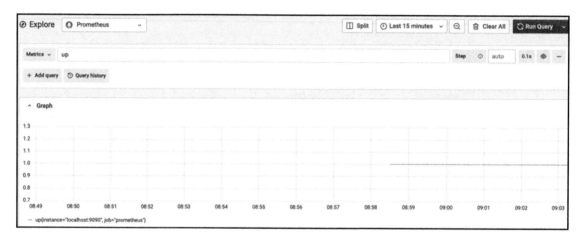

The graph shows a single series with a value of 1 and the table contains 1 in the **Value #A** field. You should also take note of the series label. In this case, it refers to the up metric, tagged with localhost:9090 for the **instance** value and prometheus for the **job** value. Going back to the configuration file, we can see where the **job** label comes from:

```
# The job name is added as a label `job=<job_name>` to any timeseries
scraped from this config.
  - job_name: 'prometheus'
```

But where does the metric itself come from, and how does Grafana know about all those metrics in the **Metrics** drop-down menu?

Every 5 seconds, Prometheus sends an HTTP request to a specific endpoint, http://localhost:9090/metrics. Go ahead, you can even open it in a browser. You should see a page filled with metrics data. Here are the first few lines:

```
# HELP go_gc_duration_seconds A summary of the GC invocation durations.
# TYPE go_gc_duration_seconds summary
go_gc_duration_seconds{quantile="0"} 7.057e-06
```

```
go_gc_duration_seconds{quantile="0.25"} 1.2362e-05
go_gc_duration_seconds{quantile="0.5"} 2.7312e-05
go_gc_duration_seconds{quantile="0.75"} 0.000259168
go_gc_duration_seconds{quantile="1"} 0.001861891
go_gc_duration_seconds_sum 0.006119489
go_gc_duration_seconds_count 36
# HELP go_goroutines Number of goroutines that currently exist.
# TYPE go_goroutines gauge
go_goroutines 39
# HELP go_info Information about the Go environment.
# TYPE go_info gauge
go_info{version="go1.13.1"} 1
...
```

As you can see, a lot of the metrics are simply a *metric name* and a *value* and are sometimes a duplicated metric name followed by a key-value pairing in braces called a **label**. In other applications, the label is called a **tag**, but it performs the same function, which is to attach a piece of metadata to the metric to distinguish between similar metrics.

This page of data is parsed, timestamped, and stored in the Prometheus database. When you launch the **Explore** tool in Grafana, the Prometheus data source plug makes a service discovery query to find out what metrics are available and based on the response, it builds a convenient menu for you.

Let's now take a look at how the go_gc_duration_seconds metric is depicted in **Explore**. Select **go** from the dropdown (**go**, in this case, refers to the initial portion of the metric name, called the metric's **namespace**). From the submenu, select gc_duration_seconds to see the metric graph:

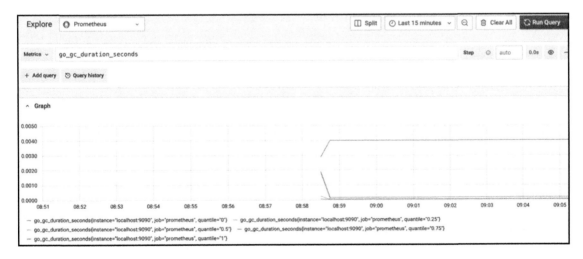

Now, we can see that each series name includes **quantile**, along with **instance** and **job**. Further down in the table, **quantile** is treated as a field, much like in a typical database or spreadsheet. This is great, but are we limited to Prometheus metrics? Not at all!

Configuring Grafana metrics

Now that we have a handle on some of the rich metrics available in Prometheus, can we get similar metrics in Grafana? Indeed, we can, but in order to do so with the Docker versions of both Prometheus and Grafana, we need to link them over the same network. That's why we brought them up as a dual container app in Docker Compose. All containers in a Docker Compose app share a single network, complete with a DNS entry, which happens to be the container name.

Let's go ahead and update the configuration with a new job that will scrape the Grafana server. Add additional lines to scrape_configs in the prometheus.yml file (also available as prometheus-grafana.yml from this book's GitHub repository):

```
scrape_configs:
  # The job name is added as a label `job=<job_name>` to any timeseries
scraped from this config.
  - job_name: 'prometheus'

    # Override the global default and scrape targets from this job every 5
seconds.
    scrape_interval: 5s

    static_configs:
      - targets: ['localhost:9090']
  - job_name: 'grafana'

    # Override the global default and scrape targets from this job every 5
seconds.
    scrape_interval: 5s

    static_configs:
      - targets: ['grafana:3000']
```

Sending an HUP signal to the Prometheus container process should force it to re-read the configuration file. Run the following command:

```
docker-compose kill -s HUP prometheus
```

Go back to the **Prometheus** page and check the targets at http://localhost:9090/targets to confirm that Grafana is now a target:

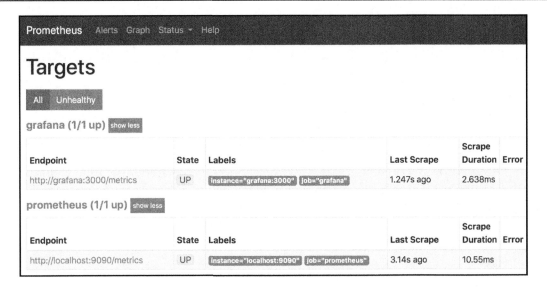

Let's go back to **Explore** and see what Grafana goodies Prometheus scraped for us.

Querying the Prometheus data source

Now that we have both Prometheus and Grafana logging metrics, let's try out some queries. I won't be able to give you a full rundown on every aspect of PromQL—the Prometheus query language—but I can help you to learn enough to be able to examine many of the server metrics that can be accessed from the Prometheus data source.

To get a better understanding of how queries work in time-series databases such as Prometheus, let's first start with a more traditional database, such as MySQL. Typically, the structure of a query looks something like this:

```
SELECT some fields
  FROM some table
  WHERE fields match some criteria
```

You get back from the query some rows, each one containing the contents of some fields. In the case of time-series databases, things work a little differently. The query has a form that is more like the following:

```
SELECT metric
  FROM some data store
  WHERE metric tags match some criteria
  AND in some time range
```

In the case of a time-series database, you get back some amount of data series, each containing metric data from the time range in question and matching any specified criteria. In general, you can think of a series as a collection of points, usually containing at least three types of information:

- A timestamp
- A metric value
- A set of key-value pairs for characterizing the data

The details differ from one time-series database to another. Some represent the value as a particular type that has a specific meaning to the database to optimize storage, searching, or aggregation. Others may store richer metadata. In any case, these three pieces of information are commonly found in some form or another across many of the current time-series databases.

Typing in a metrics query

Previously, we used **up** to determine whether Prometheus was running or not. Let's take a look at what it looks like when we run it now:

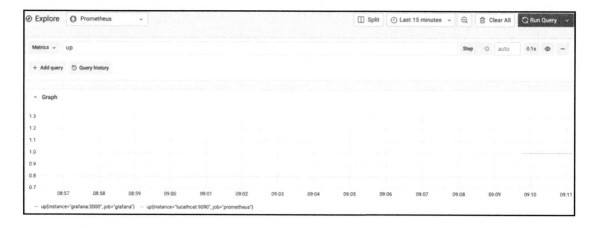

We can see that now there are two series, one of which appears to be for Grafana and the other for Prometheus. Let's go ahead and alter the query to only select the series for Grafana:

1. Type a { character into the **Metrics** text field. You will see the completed brace and a pop-up menu for selecting a label key. The data source plugin is smart enough to understand the syntax of PromQL and is helping to guide you toward making a valid query:

2. Since grafana is the name of the job we want (as seen in the data series legend), select **job** from the menu.
3. Hold down the *Shift* key. You should get a menu with the two possible options for the job. Pick **grafana** from the menu:

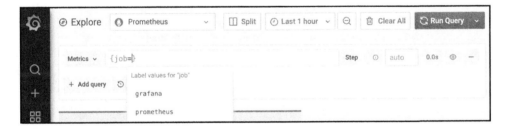

4. Click on the blue **Run Query** button or press the *Return* key (*Enter* on Windows) to execute the query.
5. You now have just the single data series corresponding to the Grafana **up** metric.

You can retrieve any of your past queries from **Query history**. Simply click on **Query history** and select a query from the **Query history** tab. Click on **Query history** again to close the tab.

There are dozens of metrics available in Grafana; let's try to query for a few more of them.

Querying for process metrics

Moving up the application stack, let's make a couple of queries to the Grafana process. First, let's query for the number of `go` routines. While it isn't as descriptive as the Linux `uptime` command, it is readily available and can give a rough indication of server load.

Before I show you the query, try to guess what it should be. You might need to refresh your memory by examining the metrics web endpoint at `http://localhost:3000/metrics`. Also, remember that we only want to see the metrics for Grafana, not both Grafana and Prometheus. Check out the `go` namespace in the **Metrics** menu, as in the following screenshot:

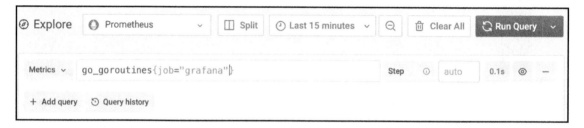

Let's also look at memory consumption, another indicator of how well the Grafana server process is performing. Running out of memory can seriously degrade performance, so you might need to build a panel with an alert for when the amount of free memory falls below a certain level. Again, try to determine what query would produce a data series for the memory consumed. Look at the `process` namespace in the **Metrics** menu:

If you guessed `process_resident_memory_bytes`, congratulations! Next up, we're going to look at how to transform our data series in new ways by incorporating the concept of aggregation into our queries.

Detecting trends with aggregations

As we continue up the stack, let's now take a look at some server performance metrics. How about an obvious web server metric? Enter `prometheus_http_requests_total` to get an idea of how many requests have been served so far:

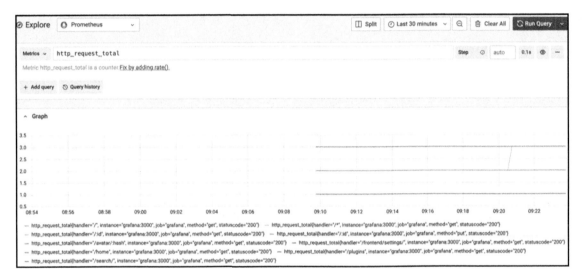

Well, this is a bit of a mess. You can't see all 22 of the time series—they're all stacked on top of each other and there's a vague warning about something monotonically increasing. As we saw in the previous section, it's no problem to apply filters—say, to filter out the GET method handlers—but then we'd still have a stack of nearly 20 individual series.

Applying aggregations to our query data

If only there were some way to combine all the individual data series into one. It turns out there is, and it's called an **aggregation**. We can actually tell Prometheus to apply an aggregation function (in this case, sum) after we specify what series we'd like to see.

While the actual query syntax differs from database application to database application, in the case of PromQL, you simply wrap parentheses around your existing query and add the word `sum` in front of it:

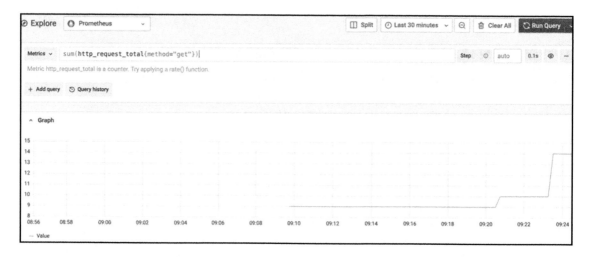

That's a rather clumsy way to describe it, however. In PromQL, `sum` is actually a function call that takes the metric query as an argument. The result of the query is passed to `sum()`, so on the Prometheus server, a new series is created by summing up the values of the data points in each series and is returned to the Grafana data source client. The power of PromQL as a query language is that you can chain these aggregations together and even combine them with the results of other queries.

But what about that *monotonically increasing* warning? First, let's clear up something that we glossed over earlier. Recall how we initially looked at the `go_goroutines` metric; you may have noticed a `TYPE` metadata string that preceded the metric on the endpoint page. You may have also noticed that the `go_goroutines` metric name was followed by the word `gauge`:

```
# HELP go_goroutines Number of goroutines that currently exist.
# TYPE go_goroutines gauge
go_goroutines 33
```

However, checking the same metadata for `http_request_total` reveals the word `counter`:

```
# HELP http_request_total http request counter
# TYPE http_request_total counter
...
```

While not every time-series database distinguishes between numerical metrics, Prometheus does, and it's important to appreciate the distinct difference between `gauge` and `counter`.

`gauge` is typically a point-in-time measurement that can fluctuate in either direction—for example, think of a thermometer reading. Gauges in software are often registered with the internal metrics system as a dump of the contents of a variable at the point that the metrics page was requested.

`counter`, on the other hand, is a cumulative measure that always increases, more like a rainfall gauge. Counters are registered in software as an increment to a running total value. Since the value is always incrementally increasing by a positive amount (monotonically), the data source plugin is warning us that unless we really care to know how much memory has been consumed to date, we might instead want to track the *rate* of increase instead.

Incidentally, Prometheus has two other metric types—`histogram` and `summary`.

So, why don't we check out the rate? Unfortunately, if you try to treat the rate as a function call that you can just drop the query into, you will run into issues because it contains an aggregation. We're going to discuss issues with aggregation in the next section. For now, we'll just select a single data series and run a rate:

1. Select **Metrics | http | http_request_total**.
2. In the table, click on the **handler** column cell containing `/search/`.
3. In the table, click on the **method** column cell containing `GET`.
4. Click on the **+** button to add an additional query.
5. In the table, also click on any **handler** column cell.
6. Type `irate(http_request_total{handler="/search/",method="get"}[5m])` into the second query.

This is what the graph should look like:

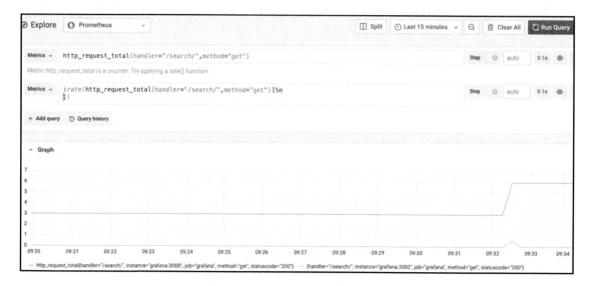

What we did was we asked Prometheus to calculate the rate that `http_request_total` changed over a 5-minute period. Since it changed very quickly, we used `irate` (**instant rate**) instead of `rate`, but they both work in similar ways. If you look very closely, you can see the rate increased momentarily as the request total increased.

This is just a taste of some of the aggregations and functions available in PromQL. Here's a list of some aggregations and functions derived from the Prometheus documentation:

- `sum`: Calculates the sum over dimensions
- `min`: Selects the minimum over dimensions
- `max`: Selects the maximum over dimensions
- `avg`: Calculates the average over dimensions
- `stddev`: Calculates the population standard deviation over dimensions
- `stdvar`: Calculates the population standard variance over dimensions
- `count`: Counts the number of elements in the vector
- `count_values`: Counts the number of elements with the same value
- `bottomk`: The smallest k elements by sample value
- `topk`: The largest k elements by sample value
- `quantile`: Calculates the φ quantile ($0 \leq \varphi \leq 1$) over dimensions

The list of functions is even longer, so be sure to consult the Prometheus documentation or the documentation for your particular data source.

Understanding the data source limitations

After seeing how powerful even relatively simple PromQL queries can be, it is tempting to think you can query and graph virtually any metric in your data source. Unfortunately, there are limitations to certain kinds of calculations, either imposed by the nature of the data or by the data source application.

It is important to remember that when you create a graph, you are entering into a trust relationship between you and your audience (which might even be you). When you place a pixel on a graph that isn't explicitly represented by a corresponding data point, you are asking your audience to accept that what you are doing is, in essence, reconstructing a signal from the underlying data.

Therefore, you have an obligation to respect the integrity of the data and not abuse that trust by manipulating the data to say things that aren't true or lead the viewer to draw erroneous conclusions.

Throughout this book, we'll come back to this theme because I believe it is necessary to not only describe the wonderful possibilities that this application provides, but also to warn you of its limitations. In this chapter, I'm going to highlight the judicious use of aggregation both in the time domain and the value domain.

Querying limits for series aggregations

The first thing to consider when querying for a new metric that we are considering for aggregation is whether or not the data can be aggregated at all. For example, examining the Grafana metrics endpoint page reveals an interesting metric:

```
# HELP go_gc_duration_seconds A summary of the GC invocation durations.
# TYPE go_gc_duration_seconds summary
go_gc_duration_seconds{quantile="0"} 9.174e-06
go_gc_duration_seconds{quantile="0.25"} 1.3627e-05
go_gc_duration_seconds{quantile="0.5"} 2.2022e-05
go_gc_duration_seconds{quantile="0.75"} 9.0476e-05
go_gc_duration_seconds{quantile="1"} 0.000340337
go_gc_duration_seconds_sum 0.001069315
go_gc_duration_seconds_count 13
```

The `go_gc_duration_seconds` metric is a Prometheus metric type called a **summary**. A summary is a built-in pre-aggregated metric that can be graphed directly. It contains a histogram with five quantiles (0%, 25%, 50%, 75%, and 100%), the sum, and the count. Typically, you cannot calculate some other aggregation of the quantiles because they only describe the distribution of the data at any point in time, so any attempt to aggregate them over time yields meaningless results.

 If you wish to determine the aggregated value of a particular quantile over time, Prometheus recommends you first do the aggregation, followed by the quantile calculation.

When you are looking at raw (unaggregated) data, you again must be aware of the limitations of the data source. For example, in the case of Prometheus, it is safe to calculate a `rate` aggregation on a counter metric because, by definition, it is monotonically increasing. However, you can also get away with aggregations on a gauge, but only if the aggregation is monotonically increasing. The rate calculation can be adjusted for resets (to `0`), but not negative (decreasing) values.

In general, you should consult the documentation for your data source if you find yourself attempting to compose multiple aggregations as there may be limits to what you can do.

Finally, and perhaps most obviously, you should try to understand what you're measuring and whether the aggregation is appropriate to the metric. You might justifiably want to work out the average over time of a gauge metric, such as `go_memstats_mcache_inuse_bytes`, but taking the sum over time is probably nonsensical.

Querying limits for time aggregations

As with the limits to series aggregations, you will need to exercise care in dealing with time aggregations. Unless you are combining multiple series into a single series, many of your aggregations will be calculated over an interval of time. Space does not permit a discussion on the nuances of how a data source such as Prometheus identifies certain data points within a time interval when making sophisticated aggregation calculations.

However, we can discuss some general concepts that hold when dealing with time-based aggregations. Primarily, the key to successfully working with time aggregation is to properly choose the size of the aggregation interval. Too big and your data could become too smooth as all the variations get averaged out; too small and missed sample points might generate anomalous values or even return an error.

Along those same lines is Grafana's display aggregation. There are only so many pixels on the screen, and if there are more points to display than pixels, Grafana will throw some of them away. Setting a fixed interval risks this issue occurring if the interval is quite small relative to the time frame—say, a 5-minute interval for a 6-month dataset. Throwing a lot of points away can impact performance, so it's important to avoid this where possible.

In order to keep things efficient, Grafana provides you with an automatically calculated time interval variable that you can insert in place of a fixed interval value. We'll be talking more about variables in later chapters, but for now, simply inserting $__interval in place of a time measurement is sufficient. For example, before, we had the following query:

```
irate(http_request_total{handler="/search/",method="get"}[5m])
```

The new query would look like this:

```
irate(http_request_total{handler="/search/",method="get"}[$__interval])
```

For more details on how Grafana manages its data display over varying time ranges, consult the Grafana documentation.

Summary

We've come to the end of our introduction to data sources and how to create queries for them. As a treat, go to **Configuration** | **Data sources** and edit your Prometheus data source configuration. You'll notice a second tab called **Dashboards**. Under that tab is a set of dashboards curated to work with a Prometheus data source.

If you import the **Grafana metrics** dashboard, you'll now have a full dashboard with a number of **Graph** and **Singlestat** panels. Some of the queries we tried out in this chapter were inspired by those dashboard panels. Open and edit them to get a look at the queries, see how they were constructed, and note the techniques that were used to extract information from the data series for use in the legend.

In fact, one of the best ways to learn a complex application such as Grafana is to simply crack open the dashboard panels from different sources and glean knowledge from the work of others. One of the more pleasant aspects of Grafana is that dashboards are not driven by a hidden API or some other trickery that makes it difficult, or even impossible, to replicate a panel. Rather, Grafana is an open application, so feel free to blatantly borrow from interesting examples you get from the community.

In the next chapter, we'll take some of the concepts we've picked up through playing around with **Explore** to do something a little more realistic. We're going to capture real weather data, store it in InfluxDB, and display it on **Graph** panels. Yes, we're going to make a little Grafana weather station!

5
Visualizing Data in the Graph Panel

In the previous chapter, we concentrated our efforts on understanding how a data source is primary to the Grafana visualization workflow. We launched a Prometheus Docker container along with a Grafana server, scraped data from both applications, and then configured a Grafana Data Source in order to connect to the Prometheus server. Finally, we used the **Explore** module to get a feel for how to make various queries to the data source and get immediate feedback in the graph display.

While **Explore** is a powerful mechanism for browsing a data source, it is somewhat limited in functionality compared to the graph panel. This is not surprising as it's mostly intended to support ad hoc, transient queries with more permanent graphs living on a dashboard. Those graphs have the advantage of providing a number of significant features that benefit presentation and alerting.

With that in mind, we're going to take what we've learned about working with data sources to the next step. We'll shift our emphasis from simply using Explore on a data source to actively crafting graph panel queries and styling the panel's display elements in order to serve our needs – to communicate a message via the visual presentation of our data. You will be taking the first steps toward learning how to acquire a dataset, storing it in a data source, and working through the challenges inherent in working with real-world data.

In our case, we're going to capture weather data from the National Weather Service and store it in an InfluxDB time series database. There is some Python scripting involved, but the code has been written to use the InfluxDB HTTP API, so there's nothing particularly esoteric to it. If you have any programming experience, this should be completely straightforward. The goal of this chapter isn't to burden you with a coding challenge, but to continue working with live data, which I hope you will find rewarding and fun.

Along the way, we'll tackle some obstacles – we'll need to write a little code to import our data and we're going to dive into the tricky concepts underlying displaying data at different time scales. By the end of this chapter, you will be able to build a nice little weather dashboard. Let's get started!

The following topics will be covered in this chapter:

- Making advanced queries
- Understanding the time series data display
- Setting vertical axes
- Working with legends

Technical requirements

Tutorial code, dashboards, and other helpful files for this chapter can be found in this book's GitHub repository at `https://github.com/PacktPublishing/Learn-Grafana-7.0/tree/master/Chapter05`.

Making advanced queries

Before we can start playing with our pretty data, we'll need to put together a simple data pipeline. Patience! This is likely to be one of the rare opportunities where you will have significant control of the data that goes into your data source. Even if you don't ever plan to involve yourself in data acquisition, it helps to know some of the techniques and issues surrounding it, if only to appreciate the work that often goes into tailoring and cleaning data so it can be analyzed or visualized.

Our plan of attack for this part of our tutorial is quite straightforward:

1. Spin up both an InfluxDB and a Grafana server.
2. Code review a simple **extraction, transformation, load** (ETL) script to gather weather data.
3. Execute the script to populate an InfluxDB database.
4. Configure an InfluxDB Data Source.

Let's get started!

Launching server Docker containers

The first step is to run a `docker-compose` script that will download the Grafana and InfluxDB containers and then launch them. The `docker-compose.yml` file is available in the `Chapter05` directory of the GitHub repository for this book.

If you haven't done so already, shut down any services you might have left running from the other chapters by executing the following command (first, change to the chapter folder where you started up the service):

```
% docker-compose down
```

Here's the short `docker-compose.yml` file:

```
version: "3"
services:
  grafana:
    image: "grafana/grafana:${GRAF_TAG-latest}"
    ports:
      - "3000:3000"
    volumes:
      - "${PWD-.}/grafana:/var/lib/grafana"

  influxdb:
    image: "influxdb:${INFL_TAG-latest}"
    ports:
      - "8086:8086"
    volumes:
      - "${PWD-.}/influxdb:/var/lib/influxdb"
```

As you can see, this is pretty simple. It does the following:

- References images for InfluxDB and Grafana.
- Opens up standard application ports for both services.
- Maps the current directory to a volume in the container to persistently store our data.
- The network connecting the pair of containers is controlled by Docker Compose so that each container can connect to the other container by using the service name.

Let's start up the containers:

```
% docker-compose up -d
Starting ch5_influxdb_1 ... done
Starting ch5_grafana_1  ... done
```

You should be able to reach the Grafana application at the usual URL of `http://localhost:3000`. We'll access InfluxDB either via our Python script or Grafana Data Source. You can confirm it is running by using a simple `curl` command:

```
% curl -i http://localhost:8086/ping
HTTP/1.1 204 No Content
Content-Type: application/json
Request-Id: da5fb265-06a1-11ea-800b-0242ac120002
X-Influxdb-Build: OSS
X-Influxdb-Version: 1.7.8
X-Request-Id: da5fb265-06a1-11ea-800b-0242ac120002
Date: Thu, 14 Nov 2019 05:44:41 GMT
```

Now that we have our applications running, let's start gathering some data.

Writing the ETL script

I selected the NWS weather observation data for a couple of reasons:

- Everybody intuitively understands the weather; rain or shine, we experience it on a daily basis.
- Most of the observational data is straightforward measurements that are typically referred to in a daily forecast, such as temperature, relative humidity, and wind speed.
- The NWS API is open and simple to understand, especially for our limited use case.

The Python script is available in this book's GitHub repository in `Chapter05/weather.py` if you want to follow along. If you want to make code changes (feel free!), you'll need to rebuild the container using the provided Dockerfile as well. The steps for this are as follows:

The first line of our `main()` function sets up the logging level:

```
def main():
    logging.basicConfig(level=logging.INFO)
```

Next, we parse the command-line options:

```
    args = process_cli()
```

The `process_cli()` function specifies the command-line options:

```
    group = parser.add_mutually_exclusive_group()
```

```
parser.add_argument('--host', dest='host', default='localhost',
                     help='database host')
parser.add_argument('--port', dest='port', type=int, default=8086,
                     help='database port')
parser.add_argument('--db', dest='database',
                     help="name of database to store data in")
parser.add_argument('--drop', dest='drop', action='store_true',
                     help='drop database')
group.add_argument('--input', dest='input_file',
type=argparse.FileType('r'),
                     help="input file")
group.add_argument('--output', dest='output_file',
type=argparse.FileType('w'),
                     help='output file')
parser.add_argument('--stations', dest='stations',
                     help="list of stations to gather weather data from")
```

Some of these command-line options are needed for connecting to a database such as our InfluxDB server, but some are specific to our little application, so let's go through them one by one:

- The `--host` option refers to the InfluxDB server, which is `localhost` by default.
- The `--port` option refers to the InfluxDB server port, which is exposed by Docker at `8086`.
- The `--db` option refers to the database in InfluxDB. As in more traditional RDBMSes, data is efficiently stored in one or more databases. For the purpose of this exercise, we'll only be working in a single database.
- The `--drop` option allows you to delete (drop) the specified database. This is useful if you start experimenting with adding a lot of data and want to reset your database to a clean state.
- The `--input` option defines a file for outputting the data we gather from the NWS.
- The `--output` option is for loading that file into our InfluxDB database. I could have combined the operation into a single one, but it's sometimes handy to see the data before loading it. Grouping the `--input` and `--output` options prevent them from being used at the same time.
- The `--stations` option is for specifying a comma-separated list of NWS weather stations. They're typically located in major airports and bear names resembling radio stations such as KSFO or KLGA.

After the niceties are out of the way, we can process our command-line options.

First up is the routine to drop the database, `drop_database`:

```
if args.drop:
    drop_database(db_host=args.host, db_port=args.port,
db_name=args.database)
```

The code for dropping a database is virtually identical to the code that creates one:

```
def drop_database(db_host, db_port, db_name):
    if not db_name:
        raise Exception('drop_database: no database specified')

    url = f"http://{db_host}:{db_port}/query"
    response = requests.post(url, params=dict(q=f"DROP DATABASE
{db_name}"))
    logging.info(response.url)
    if response.status_code != requests.codes.ok:
        raise Exception(f'drop_database:
{response.status_code}:{response.reason}')
```

In fact, the only significant change is the API call that drops the database:

1. First, check for an actual database name and error if not.
2. Build the URL for an InfluxDB API query.
3. Execute a DROP DATABASE API call.
4. If the returned status code isn't 200, raise an exception.

Let's continue in main():

```
if args.output_file:
    dump_wx_data(args.stations, args.output_file)
```

Here, we're going to handle the --output option. You'll want to run weather.py with this option first to download data from the NWS. Here's the code:

```
def dump_wx_data(stations, output):
    for s in stations.split(","):
        station_info = get_station_info(s)
    tags = [
        f'station={escape_string(station_info["station_id"])}',
        f'name={escape_string(",".join(station_info["station_name"]))}',
        f'cwa={escape_string(station_info["cwa"][0])}',
        f'county={escape_string(station_info["county"])}',
        f'state={escape_string(station_info["state"])}',
        f'tz={escape_string(station_info["timezone"][0])}'
    ]
```

The `dump_wx_data()` function takes two arguments: a `stations` list and the `output` file path. The function iterates on each station in the `stations` list. We call the `get_station_info()` function to get a dictionary of interesting data about the station. This information is compiled into a list of tags, represented as `key=value` pairs. `escape_string()` is just a utility function that places an escape character (\) ahead of certain characters required by InfluxDB to be escaped.

Let's have a look at `get_station_info()`:

```
def get_station_info(station):
    info = {}

    url = f"https://api.weather.gov/stations/{station}"
    response = requests.get(url)
    logging.info(response.url)
    if response.status_code != requests.codes.ok:
        raise Exception(f'get_station_info:
{response.status_code}:{response.reason}')

    station_properties = response.json()['properties']
    info['station_name'] = station_properties['name'].split(',')
    info['station_id'] = station_properties['stationIdentifier']
```

The first pass of the NWS API endpoint is done to gather information about the station itself, namely `name` and `stationIdentifier` (which should be the same as the station variable). As the station's name is a string containing the station city and station location separated by a comma, we split it into a list just in case we want to use only part of the name. We'll store the interesting information in the `info` dictionary.

The pattern for accessing the API is pretty straightforward:

1. Construct the URL.
2. Submit a GET or POST via the Python Requests library and save the response.
3. Examine the response status code; if it's not `ok`, raise an exception.
4. Finally, the response is decoded from the original JSON object into a Python object using the response object's `json()` method.

Next, we use the station's `county` field to get another API endpoint, which will allow us to get county information:

```
url = station_properties['county']
response = requests.get(url)
logging.info(response.url)
if response.status_code != requests.codes.ok:
    raise Exception(f'get_station_info:
```

```
{response.status_code}:{response.reason}')

county_properties = response.json()['properties']
info['county'] = county_properties['name']
info['state'] = county_properties['state']
info['cwa'] = county_properties['cwa']
info['timezone'] = county_properties['timeZone']
```

Use the `station_properties` county field as a new URL. Copy interesting county information into the `info` dictionary. The `cwa` field is useful if we want to access forecast information, which is delivered by **County Warning Area (CWA)**.

Now that we have a bunch of information about the station for our tags, let's get back to `dump_wx_data()`:

```
wx_data = get_station_obs(s)
```

Here's where we get the station's observations:

```
def get_station_obs(station):
    url = f"https://api.weather.gov/stations/{station}/observations"
    response = requests.get(url)
    logging.info(response.url)
    if response.status_code != requests.codes.no_content:
        raise Exception(f"get_station_obs:
{response.status_code}:{response.reason}")
    data = response.json()['features']
    return data
```

In this case, we'll just request the data from the endpoint and return most of the response data, namely the `features` field.

Now that we have all the observation data, let's extract the observations we're interested in, along with the timestamp for the observation itself:

```
for feature in wx_data:
    for measure, observation in feature['properties'].items():
        if not isinstance(observation, dict) or measure in ['elevation']:
            continue

        value = observation['value']
        if value is None:
            continue

        unit = observation['unitCode']

        timestamp = iso_to_timestamp(feature['properties']['timestamp'])
```

We have a couple of loops here – one that goes through a list of observations, and within that loop, another loop that picks out the actual observation data that we're interested in. The steps are as follows:

1. The observations are a list of dictionaries, so we'll skip over any dictionary fields that don't map to dictionaries, as well as the elevation field, which we're not interested in as a metric.
2. Grab the field name as our InfluxDB *measurement* name. InfluxDB treats measurements much like a traditional RDBMS table – a collection of metric data points.
3. The value is the actual metric we're storing for each data point. InfluxDB lets you store more than one metric per measurement data point, but we want the metric to carry an observation unit, and gathering all the metrics with the same unit would unnecessarily complicate the code, so we keep it simple – one metric per data point. Since each observation shares a timestamp, they'll line up nicely.
4. Convert `timestamp` from the ISO 8601 format string into a seconds-since-the-epoch InfluxDB timestamp.

We use the `dateutil` library to do the conversion for us. We do this with the `iso_to_timestamp` utility function, which wraps the `isoparse()` function:

```
def iso_to_timestamp(ts):
    return int(isoparse(ts).timestamp())
```

`Ioparse()` returns a Python `datetime` object, so we convert that using the `timestamp()` method.

Finally, we'll assemble the measurement, the comma-separated tags along with the `unit` tag, the metric, and the `timestamp` into a single data point and write it to a file:

```
data = f'{measure},{",".join(tags)},unit={unit} value={value}
{timestamp}\n'
output.write(data)
```

Finally, in `main()`, we handle the `--input` option in `load_wx_data()`:

```
if args.input_file:
    load_wx_data(db_host=args.host, db_port=args.port,
db_name=args.database, input_file=args.input_file)
```

`Load_wx_data()` performs two pretty simple tasks – it creates an InfluxDB database and then loads it with data from a file using an HTTP POST request. The code is as follows:

```
def load_wx_data(db_host, db_port, db_name, input_file):
    if not db_name:
        raise Exception(f'drop: no database specified')

    create_database(db_host=db_host, db_port=db_port, db_name=db_name)

    url = "http://{db_host}:{db_port}/write"
    data = input_file.read()
    response = requests.post(url, params=dict(db=db_name, precision="s"),
data=data)
    if response.status_code != requests.codes.no_content:
        raise Exception(f"input_wx_data:
{response.status_code}:{response.reason}")
```

As arguments, it takes the connection parameters for InfluxDB, the name of the database, and the input file:

1. Check for a database and exit if one isn't specified.
2. Create a database with the parameters. The code is virtually identical to `drop_database()` except for the API call. We can call this routine regardless of whether we have an existing database because InfluxDB won't complain if the database exists.
3. Send a POST request to write the input file to the database.
4. Check for success and fail fast so that you don't get a `204` status code.

And that's pretty much all there is to it. Now, let's go capture some data!

Running the script

Now that we've got a script ready, let's dump the data we gathered from a few stations. I've created a Dockerfile and a `requirements.txt` file so that you can build and run the script from a container. You won't need to concern yourself with downloading the appropriate Python libraries (there are only a couple anyway). In a directory that you've cloned from this book's GitHub repository, build the Docker image:

```
% docker build --pull --tag weather .
```

To see if you were successful, run the script with the `--help` option:

```
% docker run -it --rm --name weather weather --help

usage: weather.py [-h] [--host HOST] [--port PORT] [--db DATABASE] [--drop]
  [--input INPUT_FILE | --output OUTPUT_FILE] [--stations STATIONS]

read forecast data from NWS into Influxdb

optional arguments:
 -h, --help             show this help message and exit
 --host HOST            database host
 --port PORT            database port
 --db DATABASE          name of database to store data in
 --drop                 drop database
 --input INPUT_FILE     input file
 --output OUTPUT_FILE   output file
 --stations STATIONS    list of stations to gather weather data from
```

Now that we've confirmed the script works, let's download some data. We'll output our data in a file called `wx.txt` (but you can name it whatever you like). We'll pick the station for San Francisco, which happens to be at the airport called KSFO. We'll map the local directory as a volume in the container so that we can access the file the container script creates:

```
% docker run --rm -v "$(PWD):/usr/src/app" weather --output wx.txt --
stations KSFO

INFO:root:https://api.weather.gov/stations/KSFO
INFO:root:https://api.weather.gov/zones/county/CAC081
INFO:root:https://api.weather.gov/stations/KSFO/observations
```

To see if all went well, you can check the first few lines of data with the `head` command:

```
% head wx.txt
temperature,station=KSFO,name=San\ Francisco\,\ San\ Francisco\
International\ Airport,cwa=MTR,county=San\
Mateo,state=CA,tz=America/Los_Angeles,unit=unit:degC
value=15.600000000000023 1573797360
dewpoint,station=KSFO,name=San\ Francisco\,\ San\ Francisco\ International\
Airport,cwa=MTR,county=San\
Mateo,state=CA,tz=America/Los_Angeles,unit=unit:degC value=10 1573797360
windDirection,station=KSFO,name=San\ Francisco\,\ San\ Francisco\
International\ Airport,cwa=MTR,county=San\
Mateo,state=CA,tz=America/Los_Angeles,unit=unit:degree_(angle) value=200
1573797360
'''
```

Let's go ahead and load it into the InfluxDB `weatherdb` database with the `--input` option. We'll need to use *host* mode in the network in order to communicate with our InfluxDB server:

```
% docker run --rm --network host -v "$(PWD):/usr/src/app" weather --input
wx.txt --db weatherdb
```

Now, let's have a look at our data!

Configuring the InfluxDB data source

Open up your browser to the Grafana app and go to **Configuration** | **Data Sources**. Add a new data source and select **InfluxDB**. Fill out the following form fields:

- **HTTP** | **URL**: `http://localhost:8086`
- **HTTP** | **Access**: `browser`
- **InfluxDB Details** | **Database**: `weatherdb`

Your data source configuration should look like this:

Now that we have a data source, let's go to **Explore** to check out our data and confirm we can query it.

There's a good chance that when you go into **Explore**, you won't see any data. That's okay because we need to generate a query first. Many of the typical parameters in an InfluxDB query are already filled out, so it's just a matter of making a couple of menu selections.

Set the time range to **Last 24 hours**. This will give us a nice spread of data and should guarantee a time range that contains at least some data.

Let's work through the query details step by step, starting with the **FROM** clause.

If you are already familiar with SQL database queries, the **FROM** clause will seem similar. You can leave the first segment set to **default**. This refers to the *retention policy* for the database. Consult the InfluxDB documentation for more information about retention policies.

The next segment in our **FROM** clause is **measurement**. For this tutorial, we stored each observation type in its own measurement. This may not always be the case as you certainly can store multiple fields of data in a single measurement. Select a **measurement** from the dropdown. If you see a list of measurements, that is a good sign. It means our measurements were correctly stored in the database and **Explore** has helpfully queried the data source to acquire them. If you don't see any graph data, try clicking **Run Query** to force a refresh. For **measurement**, I picked **temperature**; my **Explore** display looks like this:

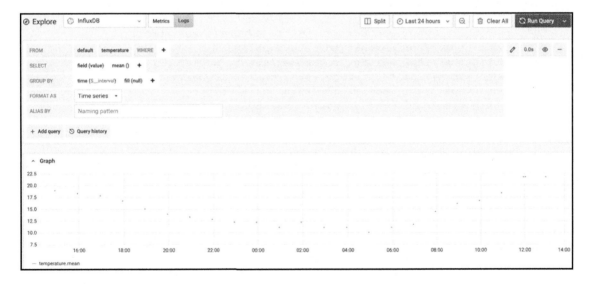

One thing that stands out is that the data is not captured at regular intervals. This isn't necessarily a bad thing, nor does it render the data unusable. Rather, it means we need to take some special care when we work with it – work that we might not ordinarily need to do if the data was more regular. That's a good thing since it forces us to grapple with some of the nuances regarding how to display time series data. In the meantime, since we have validated our pipeline, let's go big and gather some more data.

Let's delete our database so we can load it with fresh data. Ordinarily, this isn't required as InfluxDB treats a data point with the same measurement, tags, field keys, and timestamp as the same point and overwrites the field values, but we want each data series to cover the same time period, so we'll go ahead and delete the database:

```
% python weather.py --db weatherdb --drop
```

Next, we'll add a few more stations, namely Denver, CO (KDEN), St. Louis, MO (KSTL), and New York, NY (KJFK):

```
% docker run --rm --network host -v "$(PWD):/usr/src/app" weather --output
wx.txt --stations KSFO,KDEN,KSTL,KJFK

INFO:root:https://api.weather.gov/stations/KSFO
INFO:root:https://api.weather.gov/zones/county/CAC081
INFO:root:https://api.weather.gov/stations/KSFO/observations
INFO:root:https://api.weather.gov/stations/KDEN
INFO:root:https://api.weather.gov/zones/county/COC031
INFO:root:https://api.weather.gov/stations/KDEN/observations
INFO:root:https://api.weather.gov/stations/KSTL
INFO:root:https://api.weather.gov/zones/county/MOC189
INFO:root:https://api.weather.gov/stations/KSTL/observations
INFO:root:https://api.weather.gov/stations/KJFK
INFO:root:https://api.weather.gov/zones/county/NYC081
INFO:root:https://api.weather.gov/stations/KJFK/observations
```

Let's go ahead and load it into the InfluxDB weatherdb database with the --input option. We'll need to use host mode in the network in order to communicate with our InfluxDB server:

```
% docker run --rm --network host -v "$(PWD):/usr/src/app" weather --input
wx.txt --db weatherdb

INFO:root:http://localhost:8086/query?q=CREATE+DATABASE+weatherdb
...
```

Now, let's have a look at our data! You should now have four data series, covering almost 10 days of observations that include temperature, wind, and rainfall. In the next section, we'll be looking very closely at this data in order to gain an understanding of how Grafana draws data. We'll even try out different drawing styles in order to better highlight various aspects of the data display. Later, we'll work with the **Y axes** and the legend.

Understanding the time series data display

In this section, we are going to cover some important concepts surrounding time aggregation. In order to do that, we're going to craft a dashboard panel that illustrates those concepts. Along the way, we'll also be covering some of the more advanced drawing features of the graph panel.

The concepts are a bit technical, but understanding them is essential to mastering the depiction of time-based data in Grafana and other time series visualization tools:

1. Start out by creating a new dashboard and selecting **Add new panel**.
2. Set the time range to **Last 24 hours**.
3. In the **Query** tab, click on the **copy** (two pages) icon to make a copy of the current query.
4. Click the **visibility** (eye) icon for the **B** query to disable it. We'll set it in a moment.

We are going to modify the **A** query so that it singles in on a single data series – the one corresponding to the KSFO station. We're also going to remove all aggregation so that we can see the raw data points in the series. The steps are as follows:

1. Select the **temperature** measurement.
2. Select the plus sign (+) next to **WHERE**.
3. Select **station**.
4. Under **select tag value**, select **KSFO**. Note that the display shows points scattered irregularly across the time range.
5. Next to **GROUP BY**, select **time** and from the dropdown, select **Remove.** This removes **time GROUP BY** and the default **mean** aggregation.

Note that the points display has changed to lines, as shown in the following screenshot:

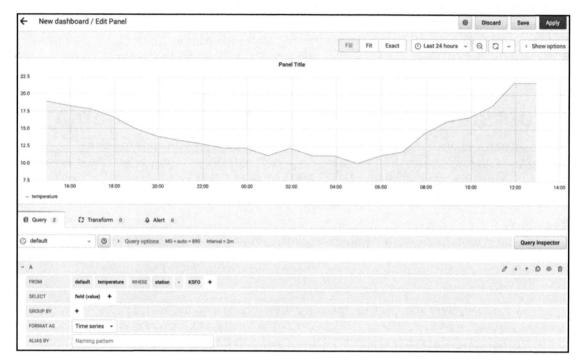

Why did the graph shift from scattered points to lines with a fill? We are going to delve into that now. Click on the visualization icon – you'll immediately note that **Draw Mode** for **Lines** does appear to be enabled. Whew, that's reassuring! You might be thinking something along the lines of, since the points display some sort of bug, if I want to also display lines, I just need to delete **time GROUP BY**. That would be fine, but what if you have thousands of points to display?

To give you a feel for that scenario, observe the following steps:

1. Click **Show options** to reveal the **Panel** tab.
2. In the **Display** section, enable **Points**.
3. Set **Area Fill** to **0** .
4. Zoom out the time range to **Last 90 days**.

Notice in the following screenshot how the points all bunch up on top of each other into blobs:

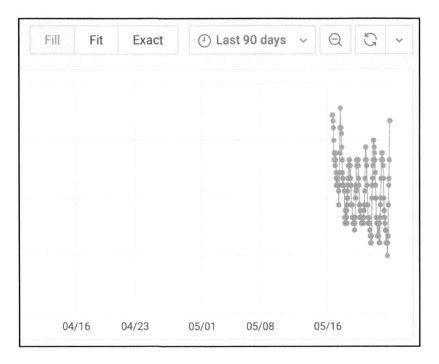

A little math would show that just tripling the number of points in the series would result in a similar problem at the 30-day range. Adding additional points would eventually cause the problem at the 1-week range, and on down to a few hours. The problem compounds when you shrink the width of the graph, such as when you pack multiple graphs in a single row of a dashboard.

It's always useful to go back to the dashboard display to examine how your graph looks in that context. It's too easy to tailor a graph in the wide-open spaces of Explore or edit mode, only to find out your beautiful graph is a mush of lines and points on the dashboard.

Displaying time-aggregated data

To solve that problem, you need to replace many of those points with a single point that represents the contribution of all of them. This is called a **time aggregation** and is used so that Grafana is always displaying a relatively constant number of points over ever-increasing time ranges.

To see how that might work, let's try to aggregate those points in time over a set interval. Looking at the space occupied by the graph, it seems like the points cover a few days, so maybe aggregating over a day is a good choice. Return to the **Queries** tab and perform the following steps:

1. Next to **GROUP BY**, select (or type the first few characters) **time ($_interval)**.
2. Change **$_interval** to **1d**.

Wait a minute! What happened to the data?

This is why we do things in a controlled scenario and not under the pressures of a production deadline. Understanding how things work will save you the nightmare of randomly clicking on various display options in the hope of getting the graph to work, but then making a potentially costly mistake.

Debugging queries with the Query Inspector

When you run into a situation like this, you do have some debugging tools at your disposal. Clicking the **Query Inspector** button opens a text box that shows the actual InfluxDB query and its results. Normally, it's just a big JSON blob of data points, but when you don't see any data, there's a good chance you've just confused InfluxDB with your query and it's complaining. Click **Refresh** to get the results of the query, as shown in the following screenshot:

Query Inspector shows you both the request and the response objects, and in this case, we want to know what came back from the query. Open all the disclosure triangles below the response to see what happened:

```
response: Object
    results:Array[1]
        0:Object
            statement_id:0
            error:"GROUP BY requires at least one aggregate function"
```

Basically, we asked InfluxDB to do a GROUP BY time, but we didn't tell it how to aggregate the grouped points into a single value. Let's go with mean. If you noticed that we're working our way toward the B query, good for you! That's pretty much what we're doing.

The **SELECT** section is where the points are selected for display. Right now, you've asked to display all the **value** field values, but we need to aggregate them. Click **+** and select (or type) **Aggregations | mean**. Yay – we got our data points back!

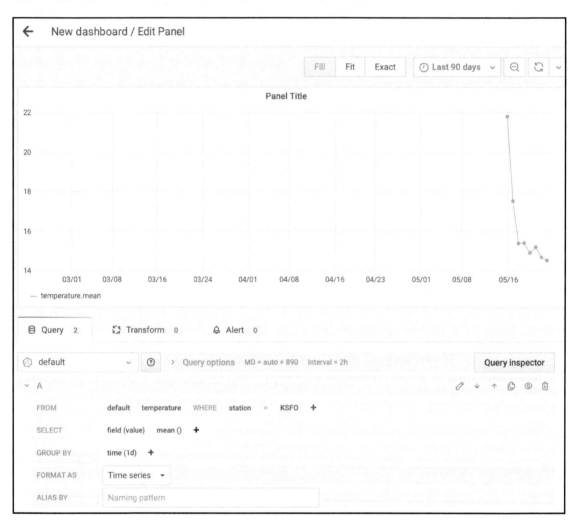

Now, zoom back into **Last 24 hours**. Yikes, what happened? Recall that we aggregated the data across a 1-day period. That means a single point now represents 24 hours, so the data is still there – the last 24 hours have just been replaced by that one point.

So, now, every time we substantially change the time range, we'll also need to adjust the interval in the time **GROUP BY**, right? Thankfully, no. Grafana can automatically calculate the time interval that covers at least the width of a single pixel, so we just need to use it in the **GROUP BY** interval. This variable is called **$_interval** and is what Grafana refers to as a *template variable*. Template variables provide a powerful means for us to add responsiveness to our graphs, and we'll be talking about them in more detail in later chapters. For now, let's just refer to the B query, which already has the time **GROUP BY** with **$interval** as the parameter.

Earlier, I said you can solve the problem of data point illegibility by simply using an aggregation with a **GROUP BY** time. Unfortunately, while that simplifies the data, technically, it represents a loss of fidelity to the original data and will have the effect of changing the appearance of data at different time range scales. This is not necessarily a bad thing, as long as you don't try to draw conclusions about the underlying data based solely on its aggregation. However, the change in appearance can be jarring if you don't know what causes it.

To give you an idea of this, let's modify the graph in order to highlight the effects of the aggregation:

1. In the **A** query, remove the **GROUP BY** time to return to the original points.
2. Enable the **B** query by clicking the eye icon.
3. Set the measurement for **B** to **temperature** and **station** to **KSFO** so that it matches query **A**.
4. Leave **SELECT** set to **mean**.
5. Set the time range to **Last 24 hours**.

The following screenshot shows what you will get as output:

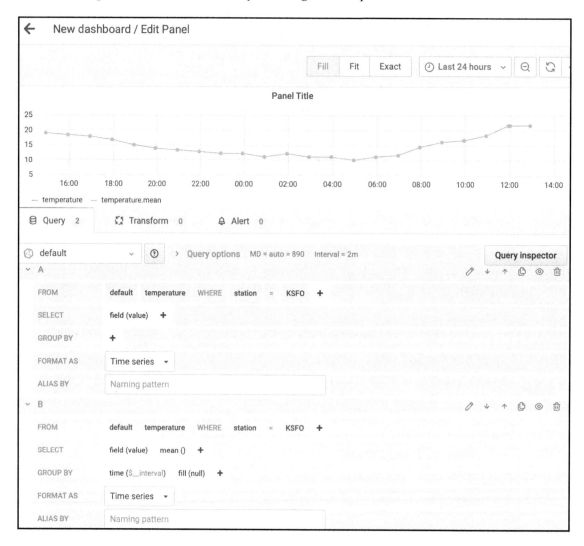

You should see a bunch of **A** query points in the same positions as the **B** query points. You can confirm this by hovering over the data point and noting that `temperature` and `temperature.mean` are identical. Now, we want to observe the changing value of **$_interval**, so while we could look at the request in the **Query Inspector**, there's an easier way of doing things: using the **ALIAS BY** field.

Observing time interval effects

ALIAS BY is the field used by Grafana to annotate the data series in the legend. If nothing is in the field, Grafana will default to constructing its own based upon the measurement and the aggregation. We're going override that with our own. Type the following into each **ALIAS BY** text field:

```
$measurement.$col
```

The legend now reads out the **measurement** value with the **SELECT** value. Now, check out the **interval** value in the **Query options** box. If you are at the 24-hour time range, at my panel width, **Interval** equals **2m**, or 2 minutes. Hovering over the points shows that they are identical. That makes sense when you examine the timestamps for the data points. Even the closest points are separated by more than 2 minutes, so each interval only contains one point to aggregate.

Despite the fact we can individually examine each data point, we'd really like to visually emphasize whether the mean value is centered over the raw data point. Go to the **Panel** tab's **Display** section and set the **Point Radius** to **3**. Now, the green points are larger, but the yellow point obscures the green point below it. Every change we make to the style of one data series is reflected in the others as well. This is a common problem, and Grafana has a clever solution – series overrides. A series override allows you to specify the drawing style of one or more by matching an override rule with the series alias value.

Let's create one for the mean temperature:

1. In the **Panel** tab, open the **Series overrides** section.
2. Click on **+ add series override**.
3. Fill the text box with `/temperature\.mean/`. This is just a **regular expression** (**regex**) that matches any alias value containing the `temperature.mean` string.
4. Click **+** , then **Points Radius | 1**.

Start progressively zooming out to **Last 90 days**. You should start to see the aggregated points start to drift further and further away from the raw data as more and more points (within the increasing interval width) contribute to the mean. Here's what they look like at 7 days:

By the time you reach 90 days, you should notice two things:

- The mean points are significantly different than the raw data around them.
- They tend to span a narrower range (sometimes referred to as **regressing to the mean**).

This is where analysts can experience a certain amount of anxiety as the graph begins to flatten out as they zoom out to wider and wider time ranges. To see how dramatic this can be, click on the temperature value label in the legend. Repeatedly clicking on the label will alternately hide and display the points corresponding to the aggregate mean points, thus giving you a better view of their relative values.

It is here that you will want to make some decisions about what kind of aggregation to display. Don't assume that mean is the only choice. If you want to emphasize the central tendency, use mean or median, while if you want to highlight an extreme, try min or max.

Setting the minimum interval

Going in the opposite direction, we need to explore a couple more aspects of the interval. Use the eye icon to hide the raw data query **A**. We're doing this as we want to see how the display is affected by the interval. You should note the points are connected by lines. Now, zoom into progressively narrower time ranges. At 7 days, you should suddenly see the lines disappear. Where did they go? Note that the **Interval** reading in **Query options** is now (in my panel size) **10m**:

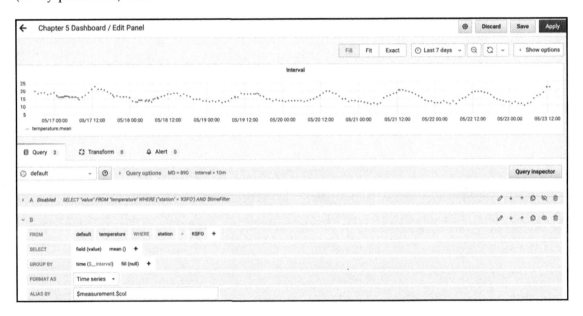

Grafana has calculated an interval that roughly covers a pixel (the smallest display element) and that interval is 10 minutes. So, in order to aggregate the values, it gathers up every data point within that range of time and calculates the mean. If there are no points in the interval, no mean is calculated and no point is displayed.

Now, when Grafana wants to connect the dots, it expects to find a pair of points that span an interval (per the definition of a line segment). Instead, **fill (null)** is setting the missing intervening points to null, which Grafana can't connect to data, so no line is generated. The points in our dataset are so sparse that as we keep narrowing our time, the interval gets smaller and the likelihood of finding any points that fall into the interval also gets smaller and smaller.

To make matters even worse, though you may not notice it, Grafana is working harder and harder for little gain. When you have a single data point in a 1-hour time range, the interval is 5 seconds, which means Grafana tries to calculate a mean $60 * 12 = 720$ times to only come up with one. To prove that is what is happening, drag a roughly 1-hour range around a single data point. Now, change the fill in the **B** query from **fill (null)** to **fill (0)**. You should now see hundreds of points (connected by lines) filling the graph from end to end:

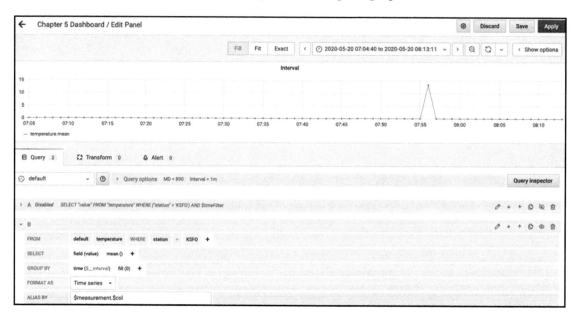

That is why we set a minimum interval to halt that calculation when it becomes pointless. Typically, if your data is regularly sampled, you'd set the minimum interval to your sample interval because you wouldn't have samples falling into a narrower interval. In the case of the NWS observation data, we don't have regular samples, so we'll rely on the precision of the data to guide us. We know the data doesn't appear to bear a timestamp with a second value, so we can infer the data is separated by no less than 1 minute. Open the **Query options** box and set **Min interval** to **1m**. You should immediately see that the number of points reduces substantially.

Now, we need to fix this because we're still generating needless points. We can tell InfluxDB that we need it to fill in missing interval points with no point at all. Set **GROUP BY** to **fill (none)**. Now, when Grafana ignores missing points, and as long as the time range contains two or more points, it knows to connect each one to the next available point, and voilà! – you have proper lines connecting your data. That's why you might have to zoom out to **Last 6 hours** or even further to start seeing lines because at that range, you are likely to see multiple points:

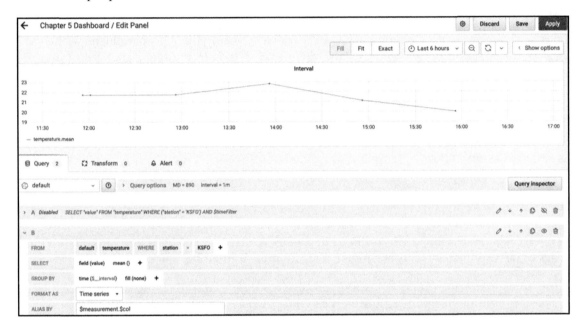

I hope this section clarifies things. It's a lot to grasp, but to a large extent, it's fundamental if you wish to successfully manage the inevitable constraints that arise when you're faced with less-than-perfect data.

Setting vertical axes

Now that we've broken down how data points are graphed horizontally in time, let's take a look at how they are graphed vertically on their **Y axes**. I'm sure whole chapters have been devoted to documenting all the ways the **Y axes** has been used and abused, from using a logarithmic scale instead of linear or vice versa to improper scale to truncation, but space doesn't permit going into all these issues.

Like any tool, we can abuse the flexibility of Grafana's **Y-axes** display. In this section, we're going to point out the opportunities for leveraging the **Y-axes** display to hopefully clarify or illuminate our data. We'll be creating a series of panels depicting various weather observations and then concentrating on different ways to adjust the Y axes, including scaling, units, and the use of multiple Y axes on a single graph.

Setting axis units

Let's start out by creating a new dashboard panel by clicking the **Add panel** icon at the top right of the dashboard, followed by **Add new panel** in the placeholder panel. Set up the query as follows:

- Time range: **Last 24 hours**
- **FROM** select measurement: **temperature**
- **GROUP BY** (use the plus icon (+) to add): **time ($_interval), tag (station), fill (none)**
- **Query options** minimum interval: **1m**

It is always good practice to assign your units as early as possible. If you don't, you could end up forgetting a crucial piece of information. For instance, failure to account for units properly has caused the loss of millions of dollars worth of space hardware. If you don't want to be responsible for losing the next Mars probe, remember the units!

How do we know the units for the temperature readings? Since they are in the low teens, it's easy to assume they are in Celsius. You could also assume the NWS uses SI units. A better approach would be to check the data tags as we deliberately included them for just such an occasion.

Click **Apply** to save the panel. Click on the title to activate the panel menu and select **Explore**. Confirm the following settings:

- Time range: **Last 3 hours**
- **FROM: default temperature**
- **SELECT: field (value) | mean ()**

- GROUP BY: **time ($_interval)** | **tag (unit)** | **fill (null)**
- **FORMAT AS**: **Table**

You should now have a spreadsheet-like table with unit and mean as the columns:

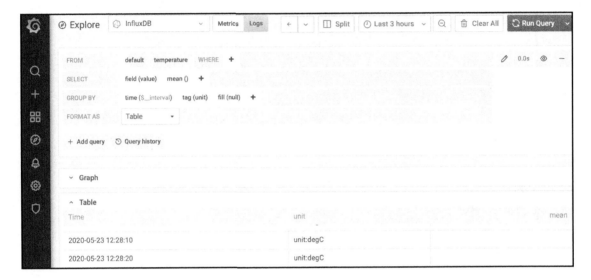

As you can see, the unit is degC or Celsius degrees. Let's go back to our graph panel and set the units:

1. Click the **Return to** panel (left arrow icon at the top) to return to the panel.
2. In the **Panel** tab, open the **Axes** section.
3. For the **Left Y** axis, set **Unit** | **Temperature** | **Celsius (°C).**

4. In the **Display** section, enable **Lines** and **Points** and set **Area Fill** to **0**. Your graph should look something like this:

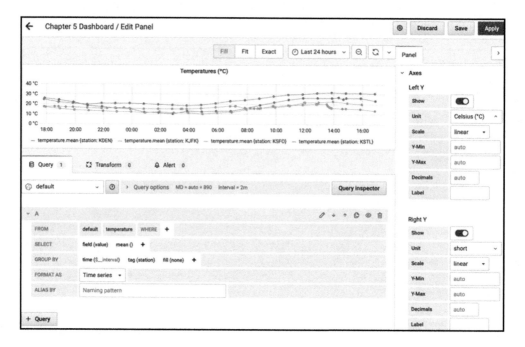

Converting into Fahrenheit

Now, suppose you live in the United States and you have to display the data in Fahrenheit. If you were momentarily tempted to just change the units to °F, I'll forgive you. Before you do that, though, you'll need to convert the data values. But before you open our weather script and start editing Python code, there is a simpler way – modify our query to do the conversion. Since the query is executed on the database server rather than in your browser, it will be quite performant. If you do need to convert all your temperature queries into Fahrenheit, you might need to consider modifying your script to do the conversion before importing instead.

In the **Queries** tab for **SELECT**, add a new operator called **Math | math**. This will append a math calculation to the aggregated value. Delete the text in the operator and type the following into the field:

```
* 9/5 + 32
```

You should see the numbers change to substantially larger values. We've converted the Celsius values into Fahrenheit. If you're curious, open **Query Inspector** to examine the actual query. Now, go back to the **Axes** section, select the **Left Y** axis, and set it to **Temperature | Fahrenheit (°F)** before you forget.

Autoscaling the Y axis

One of the things you may have noticed when you click on a single data series in the legend is that the Y axes scales automatically to accommodate the values for that series, then scales back when you display all the series. You may also have panels on your dashboard that have slightly different Y axes:

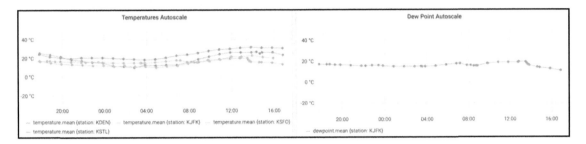

This is less than ideal for a couple of reasons:

- The scale becomes inconsistent from one data series to the next.
- It can be visually confusing if you choose to place different series in adjacent panels, each with its own scale.

Let's disable that functionality (called **autoscaling**) by anchoring our minimum and maximum Y values in the axis. Go to the **Axes** section and under **Left Y**, set the following:

- **Y-Min**: -30 (°F or °C)
- **Y-Max**: 150 (°F) or 50 (°C)

As with all such things, you should be cautious about your choice of min and max. Too wide a range and your data will get squashed into a single line. Too narrow, and Grafana will truncate the graph and leave some of your data running off the graph. You can either work empirically by determining the min and max of the data or use your best guess and start with something a bit too wide but narrow it later.

It is tempting to just scale each temperature graph with values that seem appropriate to that particular graph, but you risk confusing your viewers if one set of extreme temperatures appears to be clustered in the middle of the graph but more moderate values also appear to be clustered in the middle of the next one. Take the context into account. If there is no relevant comparison between your graphs or you only need to call attention to the values in the graph relative to other values inside the same graph, feel free to let the scale float.

Dual Y-axis display

Another common scenario is one in which you need to display data with different units in the same graph. Often, the point is to show how data is correlated or related by visualizing the linear relationship between one or more data series to the correlated one. The rise or fall of values seems to match the rise and fall (or vice versa, if there is a negative correlation) of other values. We are going to create two graphs that demonstrate this property: one for wind chill and another for relative humidity.

Graphing relative humidity

Create a new graph with the following queries:

- **A**: Measurement: **relativeHumidity**
- **A**: **WHERE | station = KSFO**
- **A**: **GROUP BY | time ($_interval) | fill (none)**
- **B**: Same as **A**, but measurement set to **temperature**
- **C**: Same as **A**, but measurement set to **dew point**

Clean up the display by opening the **Panel Display** section and setting the following:

- **Area Fill**: 0
- **Points**: **on**
- **Lines**: **on**

Now, you might (depending on the weather) see the relationship between dew point and temperature and the resulting relative humidity. It might not be that obvious because the temperature values range over 0-25, but the relative humidity value can be nearly 100. So, we're going to move the **Y axes** for relative humidity over to the right. It won't change the data; instead, it will rescale the data independent of how the left axis is scaled.

The easiest way to move a data series to the other axis is to click on the series line in the legend for `relativeHumidity.mean`. That should trigger a pop-up. The right tab is the **Y-axis** tab, so click on it and enable **Use right y-axis**. The relative humidity series should immediately rescale, as well as the temperature and dew point series. Set **Left Y Unit** to **Temperature | Celsius (°C)** and **Right Y Unit** to **Misc | Percentage (0-100)**:

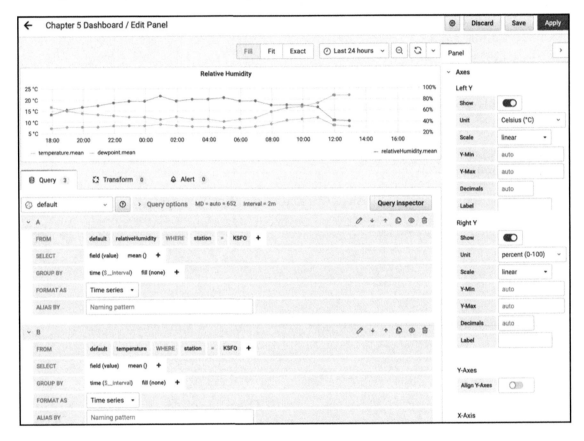

Now, you should observe that since the temperature and dew point are close to the same values, the relative humidity moves closer to 100%. Science!

Graphing wind chill

The exercise for wind chill is similar. We'll create three queries:

- **A**: Measurement: **windChill**
- **A**: WHERE | station = KDEN

- **A**: GROUP BY | time ($_interval) | fill (none)
- **B**: Same as **A**, but measurement set to **temperature**
- **C**: Same as **A**, but measurement set to **windSpeed**

Open the **Panel Display** section and set the following:

- **Area Fill**: 0
- **Points**: on
- **Lines**: on

In this case, the derived value, **windChill**, is the same unit as temperature, so we'll move **windSpeed** over to the right Y-axis:

1. Click on the **windSpeed** legend line and use its right axis.
2. Set **Left Y Unit** to **Celsius (°C)** and **Right Y Unit** to **Velocity | meter/second (m/s)**.

The following screenshot is what you will get as output:

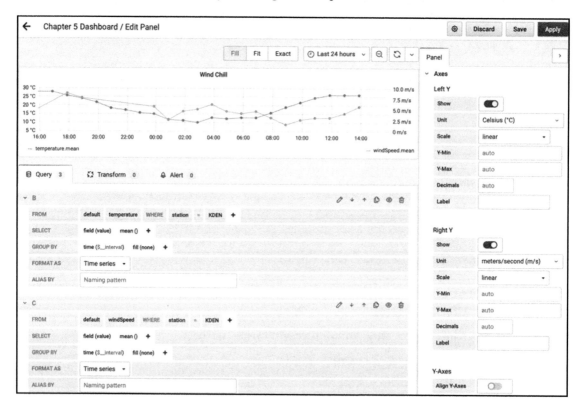

How I determined the units is left as an exercise for you.
Hint: m_s-1 should be read as meter-seconds^{-1} or meters/second.

With this feature, you can pack a lot more information onto a single graph panel. Bear in mind that the two axes will be scaled to fit the panel unless you explicitly set Y minimums and maximums, and it is natural to assume associations between the two sets of data. In the case of wind chill and relative humidity, we want to associate the values because they are physically correlated. That may not always be the case, though.

Working with legends

In the previous sections, we spent some time learning how to manage the horizontal and vertical display of our graph data. Now, we'll look at a key piece of graph display that is often overlooked: the legend. On many graphs, the legend seems like an afterthought, often floating in some non-specific whitespace where there's a convenient lack of data.

Grafana is somewhat more definitive about the legend. It lives below the graph (or to its right) and can take on a flow or a table format; that's it. However, as we've seen, the label content of the graph can be set by the **ALIAS BY** field, and that field can be matched to the series overrides. It's that functionality that we can leverage by using the legend interface.

Setting legend contents

Let's start with another graph, again for temperature. Use the following query settings:

- FROM: **temperature**
- SELECT: **field (value) mean ()**
- GROUP BY: **time ($_interval) tag (name)**
- Query options Min time interval: **1m**

Open the **Display** section and set the following:

- **Area Fill: 0**
- **Points: on**
- **Lines: on**
- **Left X Unit: Celsius (°C)**

So, now, we have a nice graph of temperatures from four different stations, but we can't really read the legend as it's down at the bottom of the graph. Let's move it and format it. Open the **Legend** section and enable **As Table** and **To the right**.

The legend now looks better, but it's taking up a lot of space. Let's go ahead and remove some of the redundancy:

1. Go to the **Panel Settings** section and enter `Mean Temperature` in the **Title** field.
2. Go to the **Queries** tab and set **ALIAS BY** to `$tag_name`.

Now, the title carries the description of the metrics and the legend just displays the station where the data was observed:

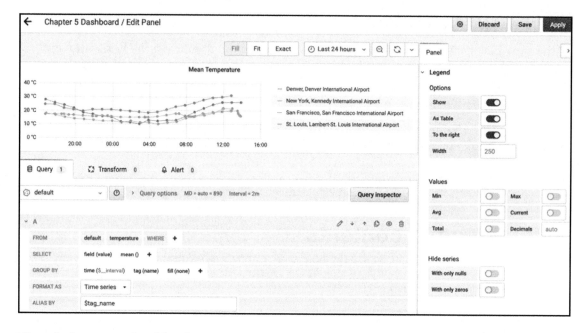

Nonetheless, you should only consider using this legend arrangement when you have the screen real estate to stretch out your graph and the legend, or the legend labels are relatively small.

Enabling legend aggregations

You've probably seen TV weather forecasters note high and low temperatures as they run down a summary of the day's weather. We can produce similar information with the graph legend. In the **Legend** section, set the following values:

- **Values**: **Min**
- **Values**: **Max**
- **Values**: **Current**

Next, we want the temperature time range to span today, which is the time from midnight to now:

1. Open the **Time range** menu dropdown.
2. On the **Absolute time range** side, click inside the **From** text box.
3. Click on today's date on the calendar widget to set the start time.
4. Enter `now` in the **To** field to set the end time.

Here's what doing this looks like:

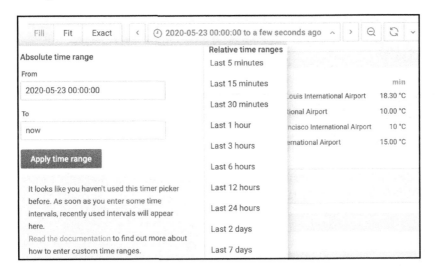

This sets the time range from midnight to now, the time period during which the high and low temperatures are determined for a given day. Alternatively, you can select **Today so far** from the **Other time ranges** list. Now, you have a little weather station!

If you want to sort the values based on a column value, simply click on the column header. Multiple clicks change the sort order and return it to the primary sort order (determined by the results of the query):

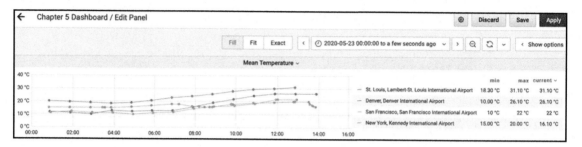

Of course, if you go back to the dashboard, you'll see how much real estate a legend takes up, especially if there are two dashboards on each row. You'll want to carefully consider whether to set a table legend on the right. If so, you might want to significantly expand the width of the panel. As an alternative, you could leave the legend formatted as a table and disable **To the right**. Now, you can leave the panel width the same and drag the panel's height down until it is tall enough to display the full table.

Summary

We've covered a lot of ground in this chapter. We wrote a simple Python ETL script to scrape data from a web-based API and import that dataset into InfluxDB. We learned key concepts behind time and field value aggregations. Then, we tried out different drawing styles and learned how to instruct Grafana on how to connect the dots when there is missing data.

We also set axis units, converted our data from one unit of measure into another, and displayed multiple series with different units on the same graph. Finally, we worked with the legend display to make it more space-efficient and aesthetically pleasing.

In the next chapter, we'll be diversifying our display panels so that they include panels that are more specialized in functionality. While these panels are somewhat more limited, they still complement the graph panel by characterizing data in truly unique ways.

Visualization Panels in Grafana

6

In the previous chapter, we took a comprehensive look at the **Graph** panel and explored a number of its powerful features. In this chapter, we're going to (mostly) set aside the **Graph** panel in favor of some of Grafana's other visualization tools.

While the **Graph** panel is indeed powerful and versatile, it isn't the only way to display data in Grafana. Sometimes, you need a different way to present your data, and other times you just want to break up the monotony of look at a grid of graphs. For these reasons, Grafana provides panels that depict data in a number of ways, and we'll examine each of them in this chapter.

First, we'll look at panels that condense data, such as the **Stat** panel and the **Gauge** and **Bar Gauge** panels. Next, we'll display geographically distributed data with the **Worldmap** panel and finally, we'll look at depicting our datasets in spreadsheet form with the **Table** panel. Initially, we'll continue with the weather data we learned to collect in Chapter 5, *Visualizing Data in the Graph Panel*, but later, we'll add another data source containing earthquake catalog data from the **United States Geological Survey (USGS)**.

The following topics will be covered in this chapter:

- Introducing the **Stat** panel
- Working with the **Gauge** panels
- Geolocating data on the **Worldmap** panel
- Structuring data fields in the **Table** panel

Technical requirements

Tutorial code, dashboards, and other helpful files for this chapter can be found in this book's GitHub repository at https://github.com/PacktPublishing/Learn-Grafana-7.0/tree/master/Chapter06.

Introducing the Stat panel

After the **Graph** panel, the **Stat** panel may well be the next most used panel for a number of reasons:

- It makes it extremely easy to see the value at a distance.
- It boils down a large dataset into a single value.
- It can feature several visually important cues.

Before we create any panels, **Stat** or otherwise, we need to get some data to display. We'll continue to use our US **National Weather Service** (**NWS**) weather data, especially as we're getting more familiar with the structure of the data.

Loading the dataset

The steps to load the dataset are as follows:

1. In order to choreograph our services, we'll be using the same `docker-compose.yml` file as we did in `Chapter 4`, *Connecting Grafana to a Data Source*:

```
version: "3"

services:
  grafana:
    image: "grafana/grafana:latest"
    ports:
      - "3000:3000"
    environment:
      GF_INSTALL_PLUGINS: grafana-worldmap-panel
    volumes:
      - "${PWD-.}/grafana:/var/lib/grafana"

  influxdb:
    image: "influxdb:latest"
    ports:
      - "8086:8086"
    volumes:
      - "${PWD-.}/influxdb:/var/lib/influxdb"
```

2. Next, we'll launch both Grafana and InfluxDB with Docker Compose:

```
$ docker-compose up -d
Creating network "ch6_default" with the default driver Creating
ch6_influxdb_1 ... done
Creating ch6_grafana_1 ... done
```

3. Build the Python container to run our scripts:

```
$ docker build --pull --tag python/ch6
```

4. Next, we'll reuse our `weather.py` script from `Chapter 5`, *Visualizing Data in the Graph Panel*, to load up the InfluxDB database with a current NWS dataset. First, we output the extracted data to a temporary file:

```
$ docker run --rm --network=host -v "$(PWD):/usr/src/app" \
        --name python python/Chapter06 bin/weather.py \
        --output data/wx.txt \
        --stations KSFO,KDEN,KSTL,KJFK
INFO:root:https://api.weather.gov/stations/KSFO
INFO:root:https://api.weather.gov/zones/county/CAC081
INFO:root:https://api.weather.gov/stations/KSFO/observations
INFO:root:https://api.weather.gov/stations/KDEN
INFO:root:https://api.weather.gov/zones/county/COC031
INFO:root:https://api.weather.gov/stations/KDEN/observations
INFO:root:https://api.weather.gov/stations/KSTL
INFO:root:https://api.weather.gov/zones/county/MOC189
INFO:root:https://api.weather.gov/stations/KSTL/observations
INFO:root:https://api.weather.gov/stations/KJFK
INFO:root:https://api.weather.gov/zones/county/NYC081
INFO:root:https://api.weather.gov/stations/KJFK/observations
```

5. Then, we send the data in the temporary file to our InfluxDB server:

```
$ docker run --rm --network=host -v "$(PWD):/usr/src/app" \
  --name python python/Chapter06 bin/weather.py \
  --input data/wx.txt \
  --db weatherdb
INFO:root:http://localhost:8086/query?q=CREATE+DATABASE+weatherdb
```

For this example, we'll be working with data from a specific station—the one at San Francisco International Airport or KSFO.

 There's nothing particularly special about the datasets I'm using in these examples. Feel free to add to or change the list to include your local stations or ones located at other places of interest.

6. Once we have our data, we add an InfluxDB data source (if Grafana doesn't already have one):

- **Name**: InfluxDB Weather
- **URL**: http://localhost:8086
- **Access: Browser**
- **Database**: weatherdb

Creating a Stat panel

The steps to create a **Stat** panel are as follows:

1. From a new or existing dashboard, create a new panel with the following query:

- **FROM: default temperature**
- **WHERE: station = KSFO**
- **SELECT: field (value)**
- **GROUP BY**: Leave empty
- **FORMAT AS: Time series**

Here's a look at our query. Note the deletion of all the aggregations in **GROUP BY**:

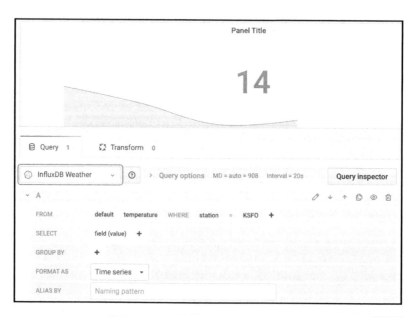

2. Now, go to the **Panel** tab and from the options in the **Visualization** section, select **Stat**. Next, let's format the panel to show the current temperature.

3. In the **Display** section, set **Value**: **Last**

Let's see what the **Panel** tab settings looks like so far:

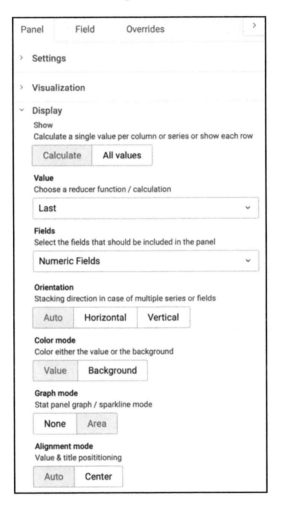

4. On the **Field** tab, we'll set the **Unit** value and the number of **Decimals**:
   - **Unit**: **Temperature | Celsius (°C)**
   - **Decimals**: 1

5. We want to delete any existing thresholds for now. Now, let's see what the **Field** tab settings should look like:

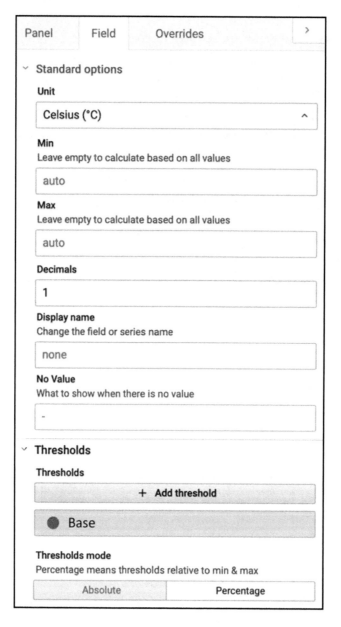

When you return to the dashboard, your panel should look something like this:

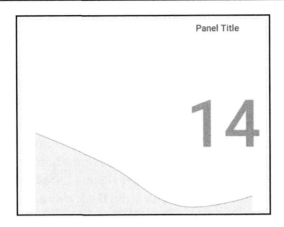

To get a better idea of how the value of the **Stat** panel relates to your data, I recommend you duplicate the panel and convert the copy into a **Graph** panel. To duplicate it, click on the drop-down menu on the panel title and select **More...** | **Duplicate**. Select **Graph** from the **Visualization** section to change the panel into a **Graph** panel. Now, when you configure the **Stat** panel, you can compare the value you see with the corresponding value in the **Graph** panel, so long as the two panels have the same query.

Here is where we come across a realization—the value of the **Stat** panel is the data aggregation. It represents the distillation of an entire data series into a single value. Previously, in our **Graph** panels, we were working with aggregations as well, but those only pertained to data groupings. In the case of **Stat**, we can certainly use an aggregation in our query, but how do we derive the stat's ultimate value?

We aggregate again in the panel itself, so the **Stat** value can be an aggregation of an aggregation. Now, as long as you don't try to create a meaningless **Stat** aggregation (such as a total of the temperatures), you should have no trouble with **Stat**; but just be careful.

Let's go through some of the settings for the **Stat** panel in order to get more familiar with them. Many of these settings will seem similar to the **Graph** panel, and indeed many of them are consistent across the panels. In fact, Grafana has unified the interface across all its panels now, so switching between the panel visualizations should be fairly seamless.

Along with the **Display** settings on the **Panel** tab, three settings on the **Field** tab for the Stat panel comprise four key settings groups:

- **Panel/Display**: Sets the display of the value and enables the sparkline
- **Field/Standard options**: Sets the unit, decimals, and min and max values
- **Field/Thresholds**: Sets the thresholds and associated colors
- **Field/Value Mapping**: Maps numerical values to text

Setting the Panel tab's display

Below the **Panel** tab **Setting** section lies the **Display** section, where the overall look of the panel can be set. The settings are described as follows:

- **Show**: Calculates either a single value or displays all the values of the query.
- **Value**: Sets the aggregation function to reduce values to a single one.
- **Limit**: Limits the number of rows displayed when **Show** is set to **All values**.
- **Orientation**: Sets the stacking orientation of multiple values to either **Vertical** or **Horizontal**, or auto-sets it based on the shape of the panel.
- **Color mode**: Sets thresholds to either the **Background** color or the **Value** and graph color.
- **Graph mode**: **None** hides and **Area** displays the sparkline graph at the bottom of the panel.
- **Alignment mode**: **Auto** sets the title and value text to span the sides of the panel and **Center** places both at the center.

If you select **All values** from the **Show** setting, you'll see a long list of each value derived from the query. You can then use the **Limit** setting to reduce the number of values displayed to something more manageable.

Setting the value aggregation

Unless your data series has only a handful of values, a long list of numbers crammed into a panel isn't going to be very useful. A better alternative is to aggregate the series into a single value. Setting **Show** to **Calculate** enables a **Value** setting where you can select from an extensive set of aggregations, which we have summarized as follows:

- **Last**: The latest value in the series
- **Last (not null)**: The current/last non-null value
- **First**: The initial value in the series
- **First (not null)**: The first non-null value
- **Min**: The minimum value
- **Max**: The maximum value
- **Mean**: The average of all the values
- **Total**: The sum of all the values
- **Range**: The difference between the minimum and maximum values
- **Delta**: Calculates the cumulative change in values

- **Step**: Calculates the minimum size between values; used with increasing counters
- **Difference**: The difference from the first to last values
- **Minimum (above zero)**: The minimum non-zero value, typically used in `log min` graphs
- **All Zeros**: Returns `true` or `false` if the data series contains all zero values
- **All Nulls**: Returns `true` or `false` if the data series contains all null values
- **Change Count**: Calculates the number of times the value changes
- **Distinct Count**: Calculates the number of distinct values

A visually impressive component of the **Stat** panel is set by the **Graph** mode. It turns on the **Area** graph, which we'll discuss next.

Setting Graph mode

Setting **Graph mode** to **Area** shows a sparkline area graph along the bottom of the panel. The **Min** and **Max** settings of **Standard options** determine the range of values plotted on the graph, which we'll cover in the next section. Setting **Color mode** to **Value** sets the graph color, as well as the value.

 The area graph is a true graph, so your query should produce a proper dataset with time and field aggregations and fill handling. Switch the **Visualization** mode to **Graph** to confirm your **Query** settings, or use **Query Inspector**.

We'll work with these settings a little later. Let's move on to the **Field** tab and look at the standard option settings.

Setting the Field tab's standard options

The standard options are a set of common standard settings to support the display of numerical data in a panel. You'll find these settings in a number of panels that can display both text and graphical elements, such as the **Stat** panel, the **Gauge** and **Bar Gauge** panels, and the **Table** panel. Here's the list of options for the **Stat** panel:

- **Unit**: Sets the unit displayed immediately after the **Show** value
- **Min**: Sets the lowest displayed value
- **Max**: Sets the highest displayed value
- **Decimals**: Sets the number of decimals in the **Show** value

- **Display name**: A text title displayed in the panel
- **No Value**: Placeholder text for when there is no value

Let's go into a little more depth about some of these settings, starting with the unit.

Setting units

The unit can be thought of as more than just the unit text to accompany the value. Indeed, if you click on the drop-down menu, you can set one of the impressive options of potential units. Another way to look at it is as a mechanism for setting some arbitrary prefix or postfix text alongside the value.

Suppose you need to display a relatively uncommon unit of measure, say kiloparsecs (3,261.56 light-years, in case you were wondering):

1. Type the abbreviation for kiloparsec, kpc, into the **Unit** field.
2. Click on the **Custom unit: kpc** dropdown text to enable the custom unit

Now, consider a situation where you have a currency abbreviation that is not in Grafana's list of currencies—say, the South African Rand (R):

1. Type in prefix:, followed by R for the unit.
2. Click on the **Custom unit: prefix: R** drop-down text to enable the custom unit.

Just below **Unit** are the **Min** and **Max** settings, which determine the values that fall into the **Area** graph.

Setting Min and Max

The **Min** and **Max** settings are intended to determine the extent of values displayed in the graph, enabled when the **Graph mode** setting under **Display** is set to **Area**. Typically, the **Stat** panel sparkline graph generated by the data series is scaled to fit into a fixed-size box within the panel itself. Since all the graph points must be scaled to fit inside the box, setting either a **Min** value or a **Max** value has the effect of establishing a window of values that will be displayed in the area graph.

This can be useful if you have data that contains extreme values as you can effectively filter the outlying values from the displayed graph. So, setting **Min** and **Max** will force Grafana to scale the total graph to fit between those values, and any values outside the range will be clipped. This is a good opportunity to check the accompanying **Graph** panel to make sure the displays are consistent.

Below the **Decimals** setting is the **Display** name. It is here where we set the *title* text for the panel.

Setting the display name

The text content of the **Display name** field is displayed as a text *title* in a specific location of the panel. In the case of the **Stat** panel, that location is either to the left if you set **Display Alignment mode** to **Auto** or cozied up next to the value if you select **Center**.

You can type any arbitrary text into the field; however, if you wish to customize it with text specific to the data series, you can also use four macro variables that are replaced by text snippets. They are as follows:

- `${__series.name}`: The contents of the **Alias By** field in the query
- `${__field.name}`: The name of the field column from the **FROM** query
- `$__cell_{N}`: The contents of the **N** table cell if the data is table-formatted
- `$__calc`: The `calc` from the **Display** section section

Let's do something colorful next. The color in the **Stat** panel is controlled by the threshold, so we'll take a closer look at the thresholds now.

Setting the Field tab thresholds

The settings in the **Thresholds** section allow you the broad flexibility to control your panel's color by mapping the panel value into one value in a series of threshold ranges, each with an associated color.

Setting a threshold is simply a matter of defining a threshold value and associating a color to it. If the display value lies above a threshold value and the threshold value above it, the panel color will be set to the threshold's color, depending on the **Color mode** setting of **Display**. If the value falls below the lowest threshold, the color is set to a fixed **Base** color.

You can create as many thresholds as you like and you have the entire color spectrum at your disposal, or if you prefer, you can use the Grafana color-picker to choose from a palette of 30 colors.

Here's a quick step-by-step guide of the process:

1. Go to the **Thresholds** section of the **Field** tab.
2. Click **+ Add threshold** to add a new threshold. Grafana will try to guess a new value and color based on the existing thresholds.

3. Click on the colored dot and select a color from the picker. If you wish to use a different color than the presets, specify a custom color from the **Custom** tab in the popup.

4. Click on the number to edit the value.

5. To delete a threshold, click on the trashcan icon.

Once you set the threshold values and their associated colors, the **Color mode** setting of the **Display** section determines whether the threshold colors the **Background** color or the **Value** text and graph.

In this section, we looked at how thresholds determine the panel color. Next, we will see how value mappings determine the panel text.

Setting the Field panel's value mappings

Finally, we'll take a peek at value mappings as they're used frequently in this and other panels. Put simply, value mappings convert numbers into text. A mapping identifies a text string with a value or a range of values. It's simple to create mappings for a **Stat** panel (or any panel that supports value mappings):

1. Select either **Value** or **Range**.

2. Set a value if **Value** is selected, or the **From** and **To** values if **Range** is selected.

3. Set the corresponding text value to be displayed.

4. Add additional mappings by clicking on **+ Add a value mapping**.

Unfortunately, value mappings do come with a limitation—you must fill in both the **From** and **To** values to get a valid range mapping. You can't have an open-ended mapping to cover values outside the range.

Building our Stat panels

Let's build a couple of panels to get an idea of how to practically use some of these settings. We'll first construct a **Stat** panel with a value mapping for the temperature to get an idea of how they work. Duplicate your initial **Stat** panel to create a new one with the same query. Make the following mappings:

- **Range** | **From**: 20 | **To**: 30 | **Text**: Hot
- **Range** | **From**: 10 | **To**: 20 | **Text**: Warm

- **Range** | **From**: 0 | **To**: 10 | **Text**: Cool
- **Range** | **From**: -10 | **To**: 0 | **Text**: Cold

The **Value mappings** section should look something like this:

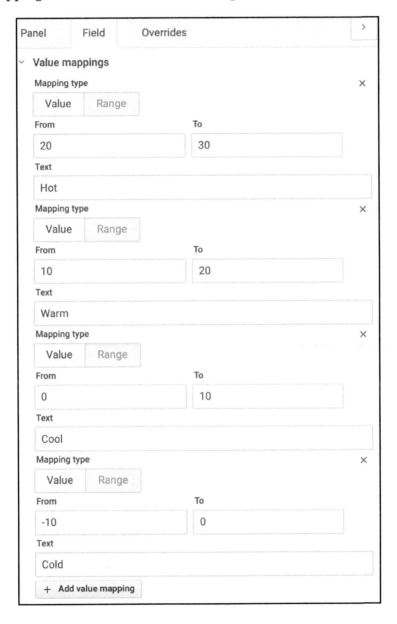

Now, instead of a mysterious number for the temperature, you can display a more user-friendly textual description:

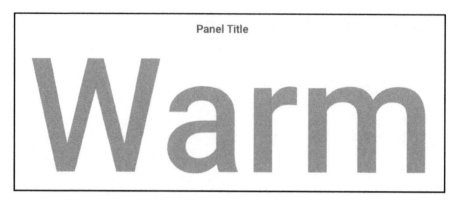

Now, let's build a fully tricked-out **Stat** panel, with thresholds, background colors, and a graph—the works! Follow these steps:

1. Create a new panel and set up the following query:

   - **FROM: default temperature | WHERE:** Leave empty
   - **SELECT: field (value) mean()**
   - **GROUP BY: time ($_interval) tag (station) fill (none)**
   - **FORMAT AS**: **Time series**
   - **ALIAS BY**: $col $measurement $tag_station
   - Query options/the **Min** interval: 1m

2. Set the title in the **Settings** section of the **Panel** tab (**Panel title**: Station temperatures)

3. On the **Panel** tab, configure the **Display** settings:

   - **Show: Calculate**
   - **Value: Last**
   - **Orientation: Auto**
   - **Color mode: Background**
   - **Graph mode: Area**
   - **Alignment mode: Center**

4. Set up the standard options on the **Field** tab:

- **Unit: Celsius (ºC)**
- **Decimals**: 1
- **Display name**: `${__series.name}`

5. Next, we'll establish some thresholds:

- **Field/Thresholds: Base Blue**
- **Field/Thresholds**: 0 (yellow)
- **Field/Thresholds**: 10 (red)

This is how my panel turned out:

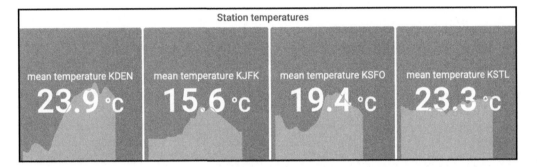

Now, try these exercises:

- With a custom time range starting from midnight of the current day (**Today so far**), create a **Stat** panel with a high temperature for the day.
- With the same time range, create a **Stat** panel to display the low temperature for the day.
- You may find that when you compare an aggregated **Stat** value with the same value in the **Graph** legend, they may not agree at large time frames. Why is that? Hint—use **Query Inspector** to examine the query sent to InfluxDB.

Here's why they may not agree. The `$__interval` variable, determined automatically by Grafana, is set on a per-panel basis. Consequently, if you compare the interval in the query for different panel types (**Graph** and **Stat**), you'll find that they calculate different intervals at large time ranges. This means that they will end up aggregating different sets of points and displaying different aggregation values. This is something to be aware of. In the next chapter, we'll see how sharing queries between different panels can be a workaround for this problem.

Working with the Gauge panel

The **Gauge** panel is intended to emulate the look of a semicircular analog graph, and it comes with a comprehensive set of controls for text and color. Along with the controls over the display and the value, there are better threshold and value mapping controls compared to those in the **Stat** panel.

To get a feel for using this gauge, let's set up a set of wind-speed gauges, one for each station.

First, let's set up a query for the wind speed for all the stations. We'll use the math operator to convert the value from the native meters per second setting to kilometers per hour:

- **FROM: default windSpeed**
- **SELECT: field (value) math (/1000 * 3600)**
- **GROUP BY: tag (station)**
- **FORMAT AS: Time series**
- Query options/the **Min** interval: 1m

Once we have our query, we'll set the look of our panel. We'll first start with the **Panel** tab, then move on to the settings on the **Field** tab.

Setting the Panel tab's display

The **Display** settings section determines the nature of what is displayed in the gauge. As with the **Stat** panel, the following controls are available:

- **Show**: Calculates a single value or displays all values of the query
- **Value**: Sets the aggregation function to reduce values to a single one
- **Limit**: Limits the number of rows displayed when **Show** is set to **All values**
- **Orientation**: Sets the stacking orientation of multiple values to either **Vertical** or **Horizontal** or auto-sets it based on the shape of the panel

Additionally, there are two threshold display switches:

- **Show threshold labels**: Displays threshold labels on the gauge perimeter
- **Show threshold markers**: Displays threshold colors on the gauge perimeter

The **Show** setting determines whether to display a single gauge displaying an aggregate value (**Calculate**) for each data series returned from the query or a single gauge for each row (**All values**) returned in a query (be careful! this can be a lot of gauges). If you choose to show all the values, the maximum number of gauges to display is set by the **Limit** field value.

The choices for **Value** when **Show** is set to **Calculate** are the same as in the **Stat** panel. For our wind gauge, we'll again use the **Last** value. We also want to see the labels and markers for our thresholds. Go ahead and set the following in the **Display** section of the **Panel** tab:

- **Show**: **Calculate**
- **Value**: **Last (not null)**
- **Show threshold labels**: **on**
- **Show threshold markers**: **on**

Setting the Field tab's standard options

Under the **Field** tab, the **Standard options** settings configure how the gauge will display its data. Here's a quick rundown of the options:

- **Unit**: Displays the unit text for the value
- **Min**: Sets the minimum gauge value
- **Max**: Sets the maximum gauge value
- **Decimal**: Sets the number of decimals to display
- **Display name**: Sets the text under each gauge
- **No Value**: Displays alternate text when there is no value

While there are several settings that you should be familiar with from the **Stat** panel, they have a distinct effect on the look of the gauge. For example, **Min** and **Max** are used to set the overall scale of the gauge. The gauge bar is drawn from the left to a position calculated to be equivalent to the value's relative distance between **Min** and **Max**.

You should take care to calibrate your gauge so that the **Min** and **Max** spread covers the general range of possible values. Setting **Min** too high or **Max** too low could result in an empty or full gauge, respectively. Setting **Min** too low or **Max** to high leaves too much empty gauge, making it useless.

Go ahead and set these standard options next:

- **Field/Unit**: **kilometers/hour (km/h)**
- **Field/Min**: 0
- **Field/Max**: 125
- **Field/Decimal**: 1
- **Field/Title**: ${__field.name}

We do want our gauges to give us some idea of how strongly the wind is blowing, so we're going to need visual cues as the wind speed rises. Let's set up some thresholds to provide those cues.

Setting the Field tab thresholds

In Grafana 7, thresholding is now unified across all panels, so the techniques for thresholding that we discussed in the **Stat** panel apply to the **Gauge** panel. Let's set up some thresholds for our wind gauge. Just to keep things interesting, we'll map the Beaufort scale to thresholds.

Starting from the bottom and working up, we set the following:

- **Base** (white)
- **2** (light blue)
- **5** (medium blue)
- **11** (blue)
- **19** (light green)
- **28** (medium green)
- **38** (green)
- **49** (medium yellow)
- **61** (dark yellow)
- **74** (light orange)
- **88** (medium orange)
- **102** (dark orange)
- **117** (red)

This is what your thresholds should look like when you're done:

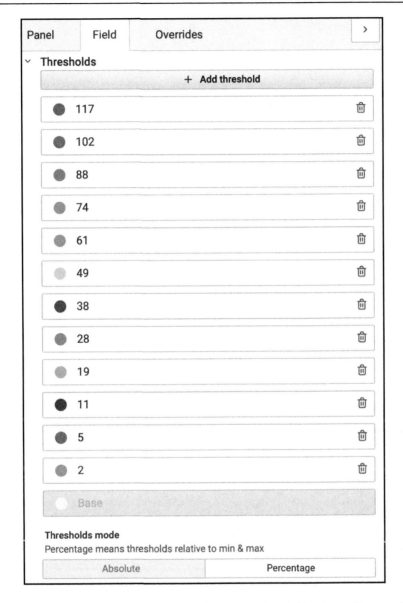

If you're reading a hard copy of this book, it might be a bit difficult to discern the gradations in color from a grayscale image. Rest assured, you will be able to download the images in glorious full color from this book's website. Details can be found in the *Preface* section of this book.

Once we have the thresholds in place, this is what our final panel looks like:

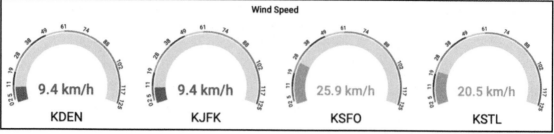

Now, let's move on from the **Gauge** panel to its close cousin—the **Bar Gauge** panel.

Adding a Bar Gauge panel

The **Bar Gauge** panel has similar functionality to the **Gauge** panel but produces its data in a substantially different form. It's designed to produce either vertical or horizontal bars whose full extent represents a maximum quantity, and the length of the rendered bar represents what proportion of the extent is covered by the value. The **Bar Gauge** panel can also depict the value's relationship to any preset thresholds through one of three visual styles.

The **Mode** setting of **Display** sets the visual style of the bar gauge and there are three choices available—**Gradient**, **Retro LCD**, and **Basic**. Let's take a closer look at each one

Setting the Gradient mode

As with all the **Bar Gauge** modes, the length of the bar is the value's relative distance between the **Min** and **Max** settings. In the case of the **Gradient** mode, the bar itself is a color gradient that smoothly transitions between each threshold color, starting from the **Base** color and proceeding up to the value's threshold color.

Setting the Retro LCD mode

Similar to the **Gradient** mode, the **Retro LCD** mode divides the bar's color gradient into a series of segments reminiscent of those on analog audio devices. The number of *illuminated* segments is determined by the value's relative distance between the **Min** and **Max** settings.

Setting the Basic mode

Finally, in the **Basic** mode, the length of the bar is still the value's relative distance between **Min** and **Max**, but the bar has a simple gradient fill set to the value's current threshold color.

Building a bar gauge

We're now going to make a bar gauge to display relative humidity. This should be fairly straightforward to grasp as we know that relative humidity is measured as a percentage from 0 to 100. First, we set up our query:

- **FROM: default relativeHumidity**
- **SELECT: field (value)**
- **GROUP BY: tag (station) tag (name)**
- **FORMAT AS: Time series**
- **ALIAS BY:** $tag_station, $tag_name
- Query options/the **Min** interval: 1m

Moving on to the display settings, we'll set some again to go with the current value, as well as setting the text and a few color thresholds:

- **Panel/Display/Show: Calculate**
- **Panel/ Display/Value: Last**
- **Panel /Display/Orientation: Horizontal**
- **Panel/Display/Mode: Retro LCD**
- **Field/Standard options/Unit: percent (0-100)**
- **Field/Standard options/Min:** 0
- **Field/Standard options/Max:** 100
- **Field/Standard options/Decimals:** 1
- **Field/Standard options/Display name:** ${__field.name}
- **Field/Thresholds: Base Blue**
- **Field/Thresholds:** 25 (yellow)
- **Field/Thresholds:** 50 (orange)
- **Field/Thresholds:** 75 (red)

If you have entered the values in the **Field** tab settings like this:

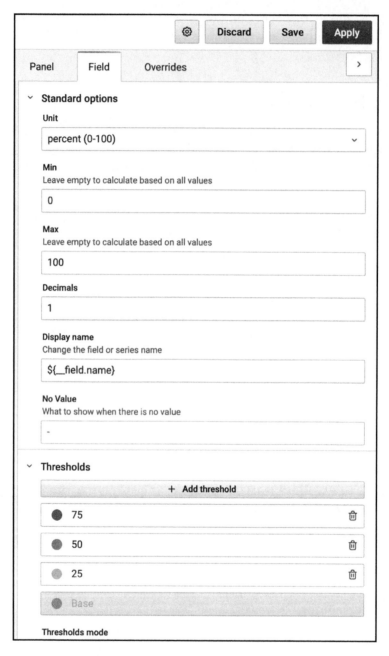

This is what your **Field** tab settings should look like:

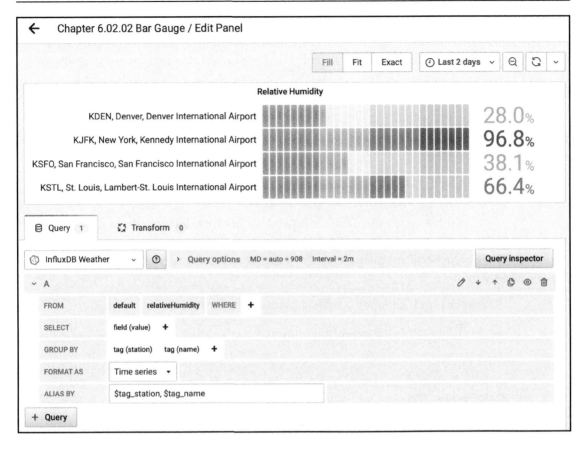

Have fun with the **Gauge** and **Bar Gauge** panels! They can prove useful not only to provide visual flair but also to complement your graphs. From a distance, the large fonts, saturated colors, and dynamic graphics serve to draw the viewer's attention. Adding the **Graph** panel then invites the viewer to take a deeper dive into the data.

Shortly, we'll be looking at the **Table** panel, another one of Grafana's built-in panels; but first, let's take a bit of an interlude from the weather and play around with a downloadable **Worldmap** panel. We'll be graphing another type of interesting natural data: earthquakes.

Geolocating data on the Worldmap panel

Up until now, we've been exclusively using graph panels that are available on Grafana out of the box. We're going to mix things up a little by bringing in a new plugin panel and visualizing a new dataset.

There are two mechanisms for installing a new plugin—the `grafana-cli` command-line tool and an environment variable setting in the Grafana configuration. Because we can easily do it in Docker Compose at the same time as we launch the service, we're going to opt for the second method. All that is required is to set the `GF_INSTALL_PLUGINS` environment variable to the list of desired plugins in our `docker-compose.yml` file and restart Grafana.

In order to visualize the location of earthquakes around the world, we'll need to install a **Worldmap** plugin panel.

1. Check the Grafana plugin directory at `https://grafana.com/grafana/plugins` to lead you to the **Worldmap** panel.
2. Click on the icon for the panel, followed by the **Installation** tab, to find the instructions for how to install the panel.
3. The instructions are intended for installation by the `grafana-cli` command-line tool:

   ```
   grafana-cli plugins install grafana-worldmap-panel
   ```

   They indicate the full name of the plugin, `grafana-worldmap-panel`.

4. Edit your `docker-compose.yml` Grafana service to include the environment variable with the `GF_INSTALL_PLUGINS` name and `grafana-worldmap-panel` as the value. The `docker-compose.yml` file is also available in the `Chapter06` folder of this book's GitHub repository:

```
grafana:
    image: "grafana/grafana:${GRAF_TAG-latest}"
    ports:
      - "3000:3000"
    environment:
      GF_INSTALL_PLUGINS: grafana-worldmap-panel
    volumes:
      - "${PWD-.}/grafana:/var/lib/grafana"
```

5. Restart your Grafana service:

   ```
   % docker-compose restart grafana
   Restarting ch6_grafana_1 ... done
   ```

If you add a new panel and check the **Visualization** section of the **Panel** tab, you will see a new **Worldmap** panel. Now, we only need to get some data.

Ingesting a new earthquake dataset

The USGS maintains a comprehensive earthquake catalog and it is freely available via a simple REST interface at `https://earthquake.usgs.gov/earthquakes/feed/v1.0/geojson.php`. The USGS provides continually updated catalogs of earthquakes, which are filtered by size over a variety of time periods ranging from 1 hour to 1 month.

To load the earthquake data, we only need to create a new Python script that is similar in structure to `weather.py` from `Chapter 5`, *Visualizing Data in the Graph Panel*. We'll call this new script `earthquake.py`, and you can find them both in the `ch6/bin` folder of the repository. Let's take a quick peek at the changes we made to `earthquake.py`.

Updating process_cli()

The first big change occurs in `process_cli()`. First, we change the parser description:

```
def process_cli():
    parser = argparse.ArgumentParser(description="read earthquake data from USGS into Influxdb")
```

Next, we replace the `--station` option to add two new options—one to select the minimum size of the earthquake and another to indicate the width of the time period covered by the catalog. Together, we'll use the values to construct our REST URL:

```
parser.add_argument("--size", dest="size",
                    choices=['significant', '4.5', '2.5', '1.0', 'all'],
                    default='significant', help="earthquake size")
parser.add_argument("--window", dest="window",
                    choices=['hour', 'day', 'week', 'month'],
                    default='hour', help="earthquake time window")
```

Updating main()

In `main()`, we'll need to create a new data dump subroutine called `dump_eq_data()`. It takes the command-line arguments for the size, window, and output file as parameters:

```
if args.output_file:
    dump_eq_data(args.size, args.window, args.output_file)
```

Adding dump_eq_data()

The code for `dump_eq_data()` is very straightforward. First, we construct a request URL from the `size` and `window` parameters and get the response:

```
def dump_eq_data(size, window, output):
    url =
f"https://earthquake.usgs.gov/earthquakes/feed/v1.0/summary/{size}_{window}
.geojson"
    response = requests.get(url)
    logging.info(response.url)
    if response.status_code != requests.codes.ok:
        raise Exception(f"dump_eq_data:
{response.status_code}:{response.reason}")
```

Next, we iterate through each feature in the response and extract the magnitude and depth for the metrics, as well as the latitude, longitude, and place name as tags:

```
for feature in response.json()['features']:
    measure = "event"

    mag = feature['properties']['mag']
    place = feature['properties']['place']
    lon, lat, dep = feature['geometry']['coordinates']
```

Assemble `tags`, `metrics`, and `timestamp`:

```
tags = [
    f"latitude={lat}",
    f"longitude={lon}",
    f"place={escape_string(place)}",
    f"magnitude={escape_string(str(mag))}"
]

metrics = [
    f"magnitude={mag}",
    f"depth={dep}",
]

timestamp = feature['properties']['time']
```

Output each event as a line in our output file:

```
data = f"{measure},{','.join(tags)} {','.join(metrics)} {timestamp}\n"
output.write(data)
```

Adding load_eq_data()

The only significant difference in our file load subroutine, called `load_eq_data()`, is the specification of time precision in milliseconds (`ms`):

```
response = requests.post(url, params=dict(db=db_name, precision="ms"),
data=data)
```

That's pretty much all there is to it! Of course, I could have written it to manage both earthquakes and the weather, but for the purpose of clarity, I kept things separate. Let's load up some data. We're going to look at all of the earthquakes over the course of a week:

```
% docker run --rm --network=host -v "$(PWD):/usr/src/app" --name python
python/ch6 \                bin/earthquake.py --size all --window week --
output data/eq.txt
% docker run --rm --network=host -v "$(PWD):/usr/src/app" --name python
python/ch6 \                bin/earthquake.py --input data/eq.txt --db
earthquakedb
```

Any `bad event` error messages can be safely ignored as they represent bad data points to be skipped.

Configuring the InfluxDB data source

Next, we need to configure a Grafana data source to our new dataset:

- **Name**: `InfluxDB Earthquake`
- **URL**: `http://localhost:8086`
- **Access**: **Browser**
- **Database**: `earthquakedb`

Now, you have a new InfluxDB data source populated with a week's worth of earthquake data. Let's see what this looks like when plotted around the world, shall we?

Setting up the Worldmap panel

As it turns out, the **Worldmap** panel can be a bit finicky, so we'll walk through the process of creating our visualization step by step. First, create a new **Worldmap** panel and assign the following values:

- **Query**: `InfluxDB Earthquake`
- **FROM**: **default event**

- **SELECT**: field (magnitude) alias (metric)
- **GROUP BY**: tag (latitude) tag (longitude) tag (place)
- **FORMAT AS**: Table

Don't worry if you get an error at this point. That's just **Worldmap** complaining because its expectations aren't being met. We'll adjust them now.

Go to **Worldmap** under the **Panel** tab and set the following:

- **Map Visual Options/Location Data**: **table**
- **Map Visual Options/Aggregation**: **current**
- **Field Mapping/Table Query Format**: **coordinates**
- **Field Mapping/Location Name Field**: **place**
- **Field Mapping/Metric Field**: **metric**
- **Field Mapping/Latitude Field**: **latitude**
- **Field Mapping/Longitude Field**: **longitude**

With any luck, you should see a bunch of colored circles of various sizes scattered around the world. If you hover over the circles, you'll see a popup with a description of the event location and the magnitude value. Let's use the thresholds to provide another visual indicator of magnitude:

- **Threshold options/Thresholds**: **2,4,6,8**
- **Threshold options/Colors**: `light green, green, yellow, orange, red`

We'll tidy up the display so that it's centered on North America and clean up the visual clutter by scaling down the circles:

- **Map Visual Options/Center**: **North America**
- **Map Visual Options/Initial Zoom**: `4`
- **Map Visual Options/Min Circle Size**: `1`
- **Map Visual Options/Max Circle Size**: `10`
- **Map Visual Options/Decimals**: `1`
- **Map Visual Options/Unit**: **(singular form)** `M`, **(plural form)** **M**
- **Map Visual Options/Show Legend**: **on**

Your panel should look something like this when you're done:

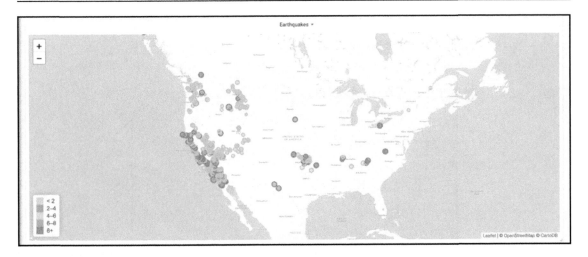

I hope you found that little digression interesting and inspiring. **Worldmap** is just one of many panels you can download from the Grafana site that improves the versatility and visual appeal of your dashboards.

Structuring data fields in the Table panel

Our last panel is one of the least graphically visual options of the panels you will encounter in Grafana. The **Table** panel provides a spreadsheet-like data grid that is useful if you want to see the rows of actual data, along with any aggregations. When rolling up your data series into an aggregation, the **Table** panel is much more useful than the **Graph** panel legend. It also gives you the capability to sort any of its columns with a single click. The number of rows can be set to give you either a fixed window of data or a scrolling list.

Comparing aggregations

To give you an idea of how the **Table** panel compares to the **Graph** panel legend, let's create a panel and have it display a set of common aggregations. Create a new panel and select a table from **Choose Visualization**. Enter these parameters for the **Query** tab:

- **Query**: InfluxDB Weather
- **SELECT**: default temperature
- **FROM**: field (value) mean ()

- **GROUP BY: time ($__interval) tag (station) tag (name) fill (none)**
- **FORMAT AS: Time series**
- Query options/the **Min** interval: `1m`

Once you've added the query, you should see the raw data fields:

Temperature	
Time ⌄	temperature.mean {name: Denver, Denver Interna...
2020-05-26 13:58:00	24 °C
2020-05-26 13:52:00	24 °C
2020-05-26 12:52:00	23 °C
2020-05-26 11:52:00	22 °C
2020-05-26 10:52:00	22 °C
2020-05-26 09:52:00	20 °C
temperature.mean {name: Denver, Denver International Airport, station: KDEN} ⌄	

The **Table** panel's interface is similar to a standard spreadsheet application:

- Sort the rows by clicking on a column.
- Adjust the column widths by dragging the column divider.
- Select a series by using the drop-down menu at the bottom of the panel.

When working with the **Table** panel, it's often best to start with the raw data and work it into the form you wish to display in the table. Since we'd like to display a set of aggregations, as in the **Graph** panel legend, we will leverage Grafana 7's new **Transform** tab to reduce each time series to an aggregation:

1. On the **Transform** tab, click on **Reduce**.
2. In the **Calculations** text field, select **Mean** from the dropdown.

This is what it should look like:

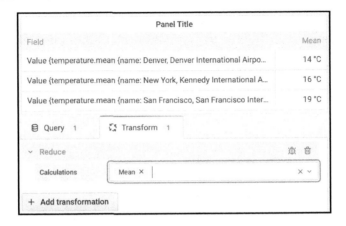

You should now see that the time values have been replaced with the series names, and the value column has been replaced with a **Mean** column. Go ahead and use the dropdown next to the **Calculations** setting to add the **Min**, **Max**, and **Last** columns.

By creating a similar **Graph** panel and enabling the legend values for the **Min**, **Max**, **Avg**, and **Current** columns in the legend, you should see identical values:

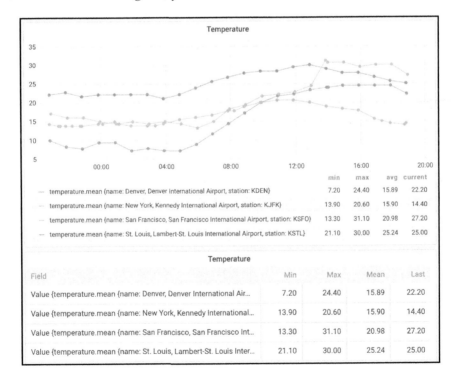

Let's go ahead and set **Unit** under **Standard options** to **Celsius (ºC)** for our table values. Now, the **Standard options** setting applies to all the column fields in the table, so if we happen to have fields with different units, we are going to need some way to set some fields with one unit and others with a different unit.

If you recall from Chapter 5, *Visualizing Data in the Graph Panel*, the look of a specific data series in the **Graph** panel can be controlled by a series override. In the **Table** panel, if we want to modify the display of a column field, we use what is called a **field override**.

Overriding field settings

Field overrides are intended to provide a generalized mechanism for formatting cells in a table and, optionally, the column headers (a special case of cells, really). Suffice to say, the process is straightforward:

1. Add an override.
2. Set a matcher for one or more field names.
3. Set one or more of the override properties found under the **Field** tab.

Let's go through an example to illustrate how to use the column styles to format multiple cells at once. We want to display a barometer reading for a number of stations, as well as the temperature. We also want to set the cell to display as a certain color depending on the barometric pressure, and we want to set a color for the text of the temperature cells.

First, we'll set up a query to pull in the data. Create a new panel and set a custom time range to start at midnight on the current day. Set up an **A** query:

- **QUERY: InfluxDB Weather**
- **FROM: default barometricPressure**
- **SELECT: field (value) mean () math (/1000)**
- **GROUP BY: time (1h) tag (station) fill (none)**
- **FORMAT AS: Time series**

Next, set up a **B** query:

- **QUERY: InfluxDB Weather** (the **A** query)
- **FROM: default temperature**
- **SELECT: field (value) mean ()**
- **GROUP BY: time (1h) tag (station) fill (none)**
- **FORMAT AS: Time series**

Just a few things to note—we're pulling in two data series, one for the barometer reading and the other for the temperature reading:

- When the tags and timestamps are the same for the datapoint in different queries, Grafana will line them up in the same row of the table.
- Unfortunately, the timestamps are all over the place, and since we only care about hourly reading, we'll roll them up in the **GROUP BY** into hour-long intervals.
- For the **A** query, we want to convert the value from pascals to kilopascals, so we'll divide the returned value by 1,000.
- We also need to pivot the table so that each column represents a series. We'll use the **Add field from calculation** option on the **Transform** tab. Set **Mode** to **Binary operation**, but leave the **Operation** fields empty. This effectively pivots the table for the purpose of performing a column-to-column operation, but without actually creating any new columns.

Your table should look like this:

| TS to Column Example ⌄ | | | | | | | |
Time	barometricPressur…	barometricPressur…	barometricPressur…	barometricPressur…	temperature.mean …	temperature.mean …	temperature.mean …	temperature.mean …
2020-05-26 09:00:00	101.80	102.44	101.19	101.32	20.00	20.00	21.70	28.30
2020-05-26 10:00:00	101.73	102.37	101.19	101.29	21.70	20.60	22.20	28.30
2020-05-26 11:00:00	101.69	102.37	101.19	101.22	22.20	20.60	22.80	29.40
2020-05-26 12:00:00	101.66	102.30	101.15	101.19	23.30	20.00	24.40	30.00
2020-05-26 13:00:00	101.66	102.27	101.12	101.15	23.90	18.90	30.85	28.90
2020-05-26 14:00:00	101.63	102.24	101.08	101.15	24.40	18.30	30.60	27.80
2020-05-26 15:00:00	101.63	102.27	101.05	101.19	24.40	17.80	29.40	27.80
2020-05-26 16:00:00	101.63	102.27	101.02	101.19	24.40	15.60	30.00	26.70
2020-05-26 17:00:00	101.63	102.30	100.98	101.22	24.40	14.70	30.00	25.60

We want to change a few things for each column field:

- The units for the temperature and barometric pressure
- The name of the fields so that the columns look more readable
- The thresholds for the cell color
- Whether the cell background or text is colored
- The number of decimals for the temperature values

First, we set **Unit** for the field with the station KDEN temperature column:

1. From the **Overrides** tab, click on **+ Add override**.
2. Click on **Filter by field** to add a new field-based override.
3. Choose the field name from the scrolling menu—in this case, **temperature.mean {station:KDEN}**.
4. Click on **+ Add override property** to add the field property to be overriden.
5. Click on **Unit** from the scrolling menu.
6. Set the units in the fields to **Temperature / Celsius (ºC)**.

Next up, we'll go ahead and change the name of the field:

1. Click on **+ Add override property** to add the field property to be overriden.
2. Click on **Display name** from the scrolling menu.
3. Set the field to **KDEN temperature**.

Now, we'll set the thresholds:

1. Click on **+ Add override property** to add the field property to be overriden.
2. Click on **Thresholds** from the scrolling menu and add two thresholds by clicking on **+ Add threshold**:
   - **Base: Blue**
   - 5: **Yellow**
   - 10: **Red**

We next set the override for **Cell display mode**:

1. Click on **+ Add override property** to add the field property to be overriden.
2. Select **Cell display mode** from the scrolling menu.
3. Set the mode to **Color text**.

The last one for this column is to set the number of decimals to **1**.

1. Click **+ Add override property** to add the field property to be overriden
2. Select **Decimals** from the scrolling menu
3. Set the value to **1**

Now, we'll do something similar for one of the barometric pressure columns. I won't go through this step by step; you just need to know the override settings:

- **Matcher | Filter by field**: **barometricPressure.mean {station:KSFO}**
- **Unit**: **Pressure | Kilopascals (kPa)**
- **Display name**: `KSFO barometer`
- **Thresholds**:
  - **Base**: **Red**
  - `100.8`: **Orange**
  - `101.8`: **Green**
- **Cell display mode**: **Background**

As an additional exercise, go ahead and finish up the rest of the columns. You'll just need to replicate the settings for each column. When you're done, you should see a table that looks something like the following:

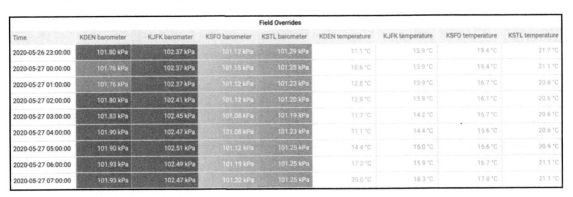

	Field Overrides							
Time	KDEN barometer	KJFK barometer	KSFO barometer	KSTL barometer	KDEN temperature	KJFK temperature	KSFO temperature	KSTL temperature
2020-05-26 23:00:00	101.80 kPa	102.37 kPa	101.12 kPa	101.29 kPa	11.1 °C	13.9 °C	19.4 °C	21.7 °C
2020-05-27 00:00:00	101.76 kPa	102.37 kPa	101.15 kPa	101.25 kPa	10.6 °C	13.9 °C	19.4 °C	21.1 °C
2020-05-27 01:00:00	101.76 kPa	102.37 kPa	101.12 kPa	101.23 kPa	12.8 °C	13.9 °C	16.7 °C	20.8 °C
2020-05-27 02:00:00	101.80 kPa	102.41 kPa	101.12 kPa	101.20 kPa	12.8 °C	13.9 °C	16.1 °C	20.6 °C
2020-05-27 03:00:00	101.83 kPa	102.45 kPa	101.08 kPa	101.19 kPa	11.7 °C	14.2 °C	16.7 °C	20.6 °C
2020-05-27 04:00:00	101.90 kPa	102.47 kPa	101.08 kPa	101.23 kPa	11.1 °C	14.4 °C	15.6 °C	20.6 °C
2020-05-27 05:00:00	101.90 kPa	102.51 kPa	101.12 kPa	101.25 kPa	14.4 °C	15.0 °C	15.6 °C	20.9 °C
2020-05-27 06:00:00	101.93 kPa	102.49 kPa	101.19 kPa	101.25 kPa	17.2 °C	15.9 °C	16.7 °C	21.1 °C
2020-05-27 07:00:00	101.93 kPa	102.47 kPa	101.22 kPa	101.25 kPa	20.0 °C	18.3 °C	17.8 °C	21.1 °C

And that does it for our **Table** panel. The **Table** panel, when coupled with the **Transform**, has a lot of potential for very sophisticated analysis. Keep an eye out on Grafana Community (`https://community.grafana.com`) for more examples of how to get the most out of the **Table** panel.

Summary

In this chapter, we looked at a number of the key plugin panels that come preinstalled with Grafana. We examined the **Stat**, **Gauge**, and **Bar Gauge** panels—panels that reduce the complexity of each data series into a single graphical or textual representation. These panels also give you a number of styling tools to augment the visual appeal and significance of your data.

We also looked at the optional **Worldmap** panel, one of the many panels that can be downloaded from Grafana Labs. The **Worldmap** panel is useful for displaying data tagged with latitude and longitude. We also showed how to represent data values visually by mapping them to a specified size and/or color.

Finally, we explored some of the capabilities of the **Table** panel. The **Table** panel is a gridded data panel, similar in appearance to a spreadsheet, that displays time-series data by row or column or in aggregation, or it simply displays tabular data. We learned how to use regular expressions to match column headers to simplify the style of cell data.

That wraps up our exploration of some of the many Grafana plugin panels; however, there are several more available for download. Now that you know how to add panels just by adding them to the startup configuration, try adding other interesting panels and exploring their capabilities as well.

In the next chapter, we're going to pull together everything we've learned so far. We going to look at how to design dashboards, and we'll create and lay out a number of panels on our dashboards. We'll also go about exploring different techniques for making our dashboard creation workflow more efficient. See you in the next chapter!

Creating Your First Dashboard
7

In the previous chapters, we've mostly concentrated on panels and how to use them and configure them. We did this pretty much exclusively on the dashboard, which is the canvas that we display our panels on. In the next few chapters, we will zoom out from the panel level to the dashboard level. We'll continue to learn more about various panels, but this will mostly be in the context of making our dashboard layouts and queries more efficient.

In this chapter, we're going to take on the task of designing a couple of dashboards – one packed with information suitable for viewing on a workstation or laptop, and another containing only key pieces of information suitable for being viewed at a glance or from a distance.

In both cases, we'll pick up some workflow techniques that can help speed up the often laborious task of creating, configuring, and laying out panels. We'll also look at ways to take our numerical data and convert it into a textual format, thereby increasing the richness of our dashboard content.

Here's what we'll cover in this chapter:

- Designing a dashboard
- Creating a high information display dashboard
- Creating a high information visibility dashboard

Let's get started!

Technical requirements

The tutorial code, dashboards, and other helpful files for this chapter can be found in this book's GitHub repository at `https://github.com/PacktPublishing/Learn-Grafana-7.0/tree/master/Chapter07`.

Designing a dashboard

Before we get started and work on a new dashboard, it's best to have a plan of action. Ask yourself a few questions:

- What information do I want to convey?
- What is the visual context for the dashboard?
- What is most important; what is least important?

Let's take a look at these questions in more detail.

Conveying information

In the case or our dashboard, we will be building a dashboard that can be used to produce a forecast of the upcoming weather. For this purpose, will need to describe the following conditions:

- Current temperature and dew point
- Barometer reading and trend – rising, falling, or steady
- Wind direction and speed
- Visibility

We also want to know the current temperature as that will help us decide what to wear, for example. The dew point is an indication of humidity (and relative comfort, depending on the temperature) and also provides an indication of how low the temperature is likely to drop. We want to know the current barometer reading and trend as that could give a forecaster an indication of an approaching low-pressure system and possibly inclement weather. The wind direction and speed can indicate the passage of weather fronts.

Determining the visual context

What is the likely context for how the dashboard is to be viewed? Will it be a computer screen on a desk or a massive display in an operations center?

In our particular case, we'd like the weather report to be available to a hypothetical weather forecaster and viewed on a relatively small screen such as a laptop or a tablet. In this case, we will be more concerned with providing high information density as it is likely to be viewed over a moderate period of time. Were the display to be on a large screen and viewed by non-practitioners, we may want to emphasize lower information density instead.

Prioritizing elements of importance

Importance works hand in hand with the visual context. If the viewer can control the display, importance dictates that the most important information appears at the top, while less important information appears lower or even below the viewable window. If the viewer doesn't have control of this, as in a kiosk display, the highest priority information might be located at the top left and lower priority information below and/or to the right, depending on how a typical view scans for reading purposes.

Let's take these concepts and apply them to our dashboard designs. First off, we will create a dashboard designed to convey as much information as possible in a relatively small area, such as a workstation monitor. Following that, we'll design a dashboard for a large-scale kiosk-type display.

Creating a high information density dashboard

In our first example, we'll be constructing a fairly detailed dashboard of graph panels. This dashboard is similar to the one you might find accompanying a metrics-driven server application. It's intended to provide a number of metric graphs that might also serve as the top layer for further drill-down exploration. In our example, we'll be assembling a series of graphs to cover the weather metrics we've scraped from the National Weather Service using the application we developed in `Chapter 5`, *Visualizing Data in the Graph Panel*.

If you've been following my instructions in the previous chapters, you're probably well aware of how much work goes into getting a panel just so, and you can be forgiven for being a little anxious about the idea of creating a lot of panels for a dashboard. It's a valid concern, and for these examples, I'm going to take you step-by-step, as well as offer some effort-saving tips where I can so that when you have to build your own dashboards, you'll be equipped with a toolbox of techniques to streamline the process.

In the next chapter, we'll be looking at even more powerful techniques for making dashboard creation even more efficient. But before we can run, we need to walk, so let's get started!

Designing the dashboard

It's often a good strategy to make a little sketch or note about what you want to do before digging in and creating a full dashboard. If you have a list of dashboards and an idea of how you'd like to lay them out, it may not seem very challenging to build up a dashboard containing 10 or even 20 panels.

For our dashboard, we have something like this in mind:

- **First row**:
    - A title panel for identifying the station
    - A current conditions panel
- **Second row**:
    - A panel for temperature-related measurements
    - A panel for moisture-related measurements
- **Third row**: A pair of panels for barometer pressure and the trend
- **Fourth row**: A set of panels for wind speed
- **Fifth row**: A panel for visibility

Let's get started by creating a new dashboard and setting the time range to **Today so far**. Don't forget to save it! Next, we'll start creating and laying out our panels, starting with our first panel, which will display the station's name.

Building a station text panel

In order to display the title information for our dashboard, we'll need to introduce a new panel: the **Text** panel. The **Text** panel is a simple panel for displaying formatted text. The text can be either in markdown or HTML format. In our case, we want a little bit more control over formatting, so we'll fill in the content in HTML format.

Create a new panel and, in the **Visualization** section, set it to a **Text** panel. For these examples, we are going to use the KSFO station for our dashboards, but feel free to use a different station if you prefer. In the **Options** section, set the following values:

- **Mode**: html
- **Text**: `<h1><center>San Francisco CA (KSFO)</center></h1>`

Change to the **Settings** section and set the **Panel title** to `Station`.

If you're familiar with HTML, you'll probably recognize the markup just centers some `H1` text. If you didn't want to center the text, you could switch to markdown mode. It's beyond the scope of this book to cover either markup language, but the panel itself provides a helpful link to get you started with markdown.

Here's the **Panel** tab in action:

Now that you have an initial panel, you'll want to be thinking about the layout. Each panel you create will end up in the top-left corner of your dashboard, so you'll want to then resize it and drag it to its ultimate position. For the layout of this dashboard, you'll be working with essentially a two-column layout, so your task will be to simply size the panel to fit half the width of the page and drag it into position in either the left or the right column.

The layout process is relatively simple. In Grafana, panel geometry is defined by two pairs of numbers: the x and y coordinates (in grid units) of the panel's top-left corner and the panel's width and height. To adjust the panel's position, simply hover over the top of a panel until it turns gray and once the pointer becomes a cross-arrow, click and drag it. To adjust its size, simply hover over the lower-right corner of the panel until the pointer becomes an arrow pointing downward-right, then click-drag.

The dashboard is defined by an invisible grid that your panel will snap to in both position and size, so you only need to drag the panel to the appropriate position and adjust the sizing with the control at the bottom-right of the panel. The grid points are fairly widely spaced, so you don't need to worry about precision – just drag the panel or the resize control until an outline appears and then release. You can use the border cue to get an idea of where a move or resize will land, as shown in the following screenshot:

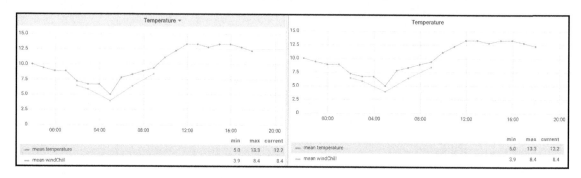

The dashboard layout manager can only move panels, so resizing or positioning a panel so that it overlaps another panel will cause the other panel to move down to get out of the way. I've found that if you want panels to stay on the same row, it's best to resize them down first, arrange them, then resize them up to fill in any empty space. It can be a little tricky to get things to look just right, but with a little practice, you'll find it almost becomes second nature to drag panels around into the layout you desire.

Modifying the weather.py script

Our next panel is our new friend the **Stat** panel. However, we'll be using it to display text describing the current conditions. We'll need to make a couple of modifications to our script in order to add the data field, but it's only a few lines. Let's look at the changes we'll make to our `weather.py` script.

We want to add a string as a metric value, so we'll need to capture the `textDescription` field from the retrieved object. But when using a string as a field value, we need to quote it first. We need to add a little routine to quote the string:

```
def quote_string(string):
    return f'"{string}"'
```

Next, we need to make a slight modification to the `dump_wx_data` routine to capture the `textDescription` field:

```
wx_data = get_station_obs(s)
for feature in wx_data:
    for measure, observation in feature['properties'].items():
        if measure in ['elevation']:
            continue
        if measure in ['textDescription']:
            value = quote_string(observation)
            unit = None
        elif isinstance(observation, dict):
            value = observation['value']
            unit = observation['unitCode']
        else:
            continue
```

Here, we did the following:

- We checked to see if the observation is an `elevation` and skip it if so. Otherwise, we capture the `textDescription` value as our value (with `textDescription` as the field key, but no associated unit tag).
- We grabbed any observations represented by a dictionary.
- We skipped over everything else.

That's all there is to it. Refer to the instructions from Chapter 5, *Visualizing Data in the Graph Panel*, for how to build the Docker container for our script; then run the commands for dumping and loading our weather data.

Building the current conditions panel

Once we've reloaded our data with the new field values, we can set up a **Stat** panel to display it. In the **Query** tab, set up the following:

- **Data source: InfluxDB Weather**
- **FROM: default textDescription**

- **WHERE: station = KSFO**
- **GROUP BY:** <empty>
- **SELECT: field(value)**

In the **Settings** section, set up the **Title: Current Conditions**

In the **Visualization** section, set up the **Visualization: Stat**

In the **Display** section, set up the following:

- **Value: Last**
- **Graph Mode: None**

In the **Field** tab, in the **Thresholds** section, set the following:

- Delete any existing thresholds (trash can icon)
- Base Color: **Custom | grey**

To get a custom gray color, do the following:

1. Click the color circle.
2. Select the **Custom** tab.
3. Type grey in the text field.

You can now lay out the two panels into an appropriate two-column style. Resize them so that they take up approximately half the page width. Give them the smallest height that will display all the content in the panel. Drag the **Station** panel to the left-hand side and the **Current Conditions** panel to the right. You might have to do a little jockeying to get both to sit next to each other with no space between them, but once you get the hang of it, you will have a fairly mastered layout, so take your time and play around with the controls.

You should end up with a row that looks like this:

We're off to a good start. Let's make this dashboard useful and put some temperatures up there!

Building the temperature panel

On to the next row! Here, we're going back to the **Graph** panel. As you're well aware, configuring the **Graph** panel can be an elaborate process involving many settings, so it will take some additional diligence to keep the panels looking and functioning consistently. I recommend that you create a general base panel with some common settings so that when you need to create a new panel, you can simply replicate your base panel and customize it.

Here's an example of a base panel that has many settings already preset. Create a **Graph** panel, go to the **Query** tab, and set up the following:

- **Data source: InfluxDB Weather**
- **GROUP BY: time ($_interval) fill (none)**
- **Query options/Min interval: 1m**

In the **Panel** tab, set up the following:

- Visualization: **Graph**
- Display/Lines: **on**
- Display/Points: **on**
- Display/Area fill: **0**
- Display/Point Radius: **1**
- Axes/Right Y/Show: **off**
- Legend/Options/Show: **on**
- Legend/Options/As Table: **on**

To replicate this panel, you have two options. If you click on the panel title, you'll get a dropdown menu with several options. You're already familiar with the **Edit** option. Clicking on **More...** yields a submenu with the **Duplicate** option. Clicking this will give you a new identical panel. The other option is to use the **Copy** option instead. Now, you can create a new panel, but you will have a new option called **Paste Copied Panel**. If you click it, you will convert the panel into an identical copy.

There is no inherent advantage to one or the other when working with panels on the same dashboard. **Copy** becomes much more useful when you need to copy a panel from one dashboard to another one.

Now, let's create our **Temperature** panel. Here, we want to track up to three different data series – one for the actual temperature and two for *perceived* temperature, that is, wind chill and the heat index. The wind chill is heavily dependent on the wind and cold temperatures, whereas the heat index is heavily dependent on humidity and high temperatures. If the temperatures are not extreme enough or there's light winds or little humidity, there won't be any readings for those series (we deliberately don't include null readings when we import the observation data).

Just in case, we'll go ahead and include queries for all three:

- **Data source: InfluxDB Weather**
- **A/FROM: default heatIndex WHERE: station = KSFO**
- **A/SELECT: field(value) mean()**
- **A/GROUP BY: time ($_interval) fill (none)**
- **A/FORMAT AS: Time series**
- **A/ALIAS BY:** $col $measurement
- **Query options/Min Interval: 1m**

Now, make two copies of the **A** query and change the **FROM** lines, as follows:

- **B/FROM: default temperature WHERE: station = KSFO**
- **C/FROM: default windChill WHERE: station = KSFO**

If **windChill** is not available from the menu, click on the field and type it in manually.

We have the series from our queries, but depending on the weather conditions, it's likely you will only see the temperature. Let's assume we will see the others if we choose a different station in the future when we set up the **Visualization**. If you've copied this panel from a base panel, as we discussed earlier, you might not have to change much:

- **Display/Lines: on**
- **Display/Points: on**
- **Display/Area Fill: 0**
- **Display/Point Radius: 1**
- **Axes/Left Y/Unit: Celsius (°C)**
- **Legend/Options/Show: on**
- **Legend/Options/As Table: on**
- **Legend/Values/Min: on**
- **Legend/Values/Max: on**
- **Legend/Values/Current: on**

You would be fine sticking with the default color scheme for the three data series but it will be consistent for all your panels, and that can get visually monotonous. We can alter the colors of the series by clicking on the series' color line in the legend. Since we probably can't do that with all three series, we'll do it with a **Series Override** instead.

We'll use the color as a bit of visual cueing, with *blue* representing *cold* for our `windChill` series, *red* representing *hot* for our `heatIndex` series, and *orange* representing *warm* for our `temperature` series. Bear in mind that these are only suggestions and that there is no right or wrong decision regarding how to represent the data visually. In your dashboards, you may find yourself choosing different colors, or you may get feedback from viewers requesting different colors. Choose the colors and styles that help you connect the story you want to tell your audience.

Create three series overrides, one for each series:

- **Alias or regex**: `/temperature/` Color | change: **orange**
- **Alias or regex**: `/windChill/` Color | change: **blue**
- **Alias or regex**: `/heatIndex/` Color | change: **red**

We chose a regex for the data series name, just in case we want to create aliases that include the column text (`mean`, for example). In this case, we only need to match the series measurement and not the entire alias.

Name the panel title **Temperature** in the **Settings** section and move on.

Building the moisture panel

For the **Moisture** panel, we'll be querying for three interrelated data series: the temperature, the dew point, and the relative humidity. The easiest thing would be to simply duplicate the **Temperature** panel and modify the copy. To make a duplicate, click on the panel's title bar and select **More...** | **Duplicate**.

After making the duplicate, go to the **Query** area and set the following queries:

- **A/FROM: default dewpoint WHERE: station = KSFO**
- **A/FROM: default relativeHumidity WHERE: station = KSFO**
- **A/FROM: default temperature WHERE: station = KSFO**

In this case, we have access to all three data series, so we can simply click on the color bar next to each series name in the legend and set the color. To prevent any conflicts, delete the Series Overrides copied over from the Temperature panel, then use the legend to set the following values:

- `mean temperature`: **red**
- `mean dewpoint`: **blue**
- `mean relativeHumidity`**: yellow**

Since the relative humidity is a completely different scale than temperature and dew point, we'll set it up to use the right Y-axis. Click on the color bar next to the `relativeHumidity` label in the legend and select the **Y-Axis** tab. Turn on **Use the right Y-axis**. Next, we'll need to set the unit for the right Y-axis (the left y-axis should be **Celsius**). In the **Visualization** area, set up the following:

- **Axes/Right Y/Show**: **on**
- **Axes/Right Y/Unit**: **percent (0-100)**
- **Axes/Right Y/Y-Min**: **0**
- **Axes/Right Y/Y-Max**: **100**

We want to lock the minimum and maximum to 0 and 100, respectively, so that the graph doesn't scale up and down depending on the range of values in the displayed time frame. When these values are set in this way, the graph is vertically scaled to fit the entire panel.

If you open up the **Series overrides** section, you'll notice that activating the right Y-axis for **mean relativeHumidity** has automatically created a series override. Since **percentage** is a quantity, we can go ahead and turn on a little fill to help reinforce that. Add **Fill: 1** to the series override for **mean relativeHumidity**. It should end up like this:

- **Alias or regex**: **mean relativeHumidity**
- **Line fill**: **1**
- **Y-axis**: **2**

Feel free to convert the alias into a regex of `/relativeHumidity/` if you wish. In case you're wondering, Grafana designates the left Y-axis as 1 and the right Y-axis as 2.

Go to the **Settings** section and set the **Panel title**: **Moisture**

With that, you've completed another row! The two rows should look similar to the following output:

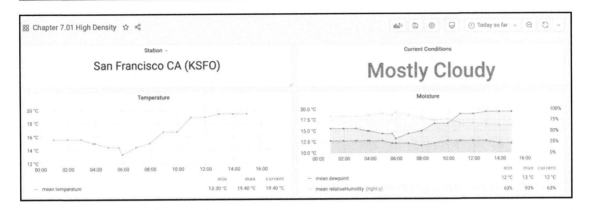

Next up, we'll work on the panels displaying barometric pressure readings.

Building the barometer panels

On this row, we're going to build two panels with slightly different views of the same data, namely the barometric pressure. To do this, we're going to create a single panel with both queries, but only one enabled. Then, in a copy of the same panel, we're going to swap the enabled queries. Just like copying the panel and tweaking the queries, this is another technique you can use to produce a number of similar panels.

Creating a barometric pressure graph panel

Create another panel (or copy your base panel) and set the following queries:

- **Data source: InfluxDB Weather**
- **A/FROM: default barometricPressure WHERE: station = KSFO**
- **A/SELECT: field (value) mean () math (/1000)**
- **A/GROUP BY: time ($_interval) fill (none)**
- **A/FORMAT AS**: Time series
- **A/ALIAS BY:** `$col $measurement`
- **B/FROM: default barometricPressure WHERE: station = KSFO**
- **B/SELECT: field (value) mean () Transformations | derivative (1h) Math | math (/1000)**
- **B/GROUP BY: time ($_interval) fill (none)**
- **B/FORMAT AS: Time series**

- **B/ALIAS BY:** `$col $measurement`
- **Query options/Min Interval:** 1m

In the query's **A SELECT** statement, we're querying for the barometric pressure. Since the NWS is sending the data in **Pascals (Pa)**, we'll divide them by 1,000 to convert this into **kilopascals (kPa)**. In the query's **B SELECT** statement, we want to calculate the rate of change in barometric pressure. The derivative will analyze the aggregated mean of barometric pressure over an interval – in this case, 1 hour – and determine the rate that it's changing. In calculus terms, we're asking InfluxDB to get the slope of the tangent to a curve that represents the pressure readings for a single hour.

If you're interested in how query **B SELECT** looks in the context of an actual InfluxDB query, text edit mode is your friend. Clicking the query's text edit mode (**pencil icon**) toggle shows you the actual query string embedded in the query object:

```
SELECT derivative(mean("value"), 1h) / 1000 FROM "barometricPressure" WHERE
$timeFilter GROUP BY time($__interval) fill(none)
```

Since this panel is only intended to show the actual barometric pressure, go ahead and disable the **B** query by clicking its **eye** icon.

Next, we'll style the graph. The style will be consistent with the temperature graphs:

- **Display/Lines: on**
- **Display/Points: on**
- **Display/Area Fill: 0**
- **Display/Point Radius: 1**
- **Axes/Left Y/Unit: Pressure | Kilopascals**
- **Legend/Options/Show: on**
- **Legend/Options/As Table: on**
- **Legend/Values/Min: on**
- **Legend/Values/Max: on**
- **Legend/Values/Current: on**

Set the **Panel title** in **Settings** as `Barometer Reading`

Creating a barometric pressure trend graph panel

For the next panel, we'll simply copy the **Barometer Reading** panel and duplicate it. In the **Query** area, disable the **A** query and enable the **B** query.

We'll need to make some adjustments to the left Y-axis to reflect a different measurement. Since the derivative we calculate is over a period of 1 hour, the true unit is kilopascals per hour. Unfortunately, Grafana doesn't provide such a unit, but we can easily create a custom unit by setting **Axes/Left Y/Unit**: `kPa/hr` | **Custom unit: kPa/hr**

Set the **Settings/Panel title**: `Barometer Trend`

That was pretty easy! The **Barometer Trend** panel is used to depict the barometer reading trend. If the derivative value is positive, that means the slope at the point is positive, so the barometer reading is rising, which is usually a sign of building high pressure and better weather. On the other hand, if the derivative value is negative, we know the pressure is dropping, which can signal an approaching low-pressure system and possible inclement weather. In the next section, we'll leverage the same derivative but convert it into a rising/falling readout.

Our dashboard rows now look like this:

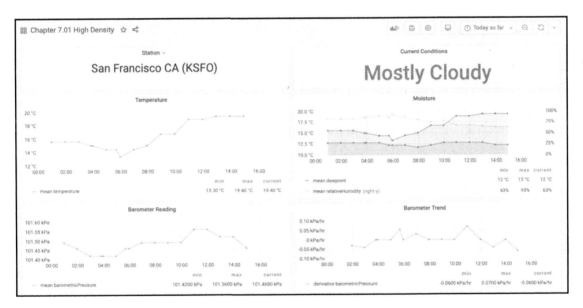

The next row of panels will cover our wind panels.

Building the wind panels

On our third row, we'll use a third technique to streamline our panel creation. In this case, we want to create two panels – one for wind speeds and another for wind direction. As we did previously, we'll create a single panel with all the necessary queries, but this time, we'll keep them enabled and use series overrides to hide the series we're not interested in.

Creating a wind speed graph panel

For the **Wind Speed** panel, we'll start by creating our panel with three queries. First, we'll set up the **A** query for wind speed:

- **Data source: InfluxDB Weather**
- **A/FROM: default windSpeed WHERE: station = KSFO**
- **A/SELECT: field (value) mean () math (/1000 * 3600)**
- **A/GROUP BY: time ($_interval) fill (none)**
- **A/FORMAT AS: Time series**
- **A/ALIAS BY:** $col $measurement

Next, we'll set up the **B** query for wind gust speed:

- **B/FROM: default windGust WHERE: station = KSFO**
- **B/SELECT: field (value) mean () math (/1000 * 3600)**
- **B/GROUP BY: time ($_interval) fill (none)**
- **B/FORMAT AS: Time series**
- **B/ALIAS BY:** $col $measurement

Finally, we'll set up the **C** query for the wind direction:

- **C/FROM: default windDirection WHERE station = KSFO**
- **C/SELECT: field (value) distinct ()**
- **C/GROUP BY: time ($_interval) fill (none)**
- **C/FORMAT AS: Time series**
- **C/ALIAS BY:** $col $measurement
- **Query options/Min interval: 1m**

In our **A** and **B** query *SELECT*s, I need to convert the wind speeds from meters/second into kilometers/hour, so I divide by 1,000 (meters in a kilometer) and multiply by 3,600 (seconds in an hour). In the case of the **C** query **SELECT**, calculating an aggregation value for a compass direction would be essentially meaningless, so we use distinct, with the understanding that wind direction is consistent in the intervening time periods between samples.

Depicting wind speed in the graph is a bit tricky. I'm opting to use points to emphasize these are spot averages; adding a line would imply the change in speed is continuous between samples, which is not necessarily the case:

- **Settings/Panel title**: `Wind Speed`
- **Display/Lines: off**
- **Display/Points: on**
- **Display/Point Radius: 4**
- **Axes/Left Y/Unit: kilometers/hour (km/h)**
- **Legend/Options/Show: on**
- **Legend/Options/As Table: on**
- **Legend/Values/Max: on**
- **Legend/Values/Current: on**

We're not that interested in minimum wind speeds as they are normally 0 anyway.

Since we may not have a `windGust` data series, it would be prudent to color the series using series overrides. We'll color the `windSpeed` series in a light purple and the `windGust` series in a dark purple to help it stand out. We'll also hide the `windDirection` series by setting a series override to hide it and remove it from the legend, as follows:

- **Alias or regex**: `/windSpeed/` Color change: **light purple**
- **Alias or regex**: `/windGust/` Color change: **dark purple**
- **Alias or regex**: `/windDirection/` Hidden Series: **true** Legend: **false**

Creating a wind direction stat panel

Now that we have a panel containing all our wind-based queries, we can leverage it to set up a wind panel for the direction. Instead of copying the **Wind Speed** panel, we just need to create a new panel or copy our base panel.

For the query, we're going to use **Dashboard Data Source** to reference the existing query from another panel on our dashboard. This plugin improves the efficiency of your dashboard by leveraging the cached data retrieved from the query in another panel. It also improves maintenance as you are changing multiple panels whenever you need to make a change to a single query they may have in common.

Dashboard Data Source is available from the **Query** dropdown in the **Queries** area. When you select **Dashboard**, you'll need to select a query set from the panel by going to the **Use results from panel** dropdown menu. Since the selections in the menu are derived from the panel titles, I recommend that you uniquely identify any panels you plan to share in this way; it will make your life easier. As we discussed previously, reference the panel results by using result from panel: `Wind Speed`

You can set the color of the data series using either the color bar in the legend or a series override. We need to set up the styles, as follows:

- **Display/Lines**: **on**
- **Display/Points**: **on**
- **Display/Point Radius**: **1**
- **Display/Area Fill**: **0**
- **Axes/Left Y/Unit**: Angle/Degrees (º)
- **Legend/Options/Show**: **on**
- **Legend/Options/As Table**: **on**
- **Legend/Options/Min**: **off**
- **Legend/Options/Max**: **off**
- **Legend/Values/Current**: **on**

I opted for turning on both the lines and points as I think it helps to make any discontinuities in wind direction stand out. Significant and sustained wind direction changes can be a sign of a frontal boundary passage. However, max and min values are inherently meaningless, so we turned them off in the legend. We'll also add our series overrides, as follows:

- **Alias or regex**: `/windSpeed/` Hidden Series: **true** Legend: **false**
- **Alias or regex**: `/windGust/` Hidden Series: **true** Legend: **false**
- **Alias or regex**: `/windDirection/` Color change: **purple**

Scrolling down a bit, this is what the bottom rows now look like:

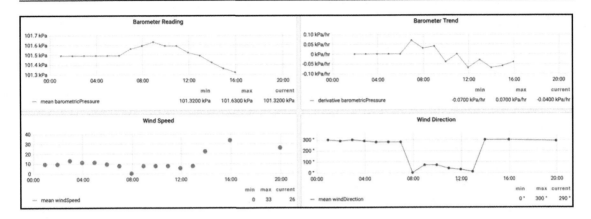

There's only one more panel to go and we're done!

Building the visibility panel

Our final panel is simply intended to depict visibility and it's straightforward to set up:

- **Query**: **InfluxDB Weather**
- **A/FROM**: **default visibility WHERE**: **station = KSFO**
- **A/SELECT**: **field (value) mean () math (/1000)**
- **A/GROUP BY**: **time ($_interval) fill (none)**
- **A/FORMAT AS**: **Time series**
- **A/ALIAS BY**: `$col $measurement`
- **Query options/Min interval**: **1m**

The value is measured in meters, so we convert it into kilometers in **SELECT**.

Since the visibility has a fixed range (10 miles or 16.09 km is considered the maximum visibility), I'm opting for a more stylized graphical representation of the visibility graph:

- **Display/Lines: on**
- **Display/Area Fill: 2**
- **Display/Line Width: 1**
- **Display/Staircase: on**
- **Axes/Left Y/Unit: kilometer (km)**
- **Axes/Left Y/Y-Max: 16.09**
- **Legend/Options/Show: on**

- **Legend/Options/Min: on**
- **Legend/Options/Max: on**
- **Legend/Values/Current: on**

We turned on the **Staircase** option to help emphasize the discrete nature of the visibility observation. Adding the fill helps reinforce the notion that visibility extends from 0 to the observation value.

As an exercise, try adding a **Wind Gust** panel in the last panel slot on the page. Here's my version (alas, there were no wind gusts at the time):

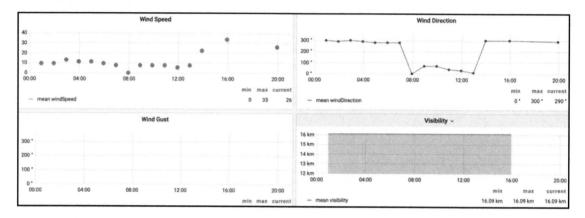

To help you work through any issues, I've included this dashboard in the GitHub repository for this book. You'll find it in the `Chapter07/dashboards` directory.

Creating a high information visibility dashboard

In this second example, we'll create a dashboard intended to provide information in a much higher level of view; that is, that of a display intended to be scanned rapidly in order for us to get a *big-picture* viewpoint. Typically, you'd see this type of dashboard in a kiosk-type context, such as in an operations center or a public informational display.

We'll be conveying a set of data that's similar to what we had in the previous section, but we'll only have a limited slice of each data series, typically the most current readings. We'll be making extensive use of the **Stat** panel as opposed to the **Graph** panel, as we did previously. The idea we're trying to convey is that the dashboard will be displayed in a context that makes details hard to read from a distance.

Designing the dashboard

What we want to do is create and arrange a set of panels that will fit on a single page as we may not have the ability to scroll around or even interact with the page (kiosk-mode). In keeping with the strategy we described previously, here's what we have in mind:

- **First row**: A panel with the station name
- **Second row**:
    - Panels for current, high, and low temperature
    - A dew point panel
- **Third row**:
    - Panels for barometer reading and trend
    - A visibility panel
- **Fourth row**:
    - A panel for the current conditions
    - Panels for wind speed, direction, and gust

In this example, we'll try to use some of what we've learned about efficient panel creation to quickly set up these panels. We'll also try to reuse some of what we built for the previous dashboard with the idea being that since we've already determined the queries, we should be able to copy over the **Graph** panels and set their **Visualizations** to **Stat** panels.

Building the station panel

Our first panel will be the **Station** panel. If you've already worked through the previous examples, copy the **Station** panel from your dashboard and create a new dashboard. You'll be doing some flipping back-and-forth between dashboards, so you may want to open them up in multiple tabs. Be sure to save your new dashboard.

In the panel, select **Paste copied panel** to set the panel. Resize the panel so that it's the full width of the window and the minimum height that still displays the text properly (about 2 grid points).

Building the temperature panels

Next, we'll set up our temperature panels. We going to squeeze four panels onto a single row, so you'll want to do some resizing. I'm working on a stock MacBook Pro screen, but that isn't necessarily a standard size for everyone. Feel free to experiment with different layouts to get a feel for what works best for your display size.

Buiding a current temperature stat panel

Copy the **Temperature** panel from the previous dashboard and paste it into a new panel. Panels always start in the top-left corner, so you'll want to get used to moving things into position immediately after creating them or building your dashboards from the bottom up!

Edit the panel and disable all the queries except for the `temperature` query. In the **Panel** tab's **Visualization** section, set the panel to **Stat.** In the **Settings** section, set the **Panel title**: `Current Temperature`

In the **Display** section, set the following value:

- **Value: Last**
- **Graph mode**: **Area**

In the **Field** tab's **Standard options** section, set the following value:

- **Standard options/Unit**: **Temperature | Celsius ºC**
- **Standard options/Decimals**: **1**

In the **Field** tab's **Thresholds** section, delete any existing thresholds and set **Base, Color: Orange**

Resize the panel to about one-third of the screen width and the height to about 4 units. As you go along, you'll resize everything to make things fit, but we can start with some general sizing so that we have room to expand.

Set this and the panel is complete.

Creating a high-temperature stat panel

Since we need two panels for the high and low temperatures, we're going to use a **Dashboard Data Source** referencing the **Temperature** query. Create a new **Stat** panel and set the query, as follows:

- **Data source: Dashboard**
- **Use results from panel**: Current Temperature

In the **Panel** tab's **Display** settings, we'll set up the panel so that it displays the highest temperature:

- **Value: Max**
- **Color mode: Value**
- **Graph mode: None**

In the **Field Standard options** settings, set the following values:

- **Unit**: ºC
- **Decimals**: 1

In the **Field Thresholds** settings, delete all the thresholds.

Set **Panel title** to **High Temperature** and resize the panel to the minimum width that comfortably displays the panel text. That's it for this panel.

Creating a low-temperature stat panel

Since the Low Temperature panel is virtually identical to the High Temperature panel, we'll just duplicate it and modify the **Panel** tab's **Display** setting as **Value: Min**

Set **Panel title** to **Low Temperature** and we're done with this panel.

Creating a dew point stat panel

The final panel in this row will be our Dew Point panel. We'll copy over the **Moisture** panel from the previous dashboard and set it up in a similar fashion to what we have for the Current Temperature panel. After copying the panel, create a new panel and choose **Paste copied panel**.

Edit the panel queries to disable all but the `dewpoint` query.

Switch the **Panel** tab's **Visualization** to **Stat** and configure it similarly to what we did for the `Current Temperature` panel:

- **Panel/Display/Value**: **Last**
- **Panel/Display/Color mode**: **Value**
- **Panel/Display/Graph mode**: **Area**
- **Field/Standard options/Unit**: **Temperature | Celsius ℃**
- **Field/Standard options/Decimals**: **1**

We'll set the sparkline blue to reference the blue we used previously for the dew point in the **Moisture** panel. Delete the thresholds in the **Field** tab's **Thresholds** menu and set **Base Color**: **Blue**

Set **Panel title** to **Dew Point** and resize it so that it fits onto the row with the other panels. At this point, your dashboard should look roughly like this:

Don't worry too much about sizing right now. When we get more panels on the dashboard, we can always scale and rearrange them to make our display more informative or aesthetically pleasing. Now, let's move on to the barometer panels.

Building the barometer panels

For the row containing the barometer panels, we will fill it with three panels, but only two of them will be barometric pressure-related. We'll fill out the row with a visibility panel. This maximizes our screen real estate utilization.

If you'd rather fill in space with an empty panel, simply use a **Text** panel and delete the panel text and title. Now, you have a handy *spacer panel* for filling in gaps or forcing other panels into tricky positions on your **Dashboard** page.

Creating a barometer reading stat panel

Moving on to the barometer panels, we'll utilize the same techniques we used previously to build our barometer reading panel. First, copy the **Barometer Reading** panel from the previous dashboard, then create a new panel on the dashboard, and then **Paste copied panel**. Check the **Query** tab on the new panel and confirm that only the **A** query (the one that queries for the mean **barometricPressure** reading) is the only enabled query. Finally, switch the panel's **Visualization** to **Stat**.

Next, we'll configure the panel's settings. We'll use kilopascals for **Unit** and the default green color as our sparkline color so that it matches the green in the original panel:

- **Panel/Display/Value: Last**
- **Panel/Display/Color mode: Value**
- **Panel/Display/Graph mode: Area**
- **Field/Standard options/Unit: Pressure | Kilopascals**
- **Field/Standard options/Decimals: 1**
- **Field/Thresholds**: <delete thresholds>
- **Field/Thresholds/Base Color: Light green**

Finally, position the panel below the **Temperature** panel and resize it so that it's roughly the same size.

Creating a barometric pressure trend stat panel

For the **Barometer Trend** panel, we'll duplicate the **Barometer Reading** panel and switch the active queries. Then we'll use a value mapping to display a text description of the trend.

Duplicate the **Barometer Reading** panel and position the next to it, if it didn't spawn there by default. Inside the **Queries** area, enable the **B** query (the one that queries for the derivative).

We'll also need to tweak the query so that it produces a slightly different value than just the derivative. Here, we want to convert the derivative so that it either produces a 1 if the derivative is positive or a -1 if the derivative is negative. The math isn't that complicated; we're just dividing the derivative by the absolute (always positive) value of the derivative. We'll use these values to create our value mappings:

- **SELECT: field (value) mean () derivative (1h) math (/abs (derivative (mean ("value"), 1h)))**

Now, let's move on to our **Settings** tabs. We should make sure to turn off the sparklines and clear the **Unit**. Now, set the following values:

- **Panel/Display/Color mode: Value**
- **Panel/Display/Graph mode: None**
- **Field/Standard options/Unit: Misc | none**

While we're on the **Field** tab, we'll create a set of three value mappings:

- Mapping Type: **Value** Value: **1** Text: `Rising`
- Mapping Type: **Value** Value: **0** Text: `Steady`
- Mapping Type: **Value** Value: **-1** Text: `Falling`

Finally, we want to color the text based on the value as well, so we'll add a pair of thresholds. We want the falling barometer to display as red and the rising barometer to display as green (use **invert** to flip the color order):

- Threshold/Base Color: **Blue**
- Threshold/Threshold: **1** Color: **Green**
- Threshold/Threshold: **-1** Color: **Red**

Set **Panel title** to **Barometer Trend** and we're done. We have some extra space to the left of our two barometer panels, so let's add a visibility panel to fill in the space.

Building the visibility panel

To create a visibility panel, we'll need to copy the **Visibility** panel from the previous dashboard. Resize it and drag it into an empty position next to the barometer panels. Let's create a little visual excitement, shall we? Switch the panel's **Visualization** to **Bar Gauge** and configure the following settings in the **Panel** tab:

- **Display/Show: Calculate**
- **Display/Value: Last**
- **Display/Orientation: Horizontal**
- **Display/Mode: Retro LCD**

In the **Field** tab, set the range of the graph and the units, as follows:

- **Field/Unit: length | kilometer (km)**
- **Field/Min: 0**
- **Field/Max: 16.09**
- **Field/Decimals: 2**

Visibility readings range from 0 to 10 miles. However, since the data returned from the query is in kilometers, we need to set the range from 0 to 16.09. We can also set a couple of thresholds to reflect the visibility extremes. Anything below 100 meters is considered zero visibility, so that will be our first threshold. The maximum visibility is 10 miles (16.09 km), so we'll set a threshold just short of that as well:

- **Thresholds/Base Color: Red**
- **Threshold/Threshold: 0.1** Color: **Light blue**
- **Threshold/Threshold: 16** Color: **Dark blue**

Set **Panel title** to **Visibility**. That completes all the editing we need to do. I'm not totally happy with the size of the displayed bar graph as it tends to draw your eye to it, so I shrank the height down to 1 unit. But now, I'm worried that will get lost next to any panels above or below it. Due to this, I will create two blank **Text** panels and placed the **Visibility** panel between them. You can see the results here:

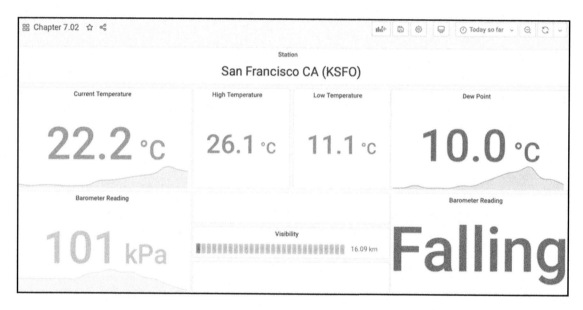

From the preceding screenshot, I can quickly see a lot of information. However, we still have the wind panels to go.

Building the wind panels

We've reached the last row on our panel, which calls for three panels to cover wind speed, direction, and gusts. We'd also like to place a panel with the current conditions on the last row. Let's start with the wind speed panel.

Creating a wind speed stat panel

We'll get our wind speed panel from the **Wind Speed** panel in our previous dashboard. Copy it and move it down to the last row at the bottom of the screen. Resize it so that it's the same width as the **Barometer Reading** panel above it and set the height so that the bottom of the panel is just inside the window. Open it for editing and disable all the queries except for the one that queries `windSpeed`.

Next, configure its **Visualization** to **Stat** and configure it as follows:

- **Panel/Display/Value**: **Last**
- **Panel/Display/Color mode**: **Value**
- **Panel/Display/Graph mode**: **Area**
- **Field/Standard options/Unit**: **Velocity | kilometers/hour (km/h)**
- **Field/Standard options/Decimals**: **1**
- **Field/Thresholds**: <delete thresholds>
- **Field/Thresholds/Base Color**: **purple**

Confirm **Panel title** is set to **Wind Speed**.

Creating a wind gust stat panel

Duplicate the **Wind Speed** panel to create the **Wind Gust** panel. It should be placed next to the **Wind Speed** panel and be the same size. Edit the queries to disable all but the queries for windGust.

Next, we'll make a tweak to the configuration. Since wind gusts are transient, it is likely there will be no wind gust data to display. In this case, it will display **No data** in big letters, which isn't particularly helpful. Let's modify the **Standard options/No Value** setting so that it says something more interesting:

- **Panel/Display/Graph mode**: **None**
- **Field/Standard options/No value**: **Steady**

Now, when there's no gust data, the display will read **Steady**, which is true. Set **Panel title** to **Wind Gust** to complete the panel.

Creating a wind direction stat panel

Our last wind panel is built the same way as the previous one – simply duplicate it. However, since a compass bearing is harder to visualize compared to compass points, we'll create a value mapping to convert the numerical display into strings.

Once you've duplicated the previous panel, disable all the queries except the one for `windDirection`. First, we'll need to make sure we've cleared most of the settings, as follows:

- **Panel/Display/Value: Last**
- **Panel/Display/Color mode: Value**
- **Panel/Display/Graph mode: None**
- **Field/Standard options/Unit: Misc | none**

Next, we'll set up the value mappings. They can be found in the **Field** tab in the **Value Mappings** section:

- **Field/Value mappings/Mapping type: range** From: **337.5** To: **22.5** Text: N
- **Field/Value mappings/Mapping type: range** From: **22.5** To: **67.5** Text: NE
- **Field/Value mappings/Mapping type: range** From: **67.5** To: **112.5** Text: E
- **Field/Value mappings/Mapping type: range** From: **112.5** To: **157.5** Text: SE
- **Field/Value mappings/Mapping type: range** From: **157.5** To: **202.5** Text: S
- **Field/Value mappings/Mapping type: range** From: **202.5** To: **247.5** Text: SW
- **Field/Value mappings/Mapping type: range** From: **247.5** To: **292.5** Text: W
- **Field/Value mappings/Mapping type: range** From: **292.5** To: **337.5** Text: NW

Whew, that was a lot of typing!

Building a current conditions panel

Our final panel is one depicting the current conditions. We don't have a panel for this one yet, so we'll need to create a **Stat** panel from scratch. Do that and set up the query, as follows:

- Data source: **InfluxDB Weather**
- FROM: **default textDescription** WHERE: **station = KSFO**
- SELECT **field(value)**
- GROUP BY: **<empty>**
- FORMAT AS: **Time series**

Here are the settings:

- Panel/Display/Value: **Last**
- Panel/Display/Color mode: **Value**

- Panel/Display/Graph mode: None
- Field/Standard options/Unit: **Misc | none**
- Field/Thresholds: Delete
- Field/Thresholds/Base Color: **Custom | grey**

Set **Panel title** to **Current Conditions** to finish editing. With this, I've left you with a bit of a challenge. You'll need to fit the **Current Conditions** panel on the last row along with the wind panels. See if you can rearrange and resize the panels to get everything to fit neatly. You may also want to adjust the font sizes to keep the text from getting cropped.

Here's my version:

I invite you to examine this dashboard screenshot and compare it to the previous one. Clearly, we can pick up important weather information at a glance. That's the intent, and I think we've succeeded. Good job!

Along with the previous dashboard, you'll find this dashboard in the GitHub repository for this book. You can find them in the `Chapter07/dashboards` directory.

Summary

That completes our exercise of working with dashboard creation and layout. Play with your dashboards' panel arrangements to see what various combinations look like. This is a good opportunity to get a better understanding of how to work with the Grafana layout manager. While you experiment with the ordering of the various panels, keep a few things in mind.

First, cultural groups can read from left to right, right to left, and from top to bottom. Know your audience and arrange your dashboard panels to reveal information in the order that your viewers typically scan. Second, use color, size, and visual contrast to draw the eye of the viewer toward the information you want to particularly highlight. Finally, depending on the context, you may want to avoid packing too much information onto a single dashboard. Too much visual information can be confusing to the viewer.

In the next chapter, we'll look at more ways to make panel creation more efficient and responsive. We'll also look at some more advanced dashboard features that can expand the scope of your dashboards by linking them together into a coherent, interactive whole.

8
Working with Advanced Dashboard Features

By now, you're probably feeling pretty comfortable with Grafana but have legitimate concerns about the effort involved. You may be thinking that the possibility of writing a lot of code to handle ETL tasks might eat into your time budget for building the dashboards. Perhaps the number of panels you will have to configure and organize on multiple dashboards seems potentially tedious, error-prone work.

In this chapter, we're going to look at how to reduce the ETL burden using off-the-shelf tools, as well as how to use templates to fill a dashboard with variants using only a single panel. We'll also show you how annotations make it possible to *drill down* into aggregated data in order to examine individual data points. Then, we'll take our dashboards and link them together with simple UI elements. Finally, we'll look at strategies for sharing our dashboards with others.

The following topics will be covered in this chapter:

- Building the data server
- Templating dashboards
- Linking dashboards
- Annotating dashboards
- Sharing dashboards

Let's get started!

Technical requirements

The tutorial code, dashboards, and other helpful files for this chapter can be found in this book's GitHub repository at https://github.com/PacktPublishing/Learn-Grafana-7.0/tree/master/Chapter08.

Building the data server

Imagine for a moment that you are working for the public works department of a major city. Throughout the day, citizens use their phones and computers to report problems via the 311 service (`https://www.open311.org/`). You've been tasked with accessing the 311 data, building dashboards, and presenting them to various stakeholders within the city government. They will want to see how many of the various types of calls are made to the system, as well as how they are distributed across the city in various council districts.

Before we can build our dashboards, we'll need to get some data. Luckily, many major cities make anonymized 311 data publicly accessible in many popular data formats, including JSON and CSV. For this exercise, we'll be working with 311 data from the city of San Francisco. This data is available via their extensive data portal at `https://data.sfgov.org/City-Infrastructure/Current-FY-Cases/iy63-pi3t`.

To get started with this exercise, open a Terminal shell window and `cd` into the `Chapter08` folder in your clone of this book's GitHub repository and download the dataset (in CSV format) from the DataSF website (or grab a copy from this book's GitHub repository). After downloading the file, we'll set up an Elasticsearch server to serve our data. Elasticsearch is part of a powerful triad of software, including Logstash and Kibana, that comprises the Elasticsearch ELK stack. Rather than writing code to import the data into Elasticsearch, we'll use Logstash to read our file and send it to the server. Here's a quick look at the `docker-compose.yml` file:

```
version: "3"
services:
  elasticsearch:
    image: docker.elastic.co/elasticsearch/elasticsearch:7.7.0
    ports:
      - "9200:9200"
    environment:
      - discovery.type=single-node
    volumes:
      - "${PWD-.}/elasticsearch:/usr/share/elasticsearch/data"

  logstash:
    image: docker.elastic.co/logstash/logstash:7.7.0
    volumes:
      - "${PWD-.}/logstash:/usr/share/logstash/pipeline"
      - "${PWD-.}/data:/data"

  grafana:
    image: grafana/grafana:latest
    ports:
      - "3000:3000"
```

```
volumes:
  - "${PWD-.}/grafana:/var/lib/grafana"
```

In this file, we first define an Elasticsearch service:

- Use the latest image version (7.7.0, at the time of writing) of Elasticsearch.
- Expose the Elasticsearch port at 9200.
- Map the /usr/share/elasticsearch/data directory in the container to a local Elasticsearch directory.

Set up a single worker node. Since you may be running Elasticsearch on a platform such as a laptop, this out-of-the-box configuration should be more than sufficient for our purposes. For Grafana, do the following:

- Use the most current image.
- Expose port 3000.
- Map /var/lib/grafana in the container to a local Grafana directory.

Finally, we need to specify the Logstash service:

- Use the latest image version (7.7.0, at the time of writing) of Logstash.
- Map the /usr/share/logstash/pipeline directory in the container to a local Logstash directory.

We won't actually run Logstash as a persistent service; instead, we are just using this service specification in Docker Compose to give Logstash access to the network our Elasticsearch and Grafana servers are running on.

Launch the services by running docker-compose:

```
% docker-compose up -d elasticsearch
% docker-compose up -d grafana
```

We specify each service individually because we don't want to spin up a Logstash service just yet. It won't hurt anything if you accidentally run all three services, but we want to control when Logstash processes the CSV file.

Before we can import our file with Logstash, we need to configure it. It is beyond the scope of this book to go into a lot of detail on the many features and capabilities of both Elasticsearch and Logstash (in fact, there are whole books available from this very publisher). In short, Logstash is designed to deliver a log-processing pipeline in a single tool, configured through a single configuration file that specifies the actions of a sequence of plugins.

A Logstash configuration includes three components: input, filters, and output. Here's a simple schematic diagram:

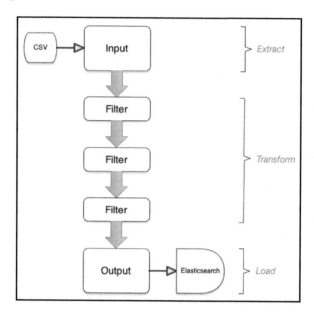

In our case, the input will be a file read in from standard input (stdin). In order to properly clean and conform our file so that it can be imported into Elasticsearch, we will configure some filters so that they can process a CSV file. Finally, the output will be to standard output (stdout, for debugging purposes) and our Elasticsearch server.

Let's walk through the configuration file; first up is the input section:

```
input {
   stdin {}
}
```

It doesn't get any more simple than this. Typically, Logstash is configured as a service that periodically looks for changes in one or more files, then reads them in for processing. We only need to run Logstash once to input a single file, so we'll use the stdin plugin so that Logstash quits after file processing is completed. Next up, we have the filter section:

```
filter {
   if "CaseID" in [message] {
     drop {}
   }
   csv {
     columns =>
```

```
["CaseID","Opened","Closed","ResponsibleAgency","Category","RequestType","A
ddress","Street",
"SupervisorDistrict","Neighborhood","PoliceDistrict","Latitude","Longitude"
,"Source","MediaURL"]
    convert => {
      "Latitude" => "float"
      "Longitude" => "float"
    }
  }
  date {
    match => ["Opened",  "MM/dd/yyyy HH:mm:ss a"]
    target => "Opened"
  }
  date {
    match => ["Closed",  "MM/dd/yyyy HH:mm:ss a"]
    target => "Closed"
  }
}
```

This is the section where the real work happens:

1. First, we check each line of the file (in Logstash, each line is treated as an event with the contents of the line stored in `message`) for the `CaseID` string, which should only be present in the header. If the line is indeed a header line, drop it from further processing.
2. Next, we configure the `csv` plugin to process each line, mapping each field in the parsed line to the corresponding element in the `columns` list (copied from the header).
3. We convert the latitude and longitude into `float` values if we want to map them.
4. By default, the `csv` plugin won't recognize the `Opened` and `Closed` fields as dates, so we will use the `date` plugin to convert them by matching the string contents of the two named date fields against the format string and store the converted date objects back in their original fields.

Once we've parsed and processed the CSV file, we'll need to ship the results to Elasticsearch. This is handled in the `output` section:

```
output {
  elasticsearch {
    hosts => "elasticsearch:9200"
    index => "data-index"
  }
  stdout {}
}
```

There are two plugins handling output: `elasticsearch` and `stdout`. The `elasticsearch` plugin is given two parameters, with `hosts` specifying the host and port for the connection to Elasticsearch and `index` specifying the destination index for the data. You can think of the Elasticsearch index as being analogous to a table in a traditional relational database. The `stdout` plugin line is optional and is included as it also prints out the same processed data it will transmit to the Elasticsearch server in the Terminal window. This output is often helpful for troubleshooting any problems that may arise when processing the data.

To load the data into Elasticsearch, run the following command:

```
% docker-compose run logstash logstash < data/Current_FY_Cases.csv
```

This command runs `logstash` from the Logstash service and redirects its input from the CSV file. The file in question is moderately sized (~325 MB), so depending on your computer's performance, it may take around 15-20 minutes to load all the rows into Elasticsearch, so take a break!

Templating dashboards

Once you've loaded the data into Elasticsearch, open up Grafana and create a new Elasticsearch data source using these options:

- **Name**: `Elasticsearch` (or whatever you prefer)
- **HTTP/URL**: `http://elasticsearch:9200`
- **HTTP/Access: Server (default)**
- **Elasticsearch details/Index name**: `data-index`
- **Elasticsearch details/pattern: No pattern**
- **Elasticsearch details/Time field name**: `Opened`
- **Elasticsearch details/Version: 7.0+**
- **Elasticsearch details/Min time interval**: `5m`

The data source page should look something like this:

You may have noticed that while we have typically been using `localhost` to access servers such as Grafana and InfluxDB, we're using `elasticsearch` in this particular case. By default, Elasticsearch is not configured to allow **Cross-Origin Resource Requests (CORS)** that would be originated from a data source via the browser. For our purposes, we want to keep to a minimal Elasticsearch configuration, so we can just switch the data source to **Server Access** mode, which forces the Grafana server to forward those requests to Elasticsearch on our behalf.

But in order to do that, we need to give it an Elasticsearch address that's visible to the server. Since we are using Docker Compose to manage networking for our services, namely Grafana and Elasticsearch, we need to configure the data source with the service name from the `docker-compose.yml` file. If you were able to successfully connect your data source to Elasticsearch, you should have seen a green message near the bottom reading **Index Ok. Time field name OK**. This indicates that the data source can access the index and identified the `Opened` field as a proper date field for use as a **Time field**.

Querying with Elasticsearch

Now that we have a functioning data source, let's build a simple **Graph** panel to get a feel for how we're going to present the data. Remember that we want to be able to look at the kinds of calls made to 311 across different neighborhoods, so let's first make a query just to get an idea of how many graffiti calls are made. You can do this in **Explore**, but we're going to build on our panel as we go, so you might want to start with a new **Graph** panel.

Go to the **Query** tab to access the Elasticsearch data source query. You'll notice its similarity to the InfluxDB **Query** tab from previous chapters. The terminology may be a little different between Elasticsearch and InfluxDB, but the concepts are very similar. Let's enter a query string into the **Query** field. Elasticsearch leverages a powerful Google-like search engine called Lucene to perform text queries, so just type in the word Graffiti and you should get a response back with all the matching data.

If you don't see anything change, make sure your query timeframe is wide enough. If you downloaded the dataset recently from DataSF, set it to **Last 7 days**; if you are using data from this book's repository, the data goes back from January 19, 2020. If your query found the data (called *documents* in Elasticsearch terminology) in your Elasticsearch server and you have the approximate time range, you should see an output similar to the following:

The next field is called **Metric**, but it is easier to think of it as an **aggregation function**. If you use **Date Histogram** for **Group by**, the specified metric in this case, Count, is calculated for each histogram bin. For **Group by**, you can modify the time interval, but let's leave it set to **auto** for now. Its date field is specified as **Opened**, which we defined when we set up the data source.

Next, let's add another **Group by** to give us a breakdown by supervisor district. Click the **+** icon to the right of the **Group by** field. This should give you another **Group by**, but by **Terms**. **Terms**, in the context of Elasticsearch, is much like the InfluxDB tag in that it represents a field of text values. Let's select **SupervisorDistrict.keyword** from the select field arrow dropdown. Since there are 11 districts in San Francisco, select **15** from the dropdown below **Top**:

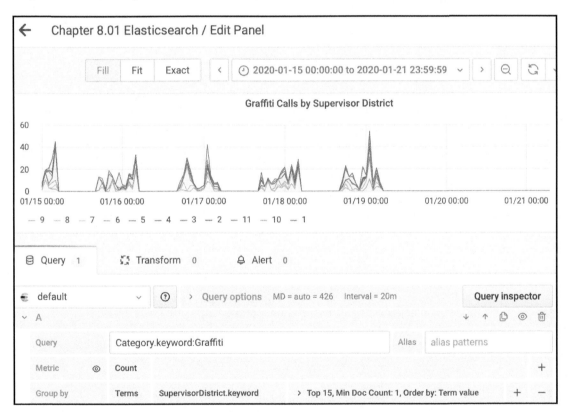

While we're at it, let's get more specific about the query. By placing `Graffiti` as the only entry in the **Query** field, we're asking Elasticsearch to find the string `Graffiti` in any of the text fields in our index. We only care about `Graffiti` as it pertains to a particular field, namely the **RequestType** field. Since we are looking at the **Graffiti** category type, we want to query the corresponding `Category.keyword` field. Enter the following in the **Query** field:

- **Query**: `Category.keyword:Graffiti`

 Let's pause for a moment to clarify something about text queries in Elasticsearch. Since we used Logstash to add our data to the Elasticsearch index without specifying the index mapping (an index configuration that works much like a database schema), Elasticsearch created one for us. For each field not otherwise specified, Elasticsearch then created two fields: a `text` field named for the field itself and a special `.keyword` version of the same field. The content in the text fields is automatically broken up (analyzed) into word-like objects called **tokens** and then indexed by those tokens. This is the way Elasticsearch supports free text searches. Keyword fields, on the other hand, are left unanalyzed, so to match a keyword field, you will need to query for the whole keyword's text.

Before we move on, let's go ahead and configure the **Panel Display** settings:

- **Bars**: **on**
- **Lines**: **off**
- **Stacking & Null value/Stack**: **on**

Configure the following setting in the **Legend** section:

- **Options/Show**: **on**

Here is what the term bars look like when they're stacked up:

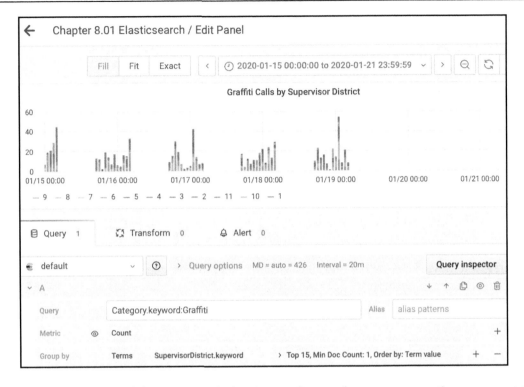

This is all well and good, but constantly having to change the query every time we want to look at a different category is going to be tedious. We're going to address this problem next.

Creating a template variable

Now that we have an idea of what our **Graph** panel might look like, we need to observe that if we were to create additional panels, one for each category of 311 call, we might need to create many panels, with each being a virtually identical panel, save for the value of the category in question. This seems tedious at best, and a potential maintenance nightmare at worst. What would happen if, say, you wanted to tailor the color scheme for the breakdowns or change the stacking options? You might end up clicking through dozens of panels, only to make a single change.

What if we could put a placeholder in our query, and then select the value of the placeholder with a menu? You could then create sort of a *template* **Graph** panel, with a placeholder for the actual query value. Here, you would enter the template variable. A *template variable* is a special string that represents a placeholder that Grafana will substitute for one or more from a set of predefined values.

Template variables have three main characteristics associated with them:

- The definition of the variable, which determines its name and the possible values.
- The insertion of the variable in various dashboard components, including panels and rows.
- The value of the variable, which, depending on the context, may be a defined constant or a user-specified selection via a drop-down menu.

The first step in working with a template variable is to define one. We'll start by defining a template variable to represent a 311 category, so let's call it `311Category`.

Open **Dashboard Settings**, select **Variables**, and click **Add Variable**. Use these settings:

- **General/Name**: `311Category`
- **General/Type**: **Query**
- **General/Label**: `311 Category`
- **Query Options/Data Source**: `Elasticsearch` (the Elasticsearch data source)
- **Query Options/Query**: `{"find": "terms", "field": "Category.keyword"}`
- **Query Options/Sort**: **Alphabetical (asc)**
- **Selection Options/Include All Option**: **on**

If you typed in the query correctly, and your timeframe encompasses a reasonable cross-section of data (at least a day or two), you should see a list of possible values under **Preview of values**:

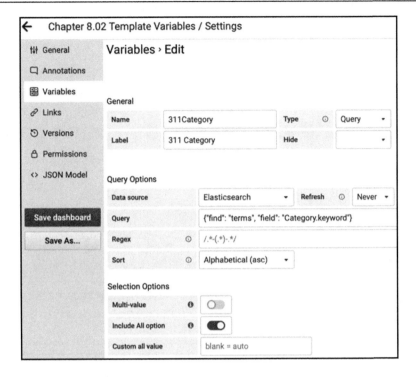

Now, let's go over these settings:

- **Name** is the actual name you will reference in the dashboard elements.
- **Label** is simply the label for the drop-down menu you will use to select the template variable's value.
- **Type** is one of several possible template variable types we'll explore. In this case, it is one that is derived via a **Data source** query.
- **Query** is a snippet of JSON that will go into an Elasticsearch query that generates the values for the template variable.

The snippet indicates the query should find the unique values (terms) for the `Category.keyword` field. The default maximum number of terms returned is 500, but if the cardinality (number of possible values) of the field is higher than a few dozen, you may want to consider setting a limit by adding the `size` key to the query:

```
{"find": "terms", "field": "Category.keyword", "size": limit}
```

- Set **Sort** to **asc** (ascending) in alphabetical order.
- Enable **Include All Option**, in case we want the option to see all the categories.

Don't forget to click **Add** or **Update** when you have finished editing the template variable. It's all too easy to click away to one of the other settings pages and, sadly, lose your changes.

Adding template variables to the graph panel

Now that we've added a template variable, we'll put it to use. First, we'll stop the query. In the **Query** field, change `Graffiti` to `$311Category`:

- **Query**: `Category.keyword:$311Category`

Let's include the variable when we set **Panel title**:

- **Title**: `$311Category by Supervisor District`

As we can see, our variable works in other places besides the query! Now that you've set up the panel, try out different values from the **311 Category** dropdown. Note how both the results and the title change in response to the variable's settings:

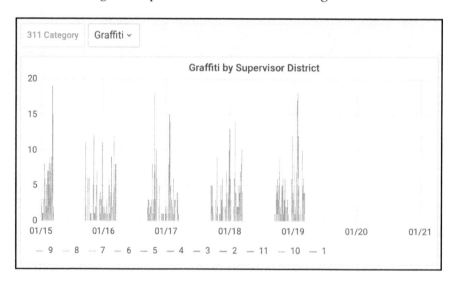

Once you've got a taste of the power of template variables, you'll begin to find all sorts of places where you can use them. When you do, your dashboards will become that much more flexible without a lot of extra effort.

Templating additional variables

Why stop here? Perhaps we could template the interval? Let's create a new variable that we will use to set different **Date Histogram** intervals. That way, we can see what the call volume looks like when aggregated across periods of time. But how do we specify possible values for time intervals? Happily, Grafana provides the answer with the `Interval` variable type. Create a new variable and call it `HistInterval`:

- **General/Name**: `HistInterval`
- **General/Type**: **Interval**
- **General/Label**: `Histogram Interval`

Feel free to modify the list of possible time intervals. There is an additional option you can activate called **Auto Option**. Turning this on will present a new interval, called **Auto**, that will automatically calculate and divide the time range into **Step count** intervals, but never create an interval smaller than **Min interval**.

Once you've set up the variable, go to the query in your panel and, in the **Then by Interval** box, open it and select **$HistInterval** from the **Interval** dropdown. The data source detects the list of **Interval** values and makes them available in the dropdown.

Try out your new panel and experiment with different intervals. You may need to adjust your time range to accommodate some of the larger intervals. Likewise, you may get an error from Elasticsearch if you set the interval time too small. Don't be alarmed – this just means that you've asked Elasticsearch to break down the graph data into too many chunks of returned data (called buckets) than it has been configured to aggregate. In a production environment, you would tune your Elasticsearch configuration to handle higher bucket counts if necessary, but for now, just scale down your time range width.

Here's what a 1-day interval across a 7-day time range might look like:

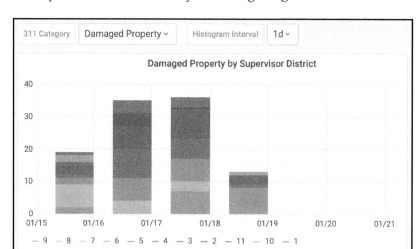

Why stop there? Behold the power of the template variable. Create a new variable called `FieldName`:

- **General/Name**: `FieldName`
- **General/Type**: **Query**
- **General/Label**: `Field Name`
- **Query Options/Data Source**: `Elasticsearch` (the Elasticsearch data source)
- **Query Options/Query**: `{"find": "fields", "type": "keyword"}`
- **Query Options/Regex**: `/(.*)\.keyword/`
- **Query Options/Sort**: **Alphabetical (asc)**

We use **Regex** to trim off the `.keyword` portion of the string. Only the text that matches the regex within the parentheses is retained. Since we removed `.keyword` from the variable, you'll need to append it when you reference the variable in your queries.

Next, we will create a new template variable that will take the result of the field name and create a variable with the terms for that field on the fly:

- **General/Name**: `FieldTerms`
- **General/Type**: **Query**
- **General/Label**: **Field Terms**
- **Query Options/Data Source**: `Elasticsearch` (the Elasticsearch data source)

- **Query Options/Query**: `{"find": "terms", "field": "$FieldName.keyword"}`
- **Query Options/Sort**: **Alphabetical (asc)**
- **Selection Options/Include All Options**: **on**

Now, update your panel query so that it uses both variables:

- **Query**: `$FieldName:$FieldTerms`

Here's an example where I selected **Category** as **Field Name** and **Abandoned Vehicle** from **Field Terms**:

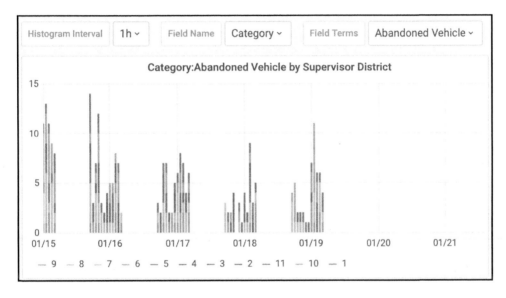

Try out different combinations of `$Field Name` and `$Field Terms` and see how it affects both the graph and the title. Also, note how the contents of the **Field Terms** dropdown changes when you pick a different **Field Name**.

Creating Ad hoc filters

Grafana has developed a special template variable that functions in a similar fashion. Called **Ad hoc filters**, it is designed to perform as a filter you would use to reduce a relatively broad query to something more specific. There is almost no setup involved in using **Ad hoc filters**. You simply specify a name and the data source that corresponds to your **Graph** panel queries. Once in place, it operates on all the queries on that dashboard. By clicking the + icon, you can continue to add **Field/Term** pairs to produce tighter filters.

Ad hoc filters can be very powerful for creating quick queries on your data source without the need to open up and edit each panel. However, you have no control over the number of possible fields and how many terms they produce, so they should be used with some caution. Here is an example that produces similar results to the preceding **Field Name/Field Terms** combination:

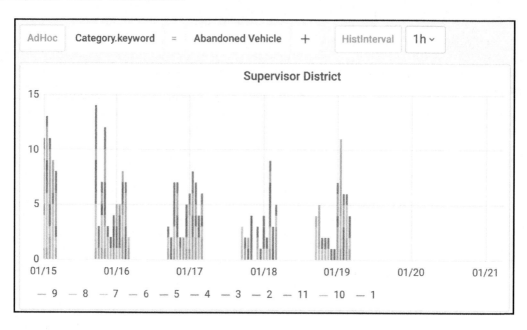

In this case, I selected `Category.keyword` when I selected **+** to create the query. Grafana automatically adds the **=** comparison operator and the dropdown containing the possible `Category.keyword` terms.

Repeating rows and panels with template variables

The dashboard layout is one of the more powerful uses for template variables. Instead of the grid layout system we looked at previously, earlier versions of Grafana used a layout model centered around lining up panels on discrete rows. The panels could vary in size, but all the panels on a row would render within the confines of the row they belonged to. This mechanic for laying out dashboards wasn't very flexible and it could be very tricky to use, but it did support a powerful feature that still exists today: repeating rows and panels.

How does a repeating row or panel work? Simply put, when you designate the repeat template variable for a row or panel, Grafana will, for each value of the variable, generate a copy of that row or panel and set the template variable to that value. You can find the repeat setting in the **General** section of each panel or row.

Let's try an example that should give you a good idea of how the repeat setting works, and also help you see how they react to different template variable settings. Start by creating a new dashboard, and on that dashboard, create a single Text panel on a single row. You can create a row by adding a new panel and selecting **Convert to row**. Open **Dashboard settings | Variables** and create a new variable:

- **General/Name:** `PanelRepeatField`
- **General/Type: Query**
- **Query Options/Data source: Elasticsearch**
- **Query Options/Refresh: Never**
- **Query Options/Query:** `{"find": "fields", "type": "keyword"}`
- **Query Options/Regex:** `/(.*)\.keyword/`
- **Query Options/Sort: Alphabetical (asc)**
- **Other options: off**

Next, create another variable for the terms:

- **General/Name:** `PanelRepeatTerms`
- **General/Type: Query**
- **Query Options/Data source:** `Elasticsearch`
- **Query Options/Refresh: Never**
- **Query Options/Query:** `{"find": "terms", "field": "$PanelRepeatField.keyword"}`
- **Query Options/Regex:** `empty`
- **Query Options/Sort: Alphabetical (asc)**
- **Selection Options/Multi-value: on**
- **Other options: off**

Now, create the second pair of these variables but name them `RowRepeatField` and `RowRepeatTerms`, respectively.

In the row, click the gear icon; you will see the dialog shown in the following screenshot:

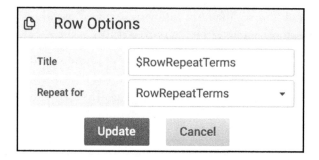

Here, set the following values:

- **Title**: $RowRepeatTerms
- **Repeat for**: RowRepeatTerms

This sets the repeat for the row. The row itself is what I will refer to as the *canonical* row. Now, go to the **Options** section in the (canonical) **Panel** tab. We're going use the **markdown Mode** text to display the variables as they're set for the panel:

```
| Variable | Value |
|--- | --- |
| _RowRepeatField_ | $RowRepeatField |
| _RowRepeatTerms_ | $RowRepeatTerms |
| _PanelRepeatField_ | $PanelRepeatField |
| _PanelRepeatTerms_ | $PanelRepeatTerms |
```

Here are the rest of the settings you need:

- **Settings/Panel title**: $PanelRepeatTerms
- **Repeat options/Repeat by variable: PanelRepeatTerms**
- **Repeat options/Repeat direction: Horizontal**
- **Repeat options/Max per row: 6**

As you can see, a panel can repeat in the vertical direction but you can only limit the number of panels in the horizontal direction:

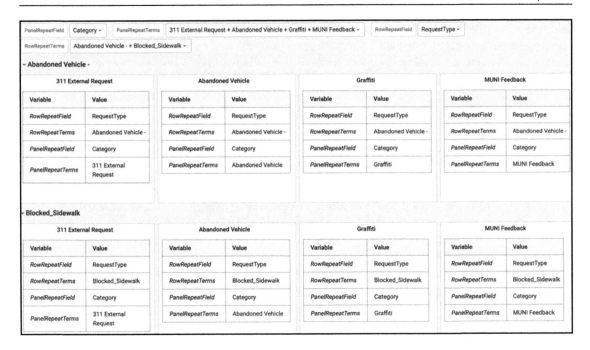

Try out the new dashboard by selecting various repeat fields and their terms. Observe how the number of rows and panels increases and decreases. Also, note how the size of the panels adjusts as the number of panels increases. You may need to tweak the canonical panel to get a nice look for the table when the panels get smaller.

Creating a new dashboard

Now, we have everything we need to begin building some dashboards. Observe that the data fields group roughly into four major types:

- Call type (**Category**, **RequestType**)
- Responsibility (**PoliceDistrict**, **ResponsibleAgency**, **SupervisorDistrict**)
- Location (**Address**, **Neighborhood**, **Street**)
- Date (**Opened**, **Closed**)

What we can do here is create a series of dashboards, each one dedicated to a **Responsibility** entity. Each dashboard will be split into two-column panels, one for each **Call** type. We will then allow the user to decide the **Group by/Terms** for the panel queries. We'll need to create several template variables to drive the dashboard, but once they're created, things should fall into place. Let's get started. First, we will need to create a dashboard. On the dashboard, we'll create some template variables.

Setting up the template variables

The first set variable will set the **Responsibility** entity for the dashboard. Since we can't query for it and it has only three possible values anyway, we'll create it as a custom variable. Custom variables are just a comma-separated list of possible values:

- **General/Name**: Entity
- **General/Type**: **Custom**
- **Custom Options/Values separated by comma**: PoliceDistrict, ResponsibleAgency, SupervisorDistrict

Here's the details for the custom variable:

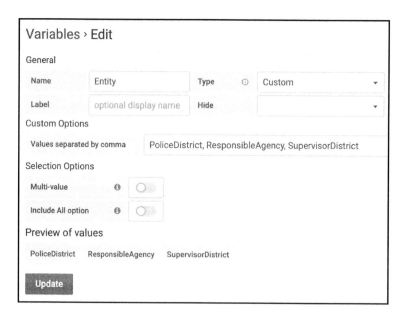

We follow up the **Entity** variable with the corresponding term's variable, which we'll call `EntityAgency`. These will be the repeat variables for the dashboard rows:

- **General/Name**: `Entity`
- **General/Type**: **Query**
- **Query Options/Data source**: `Elasticsearch`
- **Query Options/Refresh**: **Never**
- **Query Options/Query**: `{"find": "terms", "field": "$Entity.keyword"}`
- **Query Options/Sort**: **Alphabetical (asc)**
- **Selection Options/Multi-value**: **on**

Next, we'll create the two pairs of variables that represent the two columnar panels, one pair for `Category` and the other for `RequestType`:

- **General/Name**: `Category`
- **General/Type**: **Query**
- **Query Options/Data source**: `Elasticsearch`
- **Query Options/Refresh**: **Never**
- **Query Options/Query**: `{"find": "terms", "field": "Category.keyword"}`
- **Query Options/Sort**: **Alphabetical (asc)**
- **Selection Options/Multi-value**: **on**
- **Selection Options/Include All Option**: **on**

The **Group by Terms** variable needs to be set as follows:

- **General/Name**: `CategoryGrouping`
- **General/Type**: **Query**
- **Query Options/Data source**: `Elasticsearch`
- **Query Options/Refresh**: **Never**
- **Query Options/Query**: `{"find": "fields", "type": "keyword"}`
- **Query Options/Regex**: `/(.*)\.keyword/`
- **Query Options/Sort**: **Alphabetical (asc)**

`RequestType` and `RequestTypeGrouping` are pretty much the same. Just duplicate and rename the `Category` and `CategoryGrouping` variables and in the query for the `RequestType` variable replace `Category` with `RequestType`. The last variable is `AggregationInterval` for the Date Histogram, which we created previously:

- **General/Name**: `AggregationInterval`
- **General/Type**: Interval
- **Interval Options/Values**: `1m, 10m, 30m, 1h, 6h, 12h, 1d, 7d, 14d, 30d`

If you ever get stuck or lose track of all the various option settings, these dashboards will be in the GitHub repository for this book. Next up, we'll configure the panels.

Configuring the panels

Each panel will be pretty similar, with just a few differences between them, so once we've configured our first panel, we'll just copy it and make the necessary tweaks. We'll need to create a **Graph** panel, and the first order is to set up the query, as follows:

- **Data source**: `Elasticsearch`
- **Query**: `$EntityAgency AND $Category`
- **Metric**: **Count**
- **Group by/Terms**: **$CategoryGrouping.keyword**
- **Group by/Terms/Order**: **Bottom**
- **Group by/Terms/Size**: **No limit**
- **Group by/Terms/Order By**: **Term value**
- **Then by**: **DateHistogram Opened**
- **Then by/Interval**: **$AggregationInterval**
- **Query options/Min interval**: **5m**

Here, we first query for the values of the documents that match both the value of **$EntityAgency** and the value(s) of **$Category**. We **Group by** **$CategoryGrouping.keyword**, which might normally be `Category`, but could be some other grouping. We order from **Bottom** up with **No limit** so that we can see all the possible terms, and they will appear in sort order by **Term** value in proper alphabetical order (from the lowest *value* up). Finally, we set the interval to **$AggregationInterval**. For good measure, we set the minimum time interval to something reasonable, such as 5 minutes.

In the **Panel** tab, we'll turn on the bars and the legend; this is nothing too complicated:

- **Display/Bars**: on
- **Display/Lines**: off
- **Stacking and Null value/Stack**: on
- **Legend/Options/Show**: on
- **Legend/Options/As table**: on
- **Legend/Options/To the right**: on
- **Legend/Values/Avg**: on

Finally, we set up the title in **Settings**:

- **Panel title**: `$Entity ($EntityAgency) $Category by $CategoryGrouping`

That takes care of the **Category** panel. Now, let's move onto the second panel, which is much the same, but we make a few tweaks. Duplicate the **Category** panel and make these changes in the query:

- **Query**: `$EntityAgency AND $RequestType`
- **Group by/Terms**: `$RequestTypeGrouping.keyword`

Now, make the following change to the title and we're done:

- **Panel title**: `$Entity ($EntityAgency) $RequestType by $RequestTypeGrouping`

Now, we need to set up the repeating at the row level. Create a row and make sure both panels are positioned below the **Row** header. Also, make sure to resize the panels if necessary so that they share the row evenly. Here are the **Row** settings:

- **Title**: `$Entity $EntityAgency`
- **Repeat for**: **EntityAgency**

Be sure to save your dashboard and name it something relevant. When complete, the dashboard should look something like this:

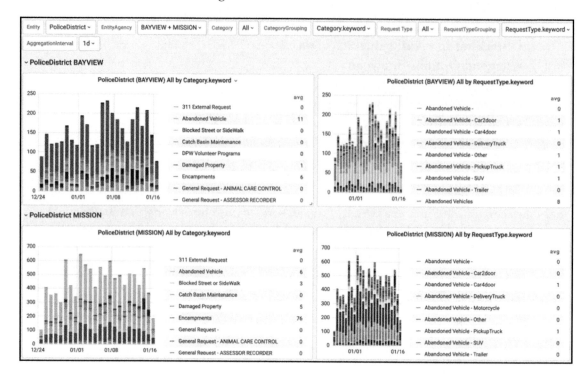

The neat thing about this is that you've effectively created three dashboards, each of which you can see by just changing that single **Entity** variable. From here, you have a few choices, depending on what works best. If you feel like your user would be happy switching between dashboards, then you could publish this as it stands. If, on the other hand, your client doesn't want to see the other dashboards, you could do one of two things:

1. *Make* a special copy of the dashboard with the client's settings for `Entity`, and then hide the `Entity` variable so it can't be changed.
2. Make a special copy of the dashboard and convert the `Entity` variable into a constant type set to the value chosen by the client.

Next, we're going to look at how to treat the dashboards as separate, but connected, via dashboard linking.

Linking dashboards

Now that you have your dashboards set up, you may have noticed that navigating between dashboards can be a bit tedious. To go to a different dashboard, you click the dashboard's name, click the Grafana logo, or click the **Dashboards** sidebar menu, and then you look for your dashboard and click on it. This isn't very efficient and makes it difficult to deploy your dashboards as a coherent site that doesn't force your users to go rummaging through a lot of dashboards that aren't relevant to them in search of the ones that are.

Fortunately, you're in luck! Grafana provides a simple, dashboard-level linking system for facilitating the creation of navigable dashboards. Dashboard linking supports intra-dashboard links via tagging, or inter-dashboard via URL. Let's see how that works for our newly created dashboards.

Adding dashboard tags

The first step will be to make a copy of the dashboard you created in the previous section. Ultimately, we're going to make three different versions of this dashboard. You can copy a dashboard by going into **Dashboard settings** and clicking **Save As...**. Then, rename the dashboard something that references the Entity variable you will choose for this dashboard.

First off, we will need to tag the dashboard. Go to **Dashboard settings→General** and set the following option:

- **Tags**: 311 Calls

The following screenshot shows the **General** panel, showing the tag settings for the dashboard:

Once we've tagged our dashboards, we'll be able to easily create dashboard links based on the tag.

Locking down a template variable

Next, we'll lock down the Entity variable. Go to **Dashboard settings→Variables** and for the Entity variable, remove all but one of the values in **Values separated by comma**. Set **Hide** to **Variable**. This step will go more smoothly if you pick the value that matches the Entity variable that was selected for the dashboard. Otherwise, you may have to do some selecting and reloading to make sure all the variables reflect the correct one for the dashboard.

Creating dashboard links

Open the **Dashboard settings→Links** menu and select **Add Dashboard Link**. Immediately, you will be presented with the option, via the dropdown, to create either a dashboard link or a URL link. Create the link with these settings:

- **Type: dashboards**
- **With tags: 311 Calls**
- **As dropdown: on**
- **Title:** `311 Calls`
- **Include/Time range: on**
- **Include/Variable values: on**

Here's a closer look at the configuration for **Dashboard Links**:

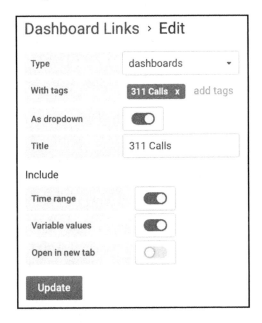

This will give you a menu that appears on the header, below the template variables. The menu will navigate you to the other dashboards that share the same tags. The settings will preserve the time range and variable values so that you don't lose your settings if you need to switch back and forth between different dashboards.

As an exercise, try to make copies of the dashboards to cover the other two entities, and link them all together. When finished, you should be able to navigate between all three; each menu should have two entries for the other two dashboards, as shown in the following screenshot:

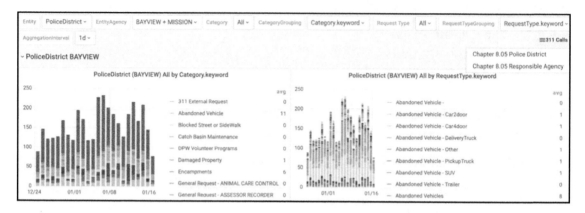

Next, we're going to move onto another advanced dashboard feature: the ability to create annotations of individual data points, both manually in the UI and automatically via an Elasticsearch query.

Annotating dashboards

Annotations are a versatile mechanism for providing highlighting individual events in the time series. By singling out a single data point at a particular time and marking it with metadata, you have the capability to *mark up* your dashboard panels with rich data such as text and tagging. Grafana provides two annotation capabilities to choose from: native Grafana annotations are created interactively and stored with the dashboard on the Grafana server, and data source annotations are created as queries to the data source, with the query and annotation configuration stored with the dashboard.

Annotating the graph panel

Since data source annotations can be resource-intensive, we'll demonstrate annotating with a single-panel dashboard. Create a new dashboard and a single **Graph** panel with the following settings:

- **Query/Data Source**: `Elasticsearch`
- **Query/Query**: **RequestType:Graffiti**

- **Panel/Display/Bars**: on
- **Panel/Display/Lines**: off
- **Panel/Display/Stacking and Null value/Stack**: on

It's not critical that you get the settings exactly right; the goal here is to just come up with a panel depicting some of our data. Once you have a working panel, manually adding annotations is quite simple:

1. Identify the appropriate moment in time.
2. On the graph, either **Option**-click and select **Add annotation** or **CMD**-click to bring up an annotation popup.
3. Fill in the text with descriptive text.
4. Add one or more tags (complete a tag by typing and then using the *Return* or *Tab* key).

An annotation is visually depicted on the **Graph** panel as a vertical dashed line with a pointer triangle, just below the graph baseline, as shown here:

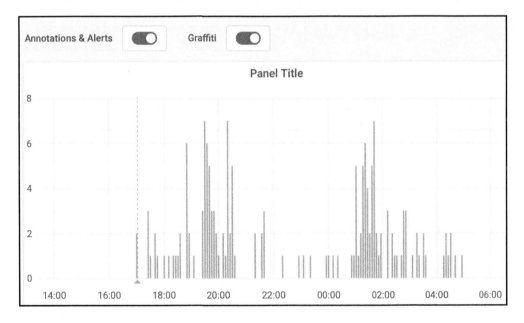

That's pretty much all there is to creating a native annotation! Next up, we'll look at how to query for our annotation data.

Querying tagged annotations

Once you've created some annotations, you'll, of course, want to be able to see and potentially query for them. To provide visibility into any native annotations, Grafana provides a built-in query, which you'll find in **Dashboard settings→Annotations**. The query is referred to as **Annotations & alerts**, and among the configuration options are the following:

- Name
- Data source
- Display enable/disable
- Hide/show query display control on the dashboard
- Annotation color
- Filtering by dashboard or tag
- Maximum number of annotations to display

So, if you toggle **Hidden** to off, you'll now see **control** on the heading, which enables and disables the query for dashboard annotations. Now, let's add a new query and see how that behaves. Earlier, I added an annotation for `Graffiti` with the following settings:

- **Description**: `Graffiti report here`
- **Tags**: `Graffiti`

Let's go to **Dashboard Settings**, open **Annotations**, and create a **New** annotation:

- **Name**: `Graffiti`
- **Data source**: **--Grafana--**
- **Enabled**: **on**
- **Hidden**: **off**
- **Color**: **red**
- **Filter by**: **Tags**
- **Tags**: `Graffiti`

When you return to your dashboard, you should see two toggle switches: one for **Annotations & Alerts** and the other for **Graffiti**. Now, toggle the **Annotations & Alerts** query off. You should now see a red annotation. Hover over the triangle; you'll see our `Graffiti` annotation. Now, swap the settings so that **Graffiti** is off and **Annotations & Alerts** is on. You should now see a blue annotation. Hovering over the annotation triangle shows the same annotation. This indicates that our annotation queries are, in fact, independent. The annotations are always there, stored in Grafana's internal database; the reason you can normally see annotations is that each dashboard contains the one annotation query dashboard filter that is both enabled and hidden.

Let's move on to querying our Elasticsearch data source for annotation data.

Creating Elasticsearch annotation queries

Along with native annotations, Grafana also allows us to leverage data sources to serve annotation queries. Unlike the native annotations, no actual annotation data is produced. Instead, the data source annotation query provides a view into the underlying data, which is then displayed by Grafana as annotations. Consequently, you wouldn't be able to produce a data source annotation query and then create a native annotation query for any of the tags generated by the data source annotation query.

The amount of data produced by a query across a large timeframe can be considerable, so be very careful when managing the scale of your queries.

In this example, we'll be creating a query for a specific annotation that is a common issue in metropolitan areas: abandoned vehicles. We'll create a query to look for abandoned cars with associated photos, then tag the annotations with the appropriate agency and embed the link in the photos in the text field. Ready?

Add a new annotation query in **Dashboard settings | Annotations**. Here are the settings:

- **Name:** `Abandoned Vehicles`
- **Data source: Elasticsearch**
- **Enabled: on**
- **Hidden: off**

- **Color**: **Orange**
- **Query**: RequestType:abandoned vehicle AND MediaURL:http
- **Field mappings/Time**: Opened
- **Field mappings/Text**: MediaURL
- **Field mappings/Tags**: Category

This is what the Elasticsearch **Annotations** query looks like:

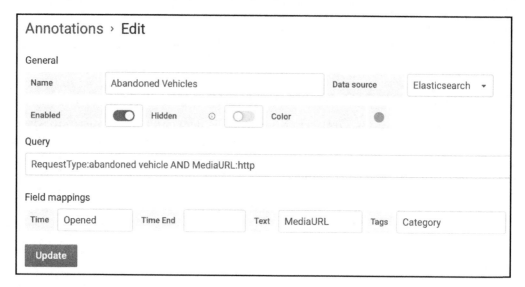

Here, the biggest difference between a native annotation query and this data source annotation query are the settings for the **Query** and **Field** mappings. The query looks for the abandoned vehicle query string in the RequestType field, as well as the http string in the **MediaURL**, indicating a URL with photos. Then, we use the field mappings to use the Opened field to set a time for the annotation (otherwise, where would we place it?), the **MediaURL** in the Text field, and create a tag using the Category field.

Once you've set up the query, look at a day or two's worth of data:

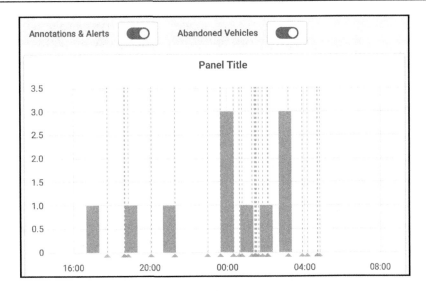

There should be a few annotations per day. Hovering over one of them reveals a URL in the Text field and the category tag. Unfortunately, the URL isn't clickable, but it does illustrate the potential for embedding rich data into an annotation.

Sharing dashboards

Now that you've created these lovely dashboards, how do you share them with the world (or your boss)? One of the first questions you must consider is the link between your dashboards and your data sources. For the sake of this book, we'll keep the data sources and the dashboards in close proximity, that is, on the same host and the same network. If you wish to share your dashboards, they will need to access your machine and possibly your network. You'll want to give some serious thought to how best to share them. Here, we'll discuss a few strategies and their pros and cons.

Sharing dashboard links

The most straightforward sharing mechanism is to simply give out a URL to your Grafana server that references the dashboard in question. Click the **Share dashboard** button (the box with an arrow coming out of it) and use the **Link** tab to create a link. If you want the dashboard to preserve the current view, make sure you enable **Current time range** and **Template variables**. Grafana will generate a custom URL you can copy and mail out.

This technique will only work if the client has access to your server and you've configured it to serve other browsers on your network. If that's not the case, you might have some difficulties. This option is most suitable for production environments where the Grafana server has been configured for multiple clients. However, the Grafana setup for this book is only able to serve to localhost at port 9200, which is essentially the computer that you're running Grafana on.

Sharing dashboards by exporting

The next best option is to export your dashboards in the hope that your client might also have access to the same data sources. You can then export to JSON and transfer the text file. Then, your clients just need to import the JSON file and make sure they've properly configured the data source(s). This is a good option if you are in an environment where you have centralized database servers and you want to transfer your dashboards for someone to review, modify, or install them on another server with the same data sources. This is how I shared the dashboards that were created for this book.

The process is quite simple: just **Share dashboards** and use the **Export** tab to save the JSON to a file or copy to a dashboard so that you can paste it into an email. The **Export for sharing externally** toggle is used when you want to share your dashboard publicly (such as on grafana.com), but want to make sure there are no explicit data source names embedded in the file. Instead, they are templated so that the importer of the dashboard file will assign them to their own data sources using a data source template variable.

Sharing dashboard snapshots

The final option is the one that is the most isolated and is for scenarios where you may have nothing more than access to a local Grafana server. For example, you may be giving a demo and have no network access or no VPN back to your data sources. The snapshot option is intended to export the dashboard and a sample dataset either to a local file or to a Grafana sharing service such as snapshot.raintank.io:

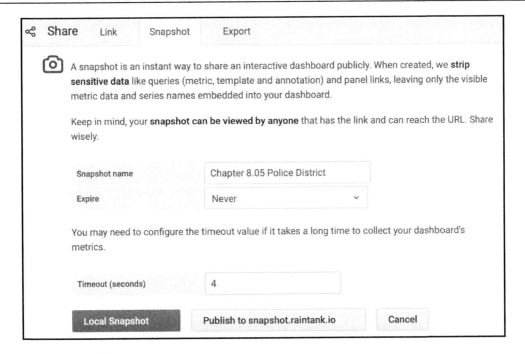

The snapshot is limited to the current timeframe, so choose one that you feel gives the best representation of the data. You will also be limited to some of the data you can show. The dashboard view is intended to be strictly read-only, so you will have no ability to edit the panels or even see the queries. The snapshot can be fairly limited, but if you are looking to give a report on a specific timeslice of data and you don't mind having some functional limitations, the snapshot can be very useful.

Summary

We've accomplished a lot in this chapter. Here, we created an Elasticsearch server and imported a realistic textual dataset with Logstash and learned about several different types of template variables, as well as how to set them up to parameterize our dashboards. Then, we applied template variables to repeat rows and panels and discovered the native annotation feature, as well as how to create annotations from an Elasticsearch query. Finally, we explored different sharing options and their pros and cons.

At this point, you have been exposed to enough of Grafana to now go off and create dashboards built around your own data sources. We've looked at two of the more popular data sources, InfluxDB and Elasticsearch, but we've only scratched the surface of their capabilities, apart from being used with Grafana. I encourage you to explore them; the more you understand how data sources manage data, the better you will be able to tailor your datasets to get the most out of Grafana.

In the next chapter, we will move on from an approach centered around analysis to one centered around alerting. We'll look at how to create alerts, tailor them to trigger at the right times, and how to connect them to various service integrations. What good are alerts if you don't know about them, right?

9
Grafana Alerting

Up to this point, we've been looking at Grafana's analytical features. In this chapter, will we move on to another important component of data visualization applications—alerting. In many typical data analysis scenarios, it is perfectly legitimate to concentrate solely on visualization. However, there are a number of scenarios that require not only using Grafana to tell stories about data but also focusing your attention and potentially triggering an action.

Before we tackle alerting, we'll take a closer look at thresholds. Thresholds, while superficially similar in concept to an alert, are significantly different. Nonetheless, they provide a good way of preparing yourself for working with alerts. They are primarily intended as visual aids, and since they don't trigger any sort of actions, you won't be waking anybody up at 3 A.M. when testing them out!

We will need some real-time data to test our thresholds and alerts on, so we'll be pulling in data acquired directly from computer hardware metrics. Our primary goal in this chapter is to learn how to set up thresholds and alerts, but to do so, we'll also need to set up a data source that can store real-time data. With real-time data, we can experiment with thresholds and alerts and get immediate feedback whenever a threshold is crossed or an alert is triggered. Finally, we'll learn how to integrate our alerts with external applications, called notification channels, so that we can receive notifications of alerts moments after they happen.

Here's what we'll be covering in this chapter:

- Setting thresholds
- Configuring alerts
- Assigning alerts to notification channels
- Troubleshooting and controlling alerts

Technical requirements

Tutorial code, dashboards, and other helpful files for this chapter can be found in the book's GitHub repository at `https://github.com/PacktPublishing/Learn-Grafana-7.0/tree/master/Chapter09`.

Setting thresholds

Before setting up our thresholds, we'll need some data. For this chapter, we'll continue to leverage our ElasticSearch/Logstash pairing, similar to the data pipeline we set up in the previous chapter. However, we'll be storing a much smaller—primarily numerical—dataset, rather than the text-driven data we used previously.

Getting this data into ElasticSearch via Logstash can get a little technical in places, but it's not unmanageable. We don't need a lot of data series to work through the threshold and alerting features, so the Logstash pipeline will be relatively straightforward. So, let's get started, shall we?

Before running any commands, first `cd` into the `Chapter09` directory of this book's repository at `https://github.com/PacktPublishing/Learn-Grafana-7.0`.

Capturing real-time data

Our dataset will be gathered directly from the computer hardware, namely the CPU and fans of a fairly standard MacBook Pro laptop. In order to capture the fan speed and CPU temperature, we'll be using a Mozilla command-line tool called `powermetrics`. Unfortunately, for our non-MacBook readers, this tool is only available on OS X, but the tools and principles will be similar for other platforms. While this example is a bit contrived, it represents a similar process repeated in thousands of data centers around the world every day. The only difference is the scale.

The `powermetrics` command is a powerful way to capture an enormous variety of data. Here is an excerpt of their description (`https://developer.mozilla.org/en-US/docs/Mozilla/Performance/powermetrics`):

> powermetrics is a Mac-only command-line utility that provides many high-quality power-related measurements. It is most useful for getting CPU, GPU and wakeup measurements in a precise and easily scriptable fashion.

Now, we don't need most of this data for our purposes. In fact, we just want two particular data fields that are monitored by the **System Management Controller** (SMC). The command-line option for gathering SMC data looks like this:

```
% powermetrics --sampler smc
```

Before you go and start typing that in, there are a few things you should know:

- The `powermetrics` command requires privileged access to various kernel data structures in order to gather its data. Consequently, you will need to run `powermetrics` with superuser privileges using the `sudo` command.
- Confirm your account has administrator privileges. On the command line, enter `sudo`, followed by your `powermetrics` command.
- In order for `powermetrics` to sample metrics at least once, specify the number of samples it should gather before exiting using the `-n` option.

 By default, the command will run indefinitely, continuously sampling data every 5 seconds until you kill it.

`powermetrics` is equipped with a number of samplers, and you can specify more than one to run; but for now, we only care about the `smc` sampler. In order to run a single sample and see what the data output looks like, execute the following command:

```
% sudo powermetrics --sampler smc -n 1
```

After a few seconds (after authenticating `sudo`), you should see some data like this:

```
Machine model: MacBookPro14,2
SMC version: 2.44f2
EFI version: 204.0.0
OS version: 19D76
Boot arguments:
Boot time: Wed Feb 5 18:23:21 2020

*** Sampled system activity (Tue Feb 11 22:08:02 2020 -0800) (5013.56ms
elapsed) ***

**** SMC sensors ****

CPU Thermal level: 0
IO Thermal level: 0
Fan: 1251 rpm
CPU die temperature: 51.60 C
```

```
CPU Plimit: 0.00
GPU Plimit (Int): 0.00
Number of prochots: 0
```

This contains everything we'll need for now. We can see that the fan is running at 1,251 rpms and the CPU die temperature (as measured by a sensor on the CPU chip) is 51.50° Celsius. Now, we could write this to a file directly and have Logstash parse the values with regular expressions. Alternatively, we could output the data in a standard format that Logstash can interpret, and convert into a data structure that we can then access to get our data.

Besides the human-readable format you see here, `powermetrics` can output to the **Property-List (p-list)** format. P-list, if you haven't already encountered it, is an XML format used by Apple to hold all kinds of structured data—most commonly, configuration files. We can have `powermetrics` write out our data in the p-list and have Logstash parse the XML for the data we need.

In order to do that, we'll need to specify the p-list output format with the `-f` option:

```
% sudo powermetrics --sampler smc -n 1 -f plist
```

Our output now looks something like this:

```
<?xml version="1.0" encoding="UTF-8"?>
<!DOCTYPE plist PUBLIC "-//Apple//DTD PLIST 1.0//EN"
"http://www.apple.com/DTDs/PropertyList-1.0.dtd">
<plist version="1.0">
<dict>
<key>is_delta</key><true/>
<key>elapsed_ns</key><integer>5010981413</integer>
<key>hw_model</key><string>MacBookPro14,2</string>
<key>smc_version</key><string>2.44f2</string>
<key>efi_version</key><string>204.0.0</string>
<key>kern_osversion</key><string>19D76</string>
<key>kern_bootargs</key><string></string>
<key>kern_boottime</key><integer>1580955801</integer>
<key>timestamp</key><date>2020-02-12T06:22:31Z</date>
<key>smc</key>
<dict>
<key>cpu_thermal_level</key><integer>0</integer>
<key>simulated_cpu_thermal_level</key><integer>0</integer>
<key>simulated_gpu_thermal_level</key><integer>0</integer>
<key>io_thermal_level</key><integer>0</integer>
<key>simulated_io_thermal_level</key><integer>0</integer>
<key>fan</key><real>0</real>
<key>cpu_die</key><real>51.59</real>
<key>cpu_die_power_target</key><real>103</real>
```

```
<key>cpu_die_fan_target</key><real>93</real>
<key>cpu_plimit</key><real>0.00</real>
<key>gpu_plimit</key><real>0.00</real>
<key>num_prochots</key><integer>0</integer>
<key>cpu_prochot</key><false/>
<key>smc_prochot</key><false/>
</dict>
</dict>
</plist>
```

This is, admittedly, more pedantic than the text version, but it should be easier for an XML parser to handle. Before moving over to the Logstash side of things, we'll need to output this data to a file on a regular basis, so we'll specify this with the −u option and set the sample interval to 1 minute using the −i option:

```
% sudo powermetrics −i 60000 −−format plist −−samplers smc −u
data/sample.plist
```

The sampling interval is measured in milliseconds, so we set the interval to 60,000 (milliseconds) for 1 minute. Since we want the command to run indefinitely, we removed the −n option. We'll be mapping a data directory for Logstash, so we'll dump the file in there.

Processing the Logstash input

Once you have powermetrics capturing data and dumping it into the file, we'll need to configure Logstash to periodically read the file and send updates to ElasticSearch. The logstash.conf file is located in the logstash directory. Let's look at the first part of the pipeline—the input:

```
input {
  file {
    mode => "tail"
    path => [ "/data/*.plist" ]
    mode => "tail"
    start_position => "end"
    codec => multiline {
      pattern => "^\0"
      negate => "true"
      what => "previous"
    }
  }
}
```

Here, we're using the Logstash `file` plugin. `file` is designed to read files in one of two modes—`read`, which simply reads the file as a whole once, or `tail`, which reads the file over and over again as it gets progressively longer, always starting from the point where it left off. In our case, we've specified `tail` because we plan to continually read the file every minute or so. Logstash will check periodically to see whether the file has changed, and if so, reads the file.

The file to read is specified by the `path` array. The file `*.plist` glob just indicates that Logstash should read any and all p-list files it finds in the `/data` directory. Specifying the start position as `end` indicates that Logstash should track where it was when it last read the file and start any subsequent readings from that position.

The trickiest part of the input configuration is the multiline codec. Normally, the default codec in Logstash treats files as a series of lines and processes each one as a separate data event. Imagine a line in a CSV file and you'll get the idea. However, in this case, we want to read the whole chunk of output from a single `powermetrics` sample. To do that, we need the `multiline` codec so that we can stitch a block of lines into a single event.

The way the `multiline` codec works is it goes through the file line by line using a regular expression to identify whether a given line belongs to the current block or to the next one. Basically, we are looking for a `sentinel` line that indicates the boundary between two blocks of lines and then we are checking to see which side of the boundary the current line belongs to. Each block is then sent on to the next phase of the Logstash pipeline as an event to be filtered and, ultimately, output.

In our case, we are searching for each **End-Of-File (EOF)**, as written by `powermetrics`, by using `match` to find a line starting (`^`) with a `nul` (`\0`) character. Setting the `negate` field to `true` indicates that it should invert the match and look for lines that *don't* match the pattern. Any line that doesn't match the pattern is then part of the group of lines previous to the matching line, as the line of a new group starts immediately after the `nul` character.

Filtering the Logstash events

Once we've properly inputted our `powermetrics` data, we need to parse the p-list and extract the fields we need. These tasks are handled in the Logstash `filter` phase:

```
filter {
  xml {
    source => "message"
    target => "doc"
    add_field => {
      "%{[doc][dict][0][key][8]}" => "%{[doc][dict][0][date][0]}"
```

```
        "%{[doc][dict][0][dict][0][key][5]}" =>
"%{[doc][dict][0][dict][0][real][0]}"
        "%{[doc][dict][0][dict][0][key][6]}" =>
"%{[doc][dict][0][dict][0][real][1]}"
    }
    remove_field => [ "doc", "message" ]
  }
  mutate {
    convert => {
      "fan" => "float"
      "cpu_die" => "float"
    }
  }
}
```

In retrospect, this choice of processing the event in a regular expression instead boils down to a judgement call. The XML parser can certainly handle the p-list, but it tends to coerce the relatively neat data structure into a series of arrays grouped by data type. Everything is pre-sorted by type, and we don't need many fields, so it's pretty straightforward to extract once you grasp what the data structure looks like.

To configure the parser, we only need to specify the field we want to read (message) and the name of the field we want to create from the parsed message. While we're at it, we want to add three fields with the add_field option.

Before tackling the parser configuration, it is simple enough to output the event in order to discern the overall structure. Here is the relevant excerpt:

```
        "doc" => {
    "version" => "1.0",
        "dict" => [
        [0] {
                "key" => [
                [0] "is_delta",
                [1] "elapsed_ns",
                [2] "hw_model",
                [3] "smc_version",
                [4] "efi_version",
                [5] "kern_osversion",
                [6] "kern_bootargs",
                [7] "kern_boottime",
                [8] "timestamp",
                [9] "smc"
            ],
                "integer" => [
                [0] "5011669967",
                [1] "1580955795"
```

```
        ],
      "string" => [
         [0] "MacBookPro14,2",
         [1] "2.44f2",
         [2] "204.0.0",
         [3] "19D76"
      ],
        "date" => [
         [0] "2020-02-11T06:32:35Z"
      ],
        "dict" => [
        [0] {
                "key" => [
                [ 0] "cpu_thermal_level",
                [ 1] "simulated_cpu_thermal_level",
                [ 2] "simulated_gpu_thermal_level",
                [ 3] "io_thermal_level",
                [ 4] "simulated_io_thermal_level",
                [ 5] "fan",
                [ 6] "cpu_die",
                [ 7] "cpu_die_power_target",
                [ 8] "cpu_die_fan_target",
                [ 9] "cpu_plimit",
                [10] "gpu_plimit",
                [11] "num_prochots",
                [12] "cpu_prochot",
                [13] "smc_prochot"
            ],
            "integer" => [
                [0] "56",
                [1] "0",
                [2] "0",
                [3] "6",
                [4] "0",
                [5] "0"
            ],
                "real" => [
                [0] "1864",
                [1] "59.47",
                [2] "103",
                [3] "93",
                [4] "0.00",
                [5] "0.00"
            ]
        }
    ]
  }
]
```

First, we need to walk through the data structure to locate the `timestamp` value. Our data is constructed from a hash of metrics (the `smc` key) nested inside a hash of metadata. Each hash key points has an array of one value. Each array entry contains a hash of arrays keyed by type name or `key`. To find the timestamp field name is simply a matter of locating it within the `doc` hash.

You'll find the timestamp field name in the `dict` hash, with an array entry of `0`, a `key` hash, and an array index of `8`. By placing the sequence of hash and array references within `%{...}`, we evaluate the contents of that particular array reference to use it as the name for `add_field`—in this case, `timestamp`. We get the value of the `timestamp` field in a similar fashion to getting the `"2020-02-11T06:32:35Z"` string.

As it happens, we don't need this particular field for the timestamp of the document that we'll create in ElasticSearch, but under other circumstances, you might need to use the embedded timestamp as it more correctly captures the capture time, rather than the ElasticSearch document creation time. In this case, they are so close, so it doesn't really matter.

We'll follow the same process to get the `fan` and `cpu_die` fields and their values (Note: the exact field array references may differ depending upon computer model). As an additional exercise, try to add a couple more fields from the p-list. After we've created new fields from our parsed XML, we'll delete it and the original message field to save a little space in our ElasticSearch index. In order to make sure we are sending `fan` and `cpu_die` to ElasticSearch with the correct type, we recast them as floats using the `mutate` plugin.

Outputting the data

The output configuration for sending our data to ElasticSearch is similar to the configuration from the previous chapter:

```
output {
  elasticsearch {
    hosts => "elasticsearch:9200"
    index => "cpu_metrics"
  }
  stdout {}
}
```

We'll send the data to ElasticSearch using the hostname and port we specified in our `docker-compose.yml` file. We've named our index `cpu_metrics`. The `stdout` plugin is used for logging/debugging.

Up to now, we've probably been writing data to our `sample.plist` file, so let's launch our Logstash, ElasticSearch, and Grafana services:

```
% docker-compose up -d
```

Within a few moments, you should have some data coming in to ElasticSearch. Next up, we need to create an ElasticSearch data source and build a couple of dashboards to visualize our dataset.

Creating an ElasticSearch data source

In this section, we create an ElasticSearch data source so that we can have a look at our data. Create the data source with the following settings:

- **Name**: `Elasticsearch CPU Metrics`
- **HTTP | URL**: `http://elasticsearch:9200`
- **HTTP | Access: Server (default)**
- **Elasticsearch details | Index name**: `cpu_metrics`
- **Elasticsearch details | Time field name**: `@timestamp`
- **Elasticsearch details | Version: 7.0+**

Save and test the data source. Now that you have a working data source, let's graph our data.

Building the dashboard panels

Create a new dashboard and add a single graph panel. We'll first create a panel to display the fan speed data. You can only set thresholds and alerts for the entire graph, so in order to set different threshold or alert levels for the CPU temperature and fan speed, we need to create a separate graph for each of them. Here's the setup for the fan speed:

1. First, we set up a query:

   - **Query source: Elasticsearch CPU Metrics**
   - **Query**: empty
   - **Metric: Average | fan**
   - **Group by: Date histogram | @timestamp | Interval: auto**

2. Set the following query options:

   - The **Min** time interval: >1m

3. Next, we set the title in the **Settings** section of the **Panel** tab:

   - **Title**: Fan Speed

4. In the **Display** section of the **Panel** tab, we need to set the graph style:

   - **Lines**: on
   - **Line Width**: 1
   - **Area Fill**: 1

5. Open the **Axes** section and set the following custom unit for the **Left Y** axis:

   - **Left Y | Unit**: rpm

6. Finally, go to the **Legend** section and set the following:

   - **Options | Show**: on
   - **Values | Current**: on

Here's what the graph should look like when you're done:

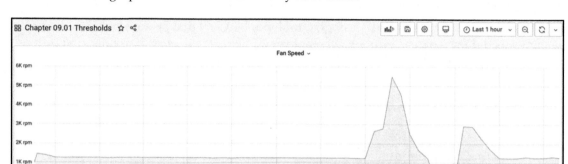

Setting thresholds

The purpose of thresholds and time regions is to provide a visual indication that the date series values have crossed into a predefined region of the graph. The threshold defines whether the data point is above or below a specified value. The time region determines when the thresholds are enabled. Once you have defined a threshold, you can then attach a visual representation to it, typically a color.

Let's set a threshold for the fan speed. Now, I'm not going to be able to tell you what an appropriate threshold for fan speed should be, but we can instead just make one up. I hereby declare that 1,000 RPMs is an appropriate threshold! OK, but what kind of threshold should we use? A threshold effectively divides the graph into two halves—the half above the threshold and the half below. What is significant about the threshold and whether you care about values on either side, or even on both sides, depends on the context.

In our case, I'm defining values below the threshold of 1,000 to be OK and values above it to not be OK. To create a threshold, go to the **Threshold** section of the **Panel** tab and click on **+ Add Threshold**. Here are the settings for creating those two thresholds:

- **T1: gt 1000, Color: critical, Fill: on, Line: on**, and **Y-axis: left**
- **T2: lt 1000, Color: ok, Fill: on, Line: off**, and **Y-axis: left**

We turned off the **T2** line so that we can see the **T1** line.

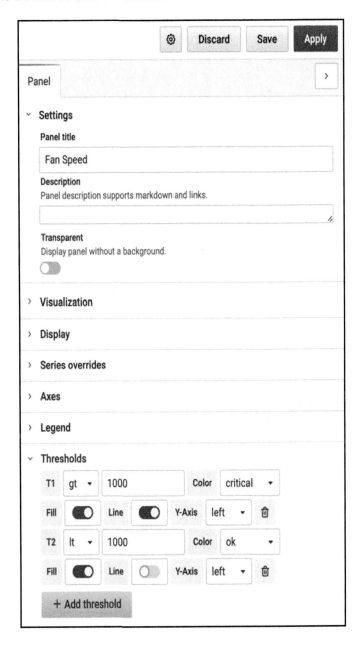

Now that we've activated the **critical** and **ok** thresholds, you also have draggable handles that you can use to move the thresholds without having to type numbers into the field:

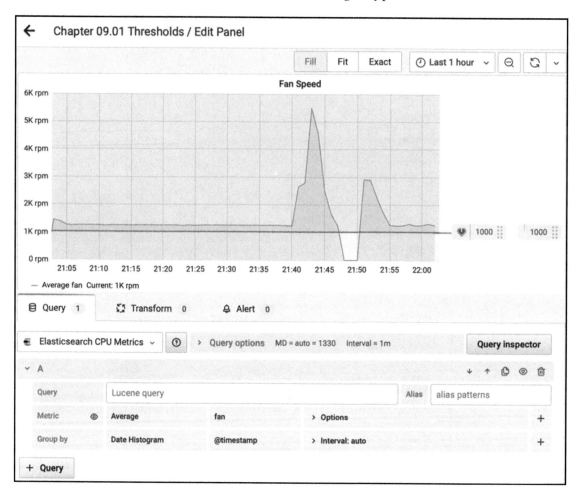

 Threshold handles are only visible from the panel editor.

Next, we'll go ahead and set up some thresholds for the CPU temperature. Make a copy of the **Fan Speed** panel and open it for editing. Modify the query:

- **Metric: Average | cpu_die**

Adjust the title in **Settings**:

- **Panel title:** CPU die Temperature

Finally, set the unit for the *Y*-axis:

- **Left Y | Unit: Celsius (°C)**

In the **Thresholds** and **Time Region** settings, let's go ahead and set a couple of arbitrary thresholds—one at 75 degrees and another at 100 degrees. We'll indicate a value above 75 to be a warning, and one above 100 to be critical:

- **T1 gt 100, Color: critical, Fill: on, Line: on,** and **Y-axis: Left**
- **T2 gt 75, Color: warning, Fill: on, Line: on,** and **Y-axis: Left**

Depending on the temperatures you record, you may or may not see the critical region, but you will still see the indicator:

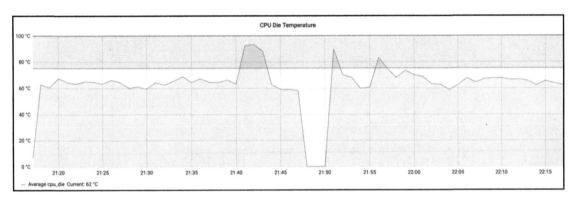

Now, let's move on to setting time regions for these thresholds.

Constraining thresholds to time regions

Setting time regions is not particularly difficult, but you do have to work in UTC time, which can be a bit of a mind bend. Let's say you don't want to worry about fan speeds after 6 P.M. because nobody is around to look at the graphs at that time to care. Open up the **Fan Speed** panel for editing and have a look at **Thresholds** and **Time Regions** in the **Panel** tab.

First, we'll need to decide what days and times of the week the region applies to. Let's block out every day from 9 A.M. to 6 P.M. for every day of the week. Here, in the Pacific time zone, 09:00 to 18:00 translates to 17:00 to 02:00 UTC the next day. Zoom out your time range to 24 hours.

Here are the time region settings for the **T1** threshold:

- **T1 | From: Any | 17:00 | To: Any | 02:00 | Color: Gray | Fill: on | Line: on**

If you have **Fill** turned on for your thresholds, I recommend you try the **Gray** color for your time regions as the overlay of a time region color on a threshold color may sometimes be confusing or misleading.

Here's a screenshot of the graph panel while editing the time region:

As an additional exercise, set a time region for the CPU temperature graph for Monday through Friday from 6 P.M. to 9 A.M. and all day on the weekends. For now, that completes our look at thresholds and time regions. Now, we're ready to look at a similar but much more powerful concept—**alerts**.

Configuring alerts

Alerts are very similar to thresholds and superficially, they may appear to be the same, but they are substantially different both in function and how they are presented on the Grafana interface. Here's a quick look at the differences:

Thresholds and Time Regions	Alerts
Primarily for visual representation	Primarily for notification triggers
Found in multiple panels	Found only in the **Graph** panels
Access in the visualization pane	Accessed through several interfaces
Many can be defined per panel	Only one per panel

Unlike a threshold, alerts have the ability to trigger notifications via what Grafana calls a notification channel. Like a panel or a data source, a **notification channel** is an integration plugin that provides a generalized interface for connecting Grafana to a third-party notification service, such as an email or PagerDuty. Currently, there are a number of notification channels available on Grafana, and more are being added over time.

Our goal in this section is to set up an alert for one of our metrics, create an email notification channel, and trigger an alert that should send out an email message.

The first step is to look at our fan speed and CPU temperature panels. You can work with an existing panel or copy an existing one. Bear in mind that alerts and thresholds are mutually exclusive at the panel level, so creating an alert will disable any thresholds you may have set. If you want to re-enable your threshold, you'll need to delete the alert.

Alert rules

In order to properly understand an alert, we need to break down the Grafana alerting system components. Alert rules are defined on the graph panel, and you can only define a single rule per panel. Rules are stored on the Grafana server, where they are evaluated continuously, so you don't need a panel to be on the active dashboard for its rule to trigger. For any given alert rule, you can have any number of notification channels.

Before we go on to define a rule for one of our panels, we need to look at how rules work in Grafana. When you define a rule, you establish the circumstances by which the rule will fire. However, in the interest of minimizing false alarms and redundant notifications, rules go through a series of phases or **states**. The set of states and the path a rule can take from one to the next is referred to as a **state machine**.

The Grafana alert state machine is very simple:

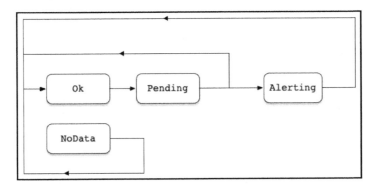

An alert can go from **Ok** to **Pending**. It can also go from **Pending** back to **Ok** or on to **Alerting**. Finally, an **Alerting** alert can go back to **Ok**. The idea is behind the **Pending** state is to allow a system that has crossed a threshold time to recover before trigging an actual alert notification. Alerts in the **Alerting** state must go back to **Ok** so that if the system were to recover, it would need to go through the **Pending** state before **Alerting**, rather than oscillating back and forth from **Alerting** to **Pending**, potentially generating many duplicate notifications. Finally, there is also a special **NoData** state, which can be triggered when the data is empty or all null.

Alerts are configured to define two moving time windows—one for determining when the state moves from **Ok** to **Alerting** and an optional second window that determines whether the state should go through a **Pending** state before going on to **Alerting**. The windows are defined as two time intervals and a threshold. If data falls below a threshold over the span of either window, the state will return to the **Ok** state.

The first step in setting up an alert is to create an alert rule. Alert rules are set in the **Alert** tab of the **Graph** panel. We'll set up an alert similar to the threshold we set earlier in this chapter. Open the **Fan Speed** panel and select the alerting (bell) subpanel. Click on **Create Alert** to create a new alert. Under **Rules**, the name of the alert is automatically derived from the title of the **Graph** panel. Feel free to change it.

This a good opportunity to reiterate the importance of maintaining good practices for titling panels and naming external artifacts such as data sources and alerts. Use alert names that describe what panel they are monitoring, so if you need to trace a problem, you won't be hunting through dashboards looking for panels. Later in this chapter, we'll examine the alert rules page—the page where all alerts are collected in one place with links to their panels.

Conditions

Next, we set how often the conditions should be evaluated for a possible alert. You want to set the **Evaluate every** field to a value that is frequent enough for the system to respond quickly to changes, but not so frequent that the Grafana and data servers are heavily loaded. Start with the default value of 1 minute. If your data updates less frequently and you can tolerate a little less responsiveness, bump up the evaluation interval. As you add alerts, keep an eye on your servers to make sure you aren't hitting them with frequent and/or heavy queries.

Next, we set the parameters for the two windows I described earlier. The first window is used to determine whether the alert should move from the **Ok** state to the **Pending** state. In a quirk of UX design, the first parameters you need to configure are below the **Rule** section in the **Conditions** section.

In the condition's WHEN clause, we set the aggregation for the time window. Most of the common aggregations are available here:

- Average (`avg`)
- Minimum (`min`)
- Maximum (`max`)
- Sum (`sum`)
- Count (`count`)
- Last (`last`)
- Median (`median`)
- Difference (`diff`)
- Percentage difference (`percent_diff`)
- Count of non-null values (`count_non_null`)

In our case, the average is sufficient. We just want to know whether the average fan speed over the time window is over 1,000. It is important to note that all series in the dataset are aggregated and evaluated and any series that crosses a threshold will trigger a state change. This means that if you have five series in your query, and only one of them triggers a state change to **Alerting**, if another series also crosses a threshold, the state will not change and no further notifications will be generated. Correspondingly, if the first series falls below the threshold while the second doesn't, the state will still continue to be **Alerting**.

The OF clause is where we set the parameters of the window: the dataset to be evaluated and the size of the time window. The dataset is set by selecting the **Query** letter in the first parameter, and the start and end of the window relative to the current time are set in the following two parameters. The width of this window doesn't need to be particularly long, but if you are monitoring a system that naturally crosses back and forth over a threshold, you may want to set the size so that it is wide enough to allow time for the system to recover from a threshold violation; that is unless you need to trigger any violations. A 5-minute window is fine for this case, so set the OF clause to **query(A, 5m, now)**.

Finally, we need to set the actual threshold value. We have a set of potential characterizations for the threshold, including the following:

- IS ABOVE
- IS BELOW
- IS OUTSIDE RANGE
- IS WITHIN RANGE
- HAS NO VALUE

In all but the last clause, you have the choice of entering values into a field or using a draggable handle. As we did previously with the threshold, we set the clause to IS ABOVE and the value to 1000. This particular condition represents only one of what could potentially be several conditions that can be logically joined together with AND or OR. Each conditional is evaluated from top to bottom and the condition is considered satisfied if the evaluation returns true.

For example, you may have a set of threshold ranges that you are monitoring, in which case you'd create a set of conditions and join them with OR so that if any one of them were violated, the logic would evaluate to true and an alert would be triggered. Alternatively, you may have a number of query datasets that all must be in violation of a threshold before an alert can be triggered, so you'd create a set of conditions—one for each query—and join them with AND.

Currently, the only condition supported by Grafana is query. This means all conditions must be based on comparing the query value to a numerical range or another threshold. This means that if you intend on creating triggers based on matching strings or checking the value of the Boolean, you should make sure the results of the query evaluate to a number. For example, to match strings, you may want to index your strings to a numbering scheme; for Booleans, you'll want to make true equal to 1 and false equal to 0.

The **For** field in the **Rules** section is a second window of time designed to provide a damper on the alert sensitivity. When conditions trigger an alert, the **For** field puts the alert in the **Pending** state, a holding pattern of sorts, for the specified length of time, just in case it might naturally return to a normal condition. If so, the state returns to **Ok**; otherwise, it goes on to **Alerting** and triggers the notifications. We'll leave our **For** field set to the default value of 5 minutes. If you're feeling impatient and want to see the alerts trigger, go ahead and remove the field value.

When the alerts trigger, you should see the state change annotations depicted in the following screenshot. Your graph will look considerably different depending on your data, but the annotations and conditions will be similar:

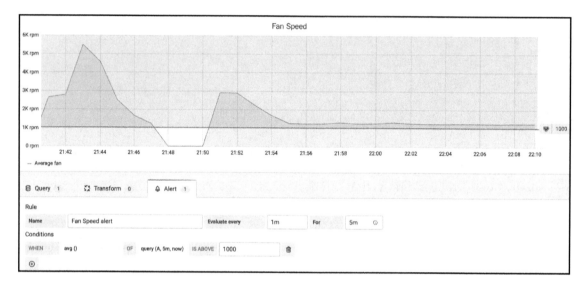

After setting up the fan speed alert, as an additional exercise, try creating a similar alert for the CPU temperature graph panel. Use conditions similar to the ones set in our earlier threshold examples.

Handling edge cases

Before we move on to creating and assigning a notification channel, we should mention the two edge case options under **No Data & Error Handling**. These are options for how to handle scenarios for when there is no data and if there are problems with the query. In either case, you may want to trigger an alert or you may want to effectively ignore the situation:

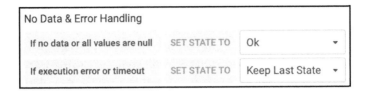

The first option, labeled **If no data or all values are null**, covers the scenario for when data is all null or there is no data all. There are four options:

- **Alerting**
- **No Data**
- **Keep Last State**
- **Ok**

The **Alerting** option allows you to trigger an alert if, for some reason, the flow of data is cut off. **No Data** will trigger a state change to the **NoData** state. Setting **Keep Last State** effectively ignores the lack of data and retains the state when the data flow is resumed. **Ok** simply resets the state to **Ok**.

The second option is labeled **If execution error or timeout** and covers scenarios where the query fails to execute, either due to an error of some kind or the server times out responding to the query. You only have two options:

- **Alerting**
- **Keep Last State**

The **Alerting** setting will cause an execution error to trigger the **Alerting** state, which can alert you to problems with the server itself. **Keep Last State** effectively ignores the error, which is useful if the server has a tendency to fail but only momentarily.

Assigning alerts to notification channels

If an alert is triggered but no one gets a notification, did anything really happen? The **notification** is the side effect of an alert, and the notification's action is executed by a **notification channel**. The notification channel is a plugin integration similar in concept to a data source. It represents a generalized interface for setting up the parameters necessary for the Grafana server to use the notification application API to pass along the alert's message. There are a number of notification channels shipped with Grafana, including emails, webhooks, PagerDuty, Slack, HipChat, and many more.

Setting up an email notification channel

Unfortunately, it is beyond the scope of this book to cover all the notification channels, but we will look at email as it is the simplest and doesn't require a third-party application. Any modern computer should have all the tools needed to set up the email notification channel. The other notification channels are covered in the Grafana documentation.

In order to set up an email, we'll first need to gather some information on how to contact and authenticate (if necessary) the **Simple Mail Transfer Protocol** (**SMTP**) email service we plan to use. We will need to find out the following:

- The SMTP server and port
- The SMTP username and password

Once we've gathered this information, we'll need to modify the Grafana configuration. By default, SMTP is disabled, so we'll need to enable it in the Grafana configuration. One possible way of modifying the configuration is to copy a sample `config` file, modify it, and restart our Grafana server. An easier way, since we're using Docker Compose to provision our containers, is to add relevant configuration environment variables. We did this in `Chapter 6`, *Visualization Panels in Grafana*, when we added a panel plugin by specifying it in the `GF_INSTALL_PLUGINS` environment variable. This time, we want to add a few more plugins to the Grafana environment in `docker-compose.yml`.

Configuring Grafana Docker containers

Let's configure Grafana Docker containers by executing the following steps.

1. The first thing we'll need do is add the appropriate email account environment variables to our `docker-compose.yml` file:

   - `GF_SMTP_ENABLED: "true"`
   - `GF_SMTP_USER: "<smtp_user>"`
   - `GF_SMTP_PASSWORD: "<smtp_password>"`
   - `GF_SMTP_HOST: "<smtp_host>:<smtp_port>"`

I need to caution you about exposing secure information such as your password in a plaintext file. Do not do this on a production server; this example is intended for educational purposes only! For myself, I generated an application-specific password intended for this purpose only, with the understanding that if my computer is compromised, I can easily revoke the password.

2. Before we can start firing off email alerts, we'll need to set up an external rendering service that will capture an image of our graph so that it can be attached to the email alert. The service is a special plugin developed by Grafana and is composed of a Node.js service and a headless Chromium browser. These two services act together to receive the URL for our graph, render it in the browser, and send an image capture back to Grafana. We'll need to add a few more environment variables:

- `GF_RENDERING_SERVER_URL`: `http://renderer:8081/render`
- `GF_RENDERING_CALLBACK_URL`: `http://grafana:3000/`
- `GF_LOG_FILTERS`: `rendering:debug`

3. In the `docker-compose.yml` file, we'll modify the existing `grafana` service:

```
grafana:
    image: "grafana/grafana:${TAG-latest}"
    ports:
      - 3000:3000
    environment:
      GF_SMTP_ENABLED: "true"
      GF_SMTP_USER: "<my@email.adddress>"
      GF_SMTP_PASSWORD: "<my_smtp_pass_here>"
      GF_SMTP_HOST: "<smtp_host_here:25>"
      GF_RENDERING_SERVER_URL: http://renderer:8081/render
      GF_RENDERING_CALLBACK_URL: http://grafana:3000/
      GF_LOG_FILTERS: rendering:debug
    volumes:
      - "${PWD-.}/grafana:/var/lib/grafana"
```

4. Add the rendering service that is simply called `renderer`:

```
renderer:
    image: grafana/grafana-image-renderer:latest
    ports:
      - 8081
```

5. Once you've edited the file, you should fully shut down your services and then bring them back up:

```
% docker-compose down
Stopping ch9_logstash_1 ... done
Stopping ch9_elasticsearch_1 ... done
Stopping ch9_grafana_1 ... done
% docker-compose up -d
Starting ch9_elasticsearch_1 ... done
Starting ch9_logstash_1 ... done
```

```
Starting ch9_grafana_1 ... done
Starting ch9_renderer_1 ... done
```

6. Now, let's create a new notification channel and try things out. Go to the alerting dropdown (bell icon) on the left sidebar and select **Notification channels** | **Add Channel** to create a new notification channel. By default, you should get an email notification channel. Configure it as follows:

- **Edit Notification Channel** | **Name**: **Email Alert**
- **Edit Notification Channel** | **Type**: **Email**
- **Edit Notification Channel** | **Default** (send on all alerts): **on**
- **Edit Notification Channel** | **Include image**: **on**
- **Edit Notification Channel** | **Disable Resolve Message**: **on**
- **Email Settings** | **Addresses**: **<email address>**

The notification channel should look similar to this:

7. We set this notification channel as the default as it is the only one we're going to use. We are enabling a nice image of the graph to go in the email message. We've disabled the **Resolve** message so that we don't get spammed. We've left **Send reminders** disabled for the same reason. Finally, we add our email address to the list.

8. Click on the **Send Test** button to confirm we've set up SMTP correctly and that we can send an email message. That's all there is to set up the notification channel. Go to the **Alert Rules** tab and click on the fan speed alert.

9. We need to associate the notification channel with our address, so go to the **Notifications** section, click on the + button next to **Send to**, and add **Email Alert**, the name of the alert we created. In the message section, type in a meaningful message about the nature of the alert and perhaps how to address it. Unfortunately, the **Message** field only accepts plaintext, I assume for security reasons.

10. Now, it's a matter of waiting for the fan speed to rise to a level above the trigger threshold. You can lower the threshold to force an alert, but if you set a **For** value, it will still take a few minutes. Once you get an alert, you should see annotations in the graph corresponding to the state changes:

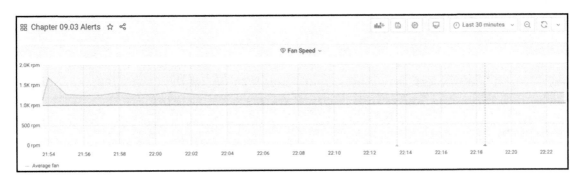

You should also get an email message with a picture of the graph and the notification message configured in the alert:

Success! You've created your first alert and received a notification message.

Troubleshooting and controlling alerts

What happens if the alert didn't fire as you expected or you didn't get an email notification? Here are some troubleshooting tips that might help you diagnose the problem.

Checking the alert history

The first step is to check **State history**. Located next to the **Test Rule** button, the **State history** button opens a pane with the current state (which you can clear if it gets too long). The state history displays the current state and up to 49 additional previous states. It might be the case that the alert has triggered but is still in a pending state, for example. Here's what a typical state history looks like:

Checking the history is a good way of getting an idea of how often your rules are firing and whether you have configured them to correctly transition from state to state, especially if you expect your alerts to switch back to **OK** when an alerting condition has reverted for the set amount of time. If you don't see the rule firing in your history, the next step is to confirm the rule configuration by testing it.

Testing the rule

The next option if you didn't get an alert notification is to confirm your alert rules are in order. The **Alert** tab has a testing facility built-in to help with diagnosing troubles. The button is located at the top right and is called **Test Rule**. Here is some of the output from a test when the alert doesn't trigger:

```
Object
firing:false
state:"ok"
conditionEvals:"false = false"
timeMs:"15.550ms"
logs:Array[3]
0:Object
message:"Condition[0]: Query"
data:Object
1:Object
message:"Condition[0]: Query Result"
data:Object
2:Object
message:"Condition[0]: Eval: false, Metric: Average fan, Value: 961.600"
data:null
```

Immediately, we can see that the firing state is `false`, indicating that the alert won't fire under these circumstances. We can also see the current state of the alert is `ok`. The objects after this represent the results of the underlying query, the result of the evaluation of the conditions with the query result, and the message summarizing the current metric.

If the current state indicates **Firing** but you didn't receive an email, it might help to double-check the notification channel. Open the notification channel's tab and select the one associated with the panel. Clicking **Send Test** should send an email out to the email address configured in the **Addresses** field.

If you still didn't get an email, check the server logs. In the Docker Compose environment, run the following:

```
% docker-compose logs --tail 50 grafana
```

This should give you an idea of what error your test might have generated. More than likely, it will reveal a problem with the Grafana server configuration, a problem with connecting to the SMTP server, or a problem with authenticating the SMTP server.

Controlling alerts

It may come about that you decide you need to disable rules for one reason or another. Perhaps it is a temporary measure during a maintenance window or perhaps you or your team are not able to handle alerts. In either case, you don't want to go through all your alerts and set their conditions so that they never trigger. Really, you just need a way to pause the alerts.

So, from the left sidebar, go to **Alerting** | **Alert Rules**. Here, you'll find all the alerts set in your panels collected in one place. This tab allows you to search for alerts by name or filter them by state. Clicking on the pause/play icon pauses and resumes the alert. If you do want to modify the rule, the settings (gear) icon will take you directly to the alert's tab. Here's a look at a couple of alert rules, one paused and the other in the firing state:

The **Alert Rules** tab serves as a great traffic control center for managing alerts, but as you can see, it is only as useful as you are diligent about naming your alerts. Develop a naming convention so that you can easily use the search feature to track down the alerts you're interested in.

Let's summarize what we have learned in this chapter.

Summary

We've come to the end of our tour of the Grafana alerting system. Using Logstash, we imported real-time hardware data via the `powermetrics` command. We took a closer look at thresholds and time regions in order to get familiar with Grafana alerts. We learned about the Grafana alerting state machine and set up threshold alerts for excessive fan speed and CPU temperature. We also configured an email notification channel for sending an alert message and triggered an alert. Finally, we explored some troubleshooting options for when things don't work the way we expect.

While it may not contain all the bells and whistles of its competitors, Grafana offers a solid system for generating notifications from data-driven alerts. Although it is configured from the **Graph** panel, the alerting rules are monitored by the Grafana server's backend. It can monitor multiple queries and logically combine a number of threshold conditions, and gracefully handles edge cases. It provides numerous, easily configurable notification channels from a diverse array of applications.

In the next chapter, we'll complete our study of Grafana's advanced features with one of its newest—Loki. Grafana Labs describes it as *"like Prometheus but with logging!"* Loki's efficient log metadata indexing features, when combined with Grafana Explore and Promtail, represent a powerful logging aggregator comparable to the venerable ElasticSearch ELK stack.

10
Exploring Logs with Grafana Loki

In this final chapter of *Section 2: Real-World Grafana*, we're going to shift gears a bit. So far, we've been operating under a dashboard-oriented paradigm in terms of how we use Grafana. This is not too unusual since Grafana has always been structured around the dashboard metaphor. Now, the development of **Explore** in Grafana 6 brings an alternative workflow – one that is data-driven and, dare I say it, exploratory.

Grafana really shines when working with numerical and some forms of textual data, but what if the data includes substantial amounts of log data? Every day, countless applications disgorge not only standard numerical metrics but also copious text logs. If you've ever enabled **debug** mode in an application, then you've seen how quickly a few meager kilobytes of information can quickly become a flood of gigabytes worth of repetitive, inscrutable gibberish. Diagnosing a problem by enabling the debugging code is more like the proverbial needle in a haystack as even a few seconds of data spans thousands of lines of text.

The goal of Grafana's Explore and other similar tools is to try to get a handle of some of that data by making searching and filtering easier, and by making it possible to associate metrics data with time-correlated log data. It's not enough for Explore to provide the ad hoc analysis; it needs to be coupled with data sources that can handle logging and metrics data. If you are familiar with Elasticsearch, then you'll know this sounds like a description of the ELK stack, which is a combination of Elasticsearch for data storage and search, Logstash for data capture, and Kibana for visualization.

Now, Grafana has dropped its hat into the ring by introducing Loki, a new project designed to provide the following (`https://grafana.com/oss/loki/`):

> "...a horizontally-scalable, highly-available, multi-tenant log aggregation system inspired by `Prometheus`. It is designed to be very cost-effective and easy to operate. It does not index the contents of the logs, but rather a set of labels for each log stream."

By combining Loki log aggregation with Prometheus metrics and Grafana visualization, Grafana is developing a software suite that could, in time, rival the venerable ELK stack. Why don't we find out more about this new product and take a glimpse at the future of Grafana?

Our ultimate goal will be to use Explore to simultaneously analyze logs and metrics. This entails setting up a number of services and getting them to talk to each other. Here's the overall plan:

1. Stand up a Loki pipeline alongside our Grafana server.
2. Collect some system logs with Promtail, a Loki agent similar in function to Elasticsearch Logstash.
3. Make any transformations to the collected log data in order to increase its utility in Explore.
4. Collect additional logging from the various services in our pipeline, including Grafana.
5. Use Prometheus to scrape the metrics from our services and use an Explore feature called **Split** to compare the logs with the time-correlated metrics.

Along the way, we'll be learning about some of the interesting Explore features that become available when you use the Loki data source.

In this chapter, we'll explore the following topics:

- Loading system logs into Loki
- Visualizing Loki log data with Explore
- Adding additional service logs
- Querying logs and metrics with Explore

Let's get started!

Loading system logs into Loki

To get started, `cd` to the `ch10` directory in your clone of this book's repository.

Our first step is to download and launch the Loki pipeline services with Docker Compose. We will use a sample `docker-compose.yml` file, which can be downloaded from the Loki GitHub repository (found at `https://github.com/grafana/loki`). By now, the `docker-compose.yml` file should seem familiar and pretty straightforward. In our initial deployment, we will set up three services: `loki`, `promtail`, and `grafana`. Let's have a quick look at the configuration for each service:

```
loki:
  image: "grafana/loki:${LOKI_TAG-latest}"
  ports:
    - "3100:3100"
  command: -config.file=/etc/loki/local-config.yaml
  networks:
    - loki
  volumes:
    - "${PWD-.}/loki:/loki"
```

First up is the Loki service itself. Loki will provide the log storage service that the data source will access to search and aggregate our logs. In the `loki` service configuration, we download the latest Docker image from the repository, expose port `3100`, and set a command-line option to use the container's local `/etc/loki/local-config.yaml` file as the configuration file. The `networks` setting creates a common network called `loki`. It's not strictly necessary to define a network as our deployment only uses a single network anyway. Finally, we'll persist the logs to a mapped volume.

Moving on to the next service, `promtail` will gather up our logs and send them to Loki. Its configuration looks as follows:

```
promtail:

  image: "grafana/promtail:${PROMT_TAG-latest}"
  ports:
    - "9080:9080"
  volumes:
    - /private/var/log:/var/log
    - "${PWD-.}/promtail:/etc/promtail"
  command: -config.file=/etc/promtail/docker-config.yaml
  networks:
    - loki
```

In this case, we have attached a local volume containing the logs. I've made a change to the volume to point to the local log directory on my version of OS X, but you may need to set this to reflect the location of your logs, depending on your operating system. This time around, we'll expose port 9080. To access a Promtail API endpoint, we can query to make sure the service is up and running correctly. Again, we'll specify a container local file for configuration.

This covers our Loki pipeline, so we'll go ahead with the Grafana service, which you should be very familiar with by now:

```
image: "grafana/grafana:${GRAF_TAG-latest}"
ports:
  - "3000:3000"
volumes:
  - "${PWD-.}/grafana:/var/lib/grafana"
networks:
  - loki
```

Now, let's launch our service stack:

```
% docker-compose up -d
Creating network "ch10_loki" with the default driver
Creating ch10_grafana_1 ... done
Creating ch10_loki_1 ... done
Creating ch10_promtail_1 ... done
```

We can use `curl` to access the endpoints for our `loki` and `promtail` services:

```
% curl -XGET http://localhost:3100/ready
Ready
% curl -XGET http://localhost:9080/ready
Ready
```

Unless Promtail was unable to locate some logs in /var/logs, you should have received the `ready` response. Let's launch Grafana and see what Loki has done with our logs.

Create a Loki data source in Grafana with these settings:

- **Name**: Loki
- **HTTP/URL**: http://loki:3100

If you are successful, you should get a message that reads, **Data source connected and labels found.**

Visualizing Loki log data with Explore

Go to **Explore** and make sure Loki is set as the data source.

Welcome to Explore! Things look quite a bit different from what you may remember from using Explore with other data sources. Let's take a quick tour of some of the basic UI features:

The features highlighted in the preceding screenshot are as follows:

1. **Log labels/Metrics Explorer**: This is where you can use the **Log labels** or **Metrics Explorer** to access log labels as they are generated or parsed from your logs. Logs can also be aggregated into metrics. Loki is architected somewhat differently than Elasticsearch in that it doesn't create a database of indexed log files. Rather, it simply associates logs with text labels, similar to metrics labels in Prometheus.

2. **Query field**: You enter log stream queries here using the LogQL query language, which is very similar to PromQL for Prometheus. Selections made from the **Log labels** dropdown will appear here as well.

3. **Metrics/Logs selector**: This switches the mode from log queries to log metrics that are created by aggregating logs over time. Use the cheat sheets as a guide on how to craft queries in the query box.

4. **Split button**: This splits the window into two queries that are side by side. For example, you can put logs on one side and metrics on the other.

5. **Time frame selection.**

6. **Run Query button**: Use this dropdown to set the refresh rate for the query.

7. **Live tail button**: This continuously displays the last few loglines matching the query. The button switches to a pause or stop selector.

8. **Line limit**: This sets a limit on the number of lines that will be displayed from a query. Defaults to 1,000 lines.

9. **Query time**: This gauges how long the query took to run. Use this to help optimize queries.

10. **Hide query.**

11. **Delete query.**

Let's have a look at the logs. From **Log labels**, select **filename** and a log file. Now, we can see how **Explore** displays both the loglines in a table and the log stream counts in a graph above it:

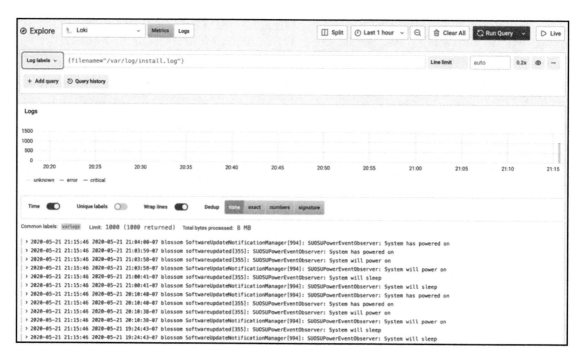

We seem to have a bit of a problem. It appears that, despite having read in logs covering a period of several hours, they appear to be all bunched up at one time period. By default, Promtail simply loads logs and sends them to Loki; it doesn't parse the timestamps or fields from the logs. We'll need to configure Promtail to break down the loglines for us, and for that, we'll need to modify its configuration.

But before we can make those modifications, we'll need to copy the original Promtail configuration file (`docker-config.yaml`) into a `promtail` directory outside the container. The easiest way to do this is to just download it from the Loki GitHub repository.

Once we've done that, we'll add additional configuration in the form of a Promtail *pipeline stage*. Pipeline stages are intended to perform data parsing and transformation, not altogether different than the `filter` section of a Logstash pipeline configuration. Pipeline stages come in four types, each performing different tasks on loglines and passing the results to the next stage:

- **Parsing stages**: Parses the **logline** and **extract** fields from parse matches
- **Transform stages**: Modifies the extracted fields
- **Action stages**: Performs some action with the extracted fields or even the logline itself
- **Filtering stages**: Drops certain stages or loglines

First, we need to add pipeline stages to our job:

```
scrape_configs:
  - job_name: system
    pipeline_stages:
```

Next, we'll construct a pipeline stage called `match`. Matches are filter stages designed to run a set of other pipeline stages on any logs that match a LogQL selector. In our case, the selector will query for the `system.log` file:

```
- match:
    selector: '{filename="/var/log/system.log"}'
```

Next, we'll parse the lines for some useful fields that we can turn into searchable labels. Here is an example line from `system.log`:

```
Feb 24 22:13:46 blossom syslogd[109]: ASL Sender Statistics
```

The first part of the line is the timestamp, followed by the hostname, the process name, a process ID in brackets, and after the colon, the message. We want to extract the timestamp and create labels for the hostname and the process name. We also want to retain the message. We don't want to create labels from the message or the process ID as they are fields with high *cardinality* or a large set of possible values, and we prefer to not overwhelm our **Log labels** explore interface with hundreds of field values.

In order to extract the fields we want, we can use a `regex` action stage:

```
- regex:
    expression: '^(?P<timestamp>[A-Za-
z]{3}\s\d{2}\s[\d:]*)\s(?P<hostname>[a-zA-
Z]+)\s(?P<processname>[\w\.]+)\[[\d+\][:\s]*(?P<output>\S.*)'
```

It's a little crazy-looking if you're not too familiar with regular expressions, but the regex will parse each line and, for each pattern, match store the matched strings in variables corresponding to timestamp, hostname, and processname. It will also store everything left over after skipping over the process ID in a variable called output. We'll take these fields and pass them on to three more pipeline stages.

The next stage is the **timestamp** action stage. It can take a string – in this case, the timestamp field parsed from the logline – and convert it into a timestamp either by matching it with a set of predefined formats or by defining a reference format string. Our timestamp field doesn't happen to fit any of the standard formats, but it is quite easy to build a format reference string that will do just fine:

```
- timestamp:
    format: "Jan 02 15:04:05"
    source: timestamp
```

The source field refers to the **match** field from our regex stage.

Next, we'll identify our hostname and processname fields as labels so we can search and/or filter on them:

```
- labels:
    hostname:
    processname:
```

Finally, we pass along the output field to the output stage, where it will become our new logline:

```
- output:
    source: output
```

And that's it! Let's have a look at our handiwork. Shut down and start up the deployment to force a reload of the configuration and log files:

```
% docker-compose down

Stopping ch10_promtail_1 ... done
Stopping ch10_grafana_1 ... done
Stopping ch10_loki_1 ... done
Removing ch10_promtail_1 ... done
Removing ch10_grafana_1 ... done
Removing ch10_loki_1 ... done
Removing network ch10_loki

% docker-compose up -d
```

```
Creating network "ch10_loki" with the default driver
Creating ch10_grafana_1 ... done
Creating ch10_promtail_1 ... done
Creating ch10_loki_1 ... done
```

Execute a query for `system.log` either using the **Log label** explorer or the query field using the query (you may need to expand your time range):

```
{filename="/var/log/system.log"}
```

Things should be quite a bit different now. You should now see a distribution of logs over time, and the logs themselves will appear to be truncated:

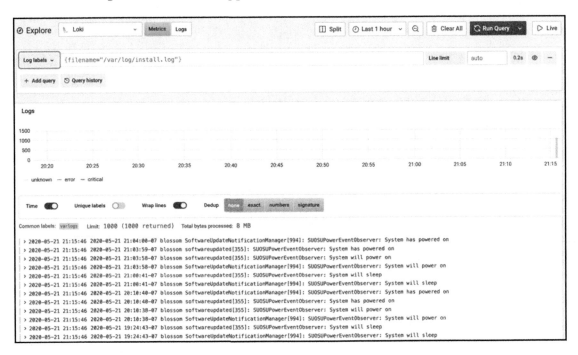

In reality, the timestamps and label fields have been parsed out and hidden, depending on whether the **Time** and **Unique labels** toggles have been switched on. To see the parsed fields, click on any of the loglines to get a detailed view of them:

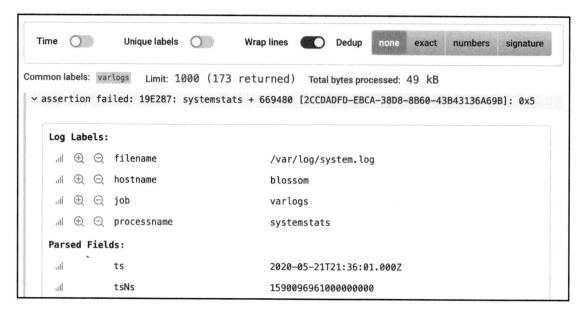

Here, you will see the `hostname` and `processname` details, along with standard representations for our `timestamp` field. Turning on the toggles reveals the labels in their original context:

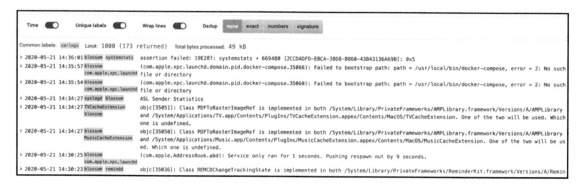

Now that we have an idea of how to work with the **Explore** panel to see our logs, let's populate it with yet more logs.

Adding additional service logs

We'd like to get Loki to not only aggregate the system logs, but also the logs our services are generating. We could adjust the Promtail configuration to look for the logs wherever they're stored by Docker, but they could be tricky to find and the container may not sync them with the filesystem in a timely enough fashion.

Luckily, the folks at Grafana have provided a log driver for Docker that can deliver logs to Loki directly, thus bypassing Promtail entirely. It requires downloading a special Loki log driver and requires adjusting the `docker-compose.yml` file so that it includes the new logging information. To download and install the driver, run the following command:

```
% docker plugin install grafana/loki-docker-driver:latest --alias loki
--grant-all-permissions
```

To confirm the installation, run the following command:

```
% docker plugin ls

ID NAME DESCRIPTION ENABLED
692bec0b6ade loki:latest Loki Logging Driver true
```

If you get `true` as output, then your plugin loaded properly and is ready to go. More information on the driver can be found in the Loki GitHub repository (`https://github.com/grafana/loki/tree/v1.3.0/docs/clients/docker-driver`).

In order to take advantage of the driver, we'll need to update our `docker-compose.yml` file and reload our containers.

To send logging information for Loki, modify the service:

```
loki:
  image: "grafana/loki:${LOKI_TAG-latest}"
  ports:
    - "3100:3100"
  command: -config.file=/etc/loki/local-config.yaml
  networks:
    - loki
  volumes:
    - "${PWD-.}/loki:/loki"
  logging:
    driver: loki
    options:
      loki-url: "http://host.docker.internal:3100/loki/api/v1/push"
```

Here, we're adding a new logging configuration to the service. We set the driver to `loki` and set the URL the driver needs to send the logs. The URL form can be found in the Promtail configuration file. Here's an excerpt:

```
clients:
  - url: http://loki:3100/loki/api/v1/push
```

Here, we configure the logging in order to set the `--log-opt` command-line option for `docker run`, which launches the container. Information on how to configure containers to use the driver can be found in the following GitHub repository: `https://github.com/grafana/loki/blob/master/docs/clients/docker-driver/configuration.md`.

In case you're wondering why we don't set the host to `loki` (the hostname for the `loki` service itself) in the service configuration, the explanation is a bit tricky. You see, the driver is set by Docker to be on the network for the Docker host, not the network internally established by Docker Compose. Effectively, it is **outside** the network we created for our services. However, Docker provides a special address for containers to access the host network: `host.docker.internal`.

We can set the configurations for the other services in a similar fashion. Here is the `promtail` service:

```
promtail:
  image: "grafana/promtail:${PROMT_TAG-latest}"
  ports:
    - "9080:9080"
  volumes:
    - /private/var/log:/var/log
    - "${PWD-.}/promtail:/etc/promtail"
  command: -config.file=/etc/promtail/docker-config.yaml
  networks:
    - loki
  logging:
    driver: loki
    options:
      loki-url: "http://host.docker.internal:3100/loki/api/v1/push"
```

And here is the `grafana` service:

```
grafana:
  image: "grafana/grafana:${GRAF_TAG-latest}"
  ports:
    - "3000:3000"
  volumes:
    - "${PWD-.}/grafana:/var/lib/grafana"
  networks:
```

```
      - loki
  logging:
    driver: loki
    options:
      loki-url: "http://host.docker.internal:3100/loki/api/v1/push"
```

To get the new logging information, shut down and restart our Docker Compose deployment:

```
% docker-compose down
Stopping ch10_promtail_1 ... done
Stopping ch10_grafana_1 ... done
Stopping ch10_loki_1 ... done
Removing ch10_promtail_1 ... done
Removing ch10_grafana_1 ... done
Removing ch10_loki_1 ... done
Removing network ch10_loki

% docker-compose up -d
Creating network "ch10_loki" with the default driver
Creating ch10_grafana_1 ... done
Creating ch10_promtail_1 ... done
Creating ch10_loki_1 ... done

% curl -XGET http://localhost:3100/ready
Ready
```

Once we've confirmed the Loki service is up and running, reloading the **Explore** page should reveal new labels corresponding to our additional logs:

Where did all those labels come from? The Loki logging driver not only delivered the logging for all our containers, but it also set labels based on the Docker container configuration, and then parsed them (as well as it could) to produce a rich set of fields for us. To get an idea of how to do this, query for the `grafana` container logs using the `compose_service` label:

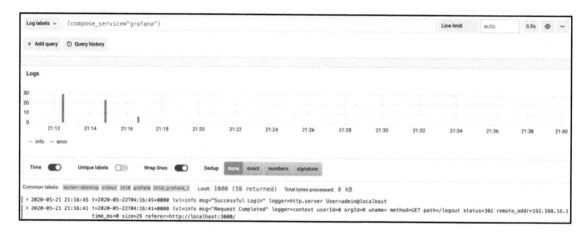

Notice how the log scraping times match the timestamps for the loglines. Now, click on one of the entries:

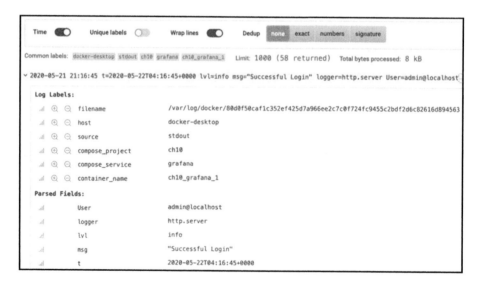

You should see a breakdown of the logline in terms of the labels and fields parsed out of the line, this time automatically by the logging driver.

Note the icons to the left of the labels. Clicking on the magnifying glasses produces either positive or negative filters based on the label. Clicking on the histogram produces a distribution of the label or field across the log query. These features allow us to quickly modify the query without the need to go up to the query field and type it in manually.

While we're here, let's take a look at the deduplication feature. Deduplication is helpful when you're looking at a stream of logs that are very similar in structure or have large chunks of repetition. Explore provides a number of deduplication strategies that can compress and summarize with varying levels of aggression. To try it out, let's look at Loki's logging capabilites. Run the following query:

```
{compose_service="loki"}
```

Older versions of Loki generated results like this (we'll get into why later):

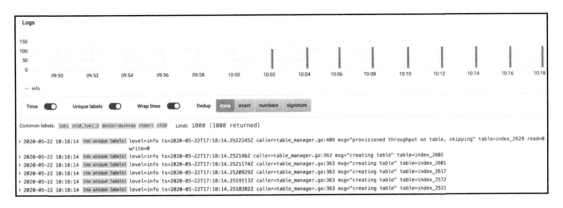

As you can see, the structure of each line is more or less identical, save for the timestamp and the values. This is a perfect case for numerical deduplication, which will identify duplication based on numerical values. Select **Dedup/numbers** to see how that works:

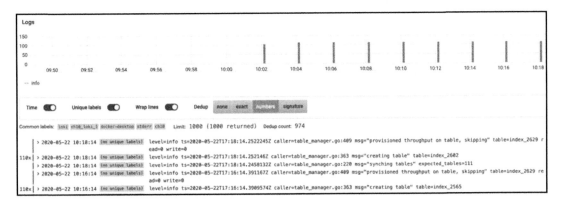

We've taken **1000** lines and reduced them by over 96%!

Now that we've seen the power of Loki log aggregation, let's couple that with Prometheus' metrics.

Querying logs and metrics with Explore

Adding Prometheus to the mix is relatively straightforward. We'll add a new Prometheus service while sending its logs to Loki to be aggregated (why not?). We'll also need to configure Prometheus to scrape the metric endpoints of our services. We did this earlier in this book, so it should be no problem for us to configure scrapers for each service.

First, let's add Prometheus to our stack:

```
prometheus:
  image: "prom/prometheus:${PROM_TAG-latest}"
  ports:
    - "9090:9090"
  volumes:
    - "${PWD-.}/prometheus:/etc/prometheus"
  command: --config.file=/etc/prometheus/prometheus.yaml
  networks:
    - loki
  logging:
    driver: loki
    options:
      loki-url: "http://host.docker.internal:3100/loki/api/v1/push"
```

We'll need to create a volume directory for Prometheus to store our configuration file (named `prometheus.yml`).

The configuration file is based on the one we developed back in `Chapter 4`, *Connecting Grafana to a Data Source*. First, we set the default scrape interval to 30 seconds:

```
global:
  # How frequently to scrape targets by default.
  scrape_interval:     30s # By default, scrape targets every 30 seconds.
```

We'll also set the scrape configuration jobs, one for each service, including Prometheus:

```
scrape_configs:
  # The job name is added as a label `job=<job_name>` to any timeseries
scraped from this config.
  - job_name: 'prometheus'
    static_configs:
      - targets: ['localhost:9090']

  - job_name: 'grafana'
    static_configs:
      - targets: ['grafana:3000']

  - job_name: 'promtail'
    static_configs:
      - targets: ['promtail:9080']

  - job_name: 'loki'
    static_configs:
      - targets: ['loki:3100']
```

We use the service names and exposed ports to set the targets for each job. Bring down and start back up your Docker Compose deployment to get the new Prometheus service:

```
% docker-compose down
Stopping ch10_grafana_1 ... done
Stopping ch10_loki_1 ... done
Stopping ch10_promtail_1 ... done
Removing ch10_grafana_1 ... done
Removing ch10_loki_1 ... done
Removing ch10_promtail_1 ... done
Removing network ch10_loki

% docker-compose up -d
Creating network "ch10_loki" with the default driver
Creating ch10_prometheus_1 ... done
Creating ch10_grafana_1 ... done
Creating ch10_loki_1 ... done
Creating ch10_promtail_1 ... done
```

You can check the Prometheus service by opening `http://localhost:9090/graph`. Next, we'll need to create a Prometheus data source with the following settings:

- **Name**: `Prometheus`
- **HTTP/URL**: `http://prometheus:9090`
- **HTTP/Access**: **Server (default)**

If Prometheus is working correctly, you should get a message along the lines of **Data source is working**. Return to **Explore** to have a look at what we've collected. We're going to use the **Split** feature to compare the log information we've gathered with the metrics we've scraped.

Here's an example based on an actual experience we encountered while writing this book. Imagine that we are monitoring our Loki service and, among the alerts, there's one based on the metric for `loki_ingester_streams_created_total`. We aren't measuring the actual total, but rather the *rate* at which the ingester streams are created, perhaps as an early warning proxy that something might be going on. After all, if there are suddenly a lot of logs to be ingested, Loki might need to create a lot of streams in a short amount of time.

Now, imagine you get an alert one day and this is what the graph looks like:

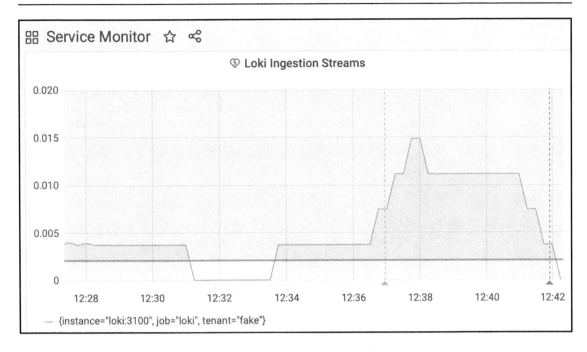

We might want to check this out. To do so, we need to select **Explore** from the panel menu to launch **Explore** with the panel query, as shown in the following screenshot:

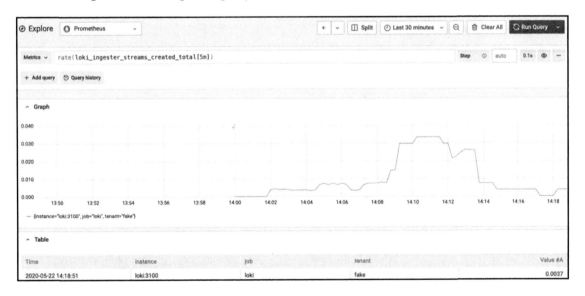

Note that the query metrics are already filled in. This doesn't really tell us anything; we need to look at the logs. This is where the **Split** feature comes in handy. We'll be able to look at logs and metrics and link them in time to look for correlations.

Let's click on the **Split** button. We now see essentially two independent **Explore** windows, so to link them by time, click on the chain icon to lock the time ranges for both windows. Now, any change in the time range in one window will be reflected in the other one as well.

In the left window, we'll load up our Loki data source and have a look at our log output. Switch to **Metrics** and enter this query:

```
{compose_service="loki"}
```

This will allow us to look at the logs generated by the Loki Docker Compose service container. Right away, we will notice something a little peculiar:

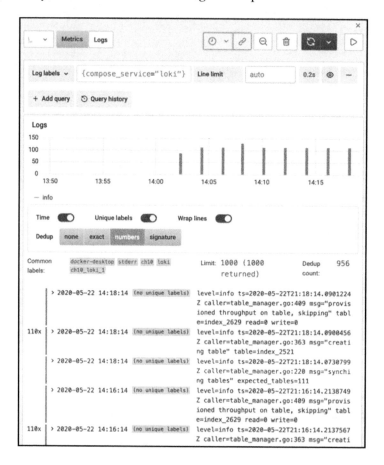

It looks like Loki is generating over 100 very similar logs every couple of minutes. This doesn't seem like a good thing, especially compared to all our other services – the primary log generator has become Loki itself! This could be a sign of some sort of bug.

As it happens, a search for `creating table` in Loki's issue tracker on GitHub yields this interesting case:

This case directly matches our problem and, as we can see, it has been fixed. All we need to do is update our service with the latest version of Loki and we should be good to go. In fact, this is the case here as the problem has, in fact, been rectified.

Hopefully, this example shows the power behind the ability to link metrics with time-correlated logging. It's a common pattern to go from an alert to an examination of the triggering metrics, and then to the corresponding logs. Having all that information at your fingertips and in the same interface can be a real time-saver, especially when you're dealing with critical incidents.

Summary

We've reached the end of `Chapter 10`, *Exploring Logs with Grafana's Loki*. In this chapter, we learned how to use **Explore** with the Loki data source to perform ad hoc analysis of logs and aggregated log metrics and we deployed a Loki pipeline to aggregate filesystem log files and, by using a custom driver, the logs generated by Docker containers. Then, we used Prometheus to collect dozens of metrics about those container services. Finally, using the Split feature, we made side-by-side comparisons of both the log and service metrics.

With that, we've also reached the end of *Section 2: Real-World Grafana*. In *Section 3: Managing Grafana*, we'll step out of our role as an end user of Grafana and into that of an administrator. We'll learn about how to manage dashboards, users, and teams. We'll also look at how to secure the Grafana server by authenticating our users with services such as OAuth2 and LDAP. Finally, we'll explore the rapidly expanding world of cloud monitoring and how Grafana fits into it.

See you soon!

Managing Grafana

3

This section is intended to highlight aspects of Grafana beyond building dashboard panels.

This section is comprised of the following chapters:

- Chapter 11, *Organizing Dashboards*
- Chapter 12, *Managing Permissions for Users and Teams*
- Chapter 13, *Authentication with External Services*
- Chapter 14, *Cloud Monitoring*

11
Organizing Dashboards

Welcome to the third and final section of *Learn Grafana 7.0*: *Managing Grafana*. By now, you've created some awesome dashboards. Maybe you've even set up valuable alerts with some of those dashboards, and now you're in the enviable position of being your team's Grafana guru. That great honor will be accompanied by great responsibilities. You're now the de facto manager of your Grafana server and all the requisite administrative tasks that come along for the ride.

In this section of this book, we'll cover some of the more common aspects of Grafana management, from keeping your dashboards tidy to managing and authenticating your users and teams, to monitoring your applications in the cloud. In *Section 2: Real-World Grafana*, we used various realistic scenarios to drive the descriptions and the associated exercises. In this section, we will present the material in a more straightforward how-to style, and along the way, cover use cases, tips, and guidelines.

We'll start by looking at some strategies for managing the broad but common problem of dashboard proliferation in this chapter, then proceed through more esoteric problems such as user management (Chapter 12, *Managing Permissions for Users and Teams*) and authentication using services such as Okta and LDAP (Chapter 13, *Authentication with External Services*) before ultimately culminating in a survey of current cloud monitoring integrations such as AWS and Azure (Chapter 14, *Cloud Monitoring*).

By the end of this chapter, not only should you have a good understanding of the run-of-the-mill aspects of managing dashboards, compiling them into playlists and cataloging them on dashboard panels, but you should have learned about strategies for naming dashboards, organizing them into folders, and managing your site as it scales up.

In this chapter, we will have a look at the following topics:

- Naming dashboards and creating folders
- Starring and tagging dashboards
- Dashboard playlists
- Dashboard list panel

Technical requirements

The tutorial code, dashboards, and other helpful files for this chapter can be found in this book's GitHub repository at `https://github.com/PacktPublishing/Learn-Grafana-7.0/tree/master/Chapter11`.

Let's get started!

Managing dashboards and folders

By now, you've probably created at least a handful of dashboards, if only to work through the examples in this book. Ideally, you're well on your way to creating many more, along with other members of your team, unit, and even your entire company. What you'll quickly find – if you haven't already – is that you've ended up with a number of dashboards in various stages of development and potentially connecting to a number of data sources, all of them lying around in the dashboard display.

Conceptually, Grafana provides four classification schemes aimed at helping you identify dashboards to satisfy common organizational needs. The first is what I call a **significance-based** scheme, which identifies the most important dashboard through a **starred** or **favorited** designation. The second is a **structure-based** scheme, which places dashboards into an arbitrary hierarchical structure of folders. The third scheme is a **nomenclature-based** scheme, or the naming convention by which we determine how best to name dashboards. The fourth and final scheme is **semantic-based** in that we attach labels or tags to dashboards, giving them whatever meaning we might desire.

Naming a dashboard

Here's how to name (or rename) a dashboard:

1. Open the dashboard.
2. Select the gear icon for **Dashboard settings**.
3. Make sure the **General** tab is selected.
4. Type a name into the **Name** field.
5. Click on **Save dashboard**.
6. Return to the dashboard.

Here's an example of editing the name of the dashboard and setting it to `My Excellent Dashboard`:

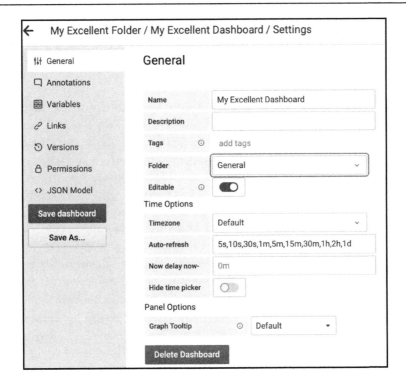

Whenever you make a change to the dashboard settings, remember to make the long UX journey to the left-hand side of the page and click on **Save dashboard**. If you return to the dashboard without saving the change, there is always the possibility that Grafana won't catch it when you try to load a different one.

 Get into the habit of typing a little comment whenever you save so that if you need to roll back to an earlier version, you'll have a way of tracking your changes. Under some legal circumstances, you might be required to maintain an audit trail of your dashboard changes, so it's a good idea to get into the practice of commenting on your saves.

Dashboard naming tips

The first opportunity you will get to organize your dashboards is when you first create and then save your dashboard. At that point, you will be forced to make a decision about what you want to name it. A lot of people, myself included, will be much more interested in building the dashboard than coming up with a proper name. Unfortunately, that tendency leads to a lot of *Dashboard 1*, *Dashboard 2*, and *Dashboard 4* copy dashboards.

These less-than-creative names fail for a number of reasons: they don't describe the content of the dashboard either to your future self or to your audience, or they tend to collide with other lazily named dashboards. Here are a few of my opinionated suggestions for constructively naming them:

- **Do use a name that accurately describes the contents of the dashboard**: For example, Total CMMR Income From Region 2, Server Room Climate Monitors, Minneapolis 311 Calls-Real Time, and so on.
- **Do try to adhere to some form of naming convention so that they are easy to scan in lists**: For example, Financial Analysis, SEC Model 2012-10, Daugherty, Sales Profile, Refreshed Customers AUNZ, Jones, and so on. Here, we're placing the broadest scope of the dashboard first, followed by a more specific description, followed by the owner. You might also do this with tagging and folders, but it does make it quicker to find the dashboard from a lengthy list.
- **Do consider using template variables to combine dashboards that differ by a single variable**: For example, like a department, business unit, or region – rather than name multiple similar dashboards with specific names.
- **Don't try to encode a hierarchical dashboard structure by naming convention**: For example, Global Sales-Regional-NE Texas, Global Sales-Regional-SW Texas, and so on. Place the dashboards into nested folders and set up labels to reflect the tiers of your hierarchy.
- **Don't try to use the name for version control**: For example, Housing Analysis 2021.v22. Grafana tracks all dashboard saves, and you can always revert to an earlier version from the **Dashboard settings | Versions** page. Remember to add a comment to your saves so that you know what the version changed.

These suggestions should not be interpreted as requirements; you might find it easier to do some of these but not others. You may not even have the ability to implement the kind of naming conventions you'd like. However, if you do have the opportunity to set up standards, try to maintain them as consistently as possible. It's better to try and maintain some level of control with a few outliers as opposed to an unmanageable free-for-all that you are forced to clean up later.

Working with dashboard folders

After naming the dashboards, arranging them into specific folders is the next mechanism for keeping things organized and tidy. Not only do folders keep your dashboards in some form of structured storage, but they also provide a means by which you can establish access controls to your dashboards. We'll discuss access control in more detail in the next chapter.

In the meantime, let's go over some common folder-related tasks:

1. Creating dashboard folders
2. Adding dashboards to folders
3. Deleting folders

Finally, we'll also go over some tips for keeping dashboards and folders tidy and manageable.

Creating a dashboard folder

There are two routes to dashboard folder creation. The first is via the left sidebar:

1. From the **Create** left sidebar, select **Folder.**
2. Type the folder's name into the **Name** field.
3. Click **Create.**

The second is via the **Dashboards** left sidebar:

1. From the **Dashboards** side menu, select **Manage.**
2. Select **New Folder.**
3. Type the folder's name into the **Name** field.
4. Click **Create.**

In both cases, you will land on the **Manage** tab of the **Dashboards** page, as shown in the following screenshot:

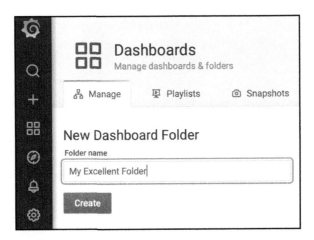

Once you've created a folder, you'll want to put something in it. We'll cover adding dashboards to a folder next.

Adding dashboards to a folder

When a folder is created, by default, it is located in the `General` folder. You can always move it from there, provided you have the permissions.

There are two methods for adding a dashboard:

- Dashboard-centric
- Folder-centric

The dashboard-centric method places a single dashboard in a folder by editing it:

1. Load a dashboard and open its **Dashboard Settings.**
2. Make sure **General** is the active tab.
3. Select the **Folder** from the drop-down.
4. Save the dashboard. If you return to the dashboard without saving, the location will appear to have changed, but it may not persist if you open a different dashboard.
5. Return to the dashboard and confirm the new dashboard location in the dashboard navigation menu.

Selecting the folder from the drop-down can be seen in the following screenshot:

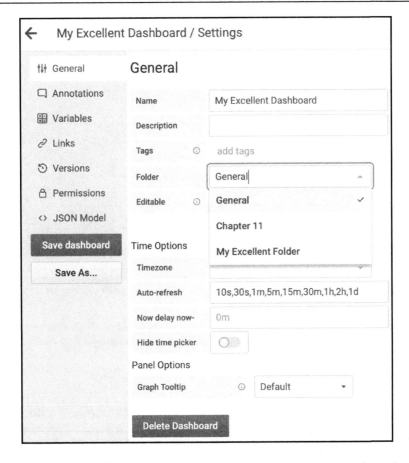

The folder-centric method collects one or more dashboards and moves them into a designated folder:

1. Select **Manage** from the **Dashboard** side menu.
2. Create a **New Folder** if one doesn't already exist.
3. Select the dashboards you wish to place into the folder.
4. Click **Move.**

5. Select the folder from the **Choose Dashboard Folder** drop-down:

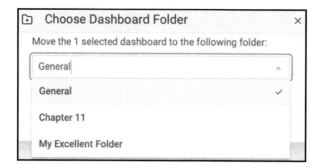

This method is clearly the one to use if you need to move a lot of dashboards around. What if you get tired of your folder? Next, we'll find out how to delete a folder.

Deleting folders

In Grafana, deleting folder is a fairly high-risk move, so do it with the utmost of caution as a folder delete also deletes its contents. Follow these steps to do this:

1. Select **Manage** from the **Dashboard** side menu.
2. Select the folder to delete.
3. Select **Delete**. You will see a warning if the folder contains dashboards:

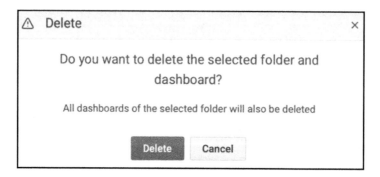

This is a very risky procedure, so you may want to consider tagging (with a **Delete** tag, for example) the dashboards you want to delete and evacuating everything from the folder before deleting it.

Guiding dashboard folder management

Here are a few suggestions when it comes to managing dashboard folders:

- **Do** embrace folders, opting for depth over breadth. Fewer top-level folders will make it easier to find and work with dashboards.
- **Do** think about the overall folder structure for your dashboards and settle for the one that offers the most utility. If you have a larger organization, it might be better to create a folder structure that partitions by department or business unit, and then allow each to create their own hierarchies. Alternatively, you might be a member of a small team that creates dashboards within an ongoing set of projects, perhaps with a folder devoted to each project.
- **Don't** redundantly embed hierarchy in folder names; for example, A/Project A-Database Queries/Project A-Database Queries-Queries per Server. Just name each folder and dashboard for its place in the hierarchy since the *navbar* breadcrumbs will depict the hierarchy; that is, Project A/Database Queries/Queries per Server.
- **Don't** duplicate dashboards into multiple folders. This approach will prove to be a maintenance nightmare. If you are tempted to put the same dashboard into multiple folders by performing duplication, consider tagging the dashboard with multiple tags instead, or consider the possibility of using template variables if the dashboard is minimally altered after being placed in the different folders.

In the next section, we'll look at starring and tagging dashboards.

Starring and tagging dashboards

Our previous sections mostly dealt with the key structural aspects of a dashboard: the name and its location in a specific folder. We will now turn to more semantic aspects, ones that are best described in terms of dashboard metadata, namely dashboard stars and labels. As we saw in `Chapter 8`, *Working with Advanced Dashboard Features*, dashboard tags prove useful when linking dashboards, but that's not the case for tags or stars, as we're about to find out.

Marking dashboards as favorites

Starred dashboards are mostly useful for when you want to highlight certain dashboards as important or otherwise memorable to you. They can be for bookmarking frequently accessed dashboard or for marking dashboards as needing some kind of special attention.

 Dashboard stars are part of a user's preferences, so starring a dashboard won't make it starred to other users.

Starring dashboards is even easier:

1. Load up a dashboard.
2. Click the star icon to **Mark as favorite**, as shown in the following screenshot:

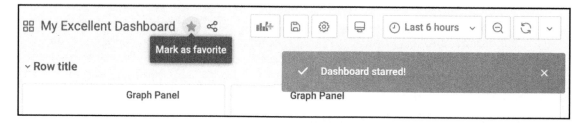

Alternatively, you can click the star next to any dashboard on a **Dashboard List** panel.

Tagging dashboards

Dashboard tags are vastly more powerful than stars. You can tag each dashboard with any number of tags. These tags can be leveraged for many important functions, including grouping, searching, and filtering. We saw tags in action when we created dashboard links back in Chapter 8, *Working with Advanced Dashboard Features*.

You will find dashboard tags used in several places, such as the following:

- Dashboard links
- Dashboards manage tab
- Dashboards playlists tab
- Dashboard list panel

Let's go over common tag functions, namely adding and deleting tags.

Adding tags

Currently, there is only one mechanism for adding tags:

1. Open a dashboard for editing.
2. Select the dashboard's settings.
3. Make sure you're viewing the **General** tab.
4. Type the tag name into the field.
5. Type ENTER or TAB to add one or more tags.
6. Click **Save dashboard**.
7. Return to the dashboard.

Here, we're adding the excellent tag:

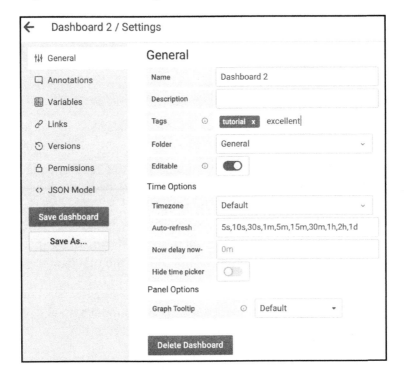

Refer back to Chapter 8, *Working with Advanced Dashboard Features*, for details on how to use tags to link dashboards. As we've seen, tags are very useful, but creating them can be tedious as they can only be added on a per-dashboard basis. Sadly, deleting them isn't much easier.

Deleting tags

Unfortunately, there is no explicit mechanism for managing tags, either to create them or to delete them. If you want to get rid of a tag, you will need to go through every tagged dashboard and delete it manually.

Building and running dashboard playlists

A dashboard playlist is a selection of dashboards that can be played in a looped sequence. Any dashboard can appear in such a playlist. A playlist consists of one or more dashboards displayed in a sequence, separated by a specified interval. They're typically used to create an automated display cycle of dashboards for unattended venues such as kiosks or operation centers.

Creating a playlist

Before we can start running a playlist, we'll need to create one. The **Playlists** tab can be found on the **Dashboards** management page. Follow these steps:

1. From the left sidebar, select **Dashboards | Playlists**.
2. Click **New Playlist.**
3. Set a **Name** for the playlist. You will not be able to **Create** the playlist until you set a **Name**.
4. Set the time **Interval** between dashboards.
5. Click **+** to add a playlist for each dashboard you wish to add to the playlist. You can also add starred dashboards, or all dashboards bearing a specified tag.
6. Click ↑↓ to adjust the order of the dashboards in the playlist.
7. Click **Create**.

Here is an example of the playlist page after selecting a dashboard for the playlist:

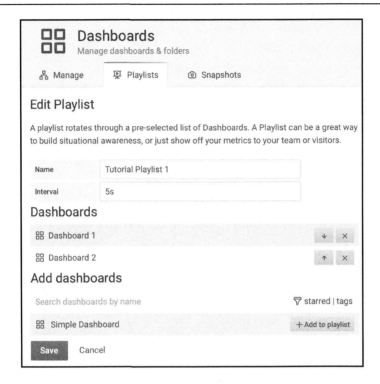

 As the number of dashboards grows, it could become more difficult to find dashboards for playlists, so consider naming conventions, tags, or stars so that you can filter on them when you create or edit playlists.

In the next few sections, we'll go into a little more detail about how to run playlists, especially in their various display modes. These modes are designed to gradually screen real estate that is typically devoted to controls such as the sidebar and the time range picker.

Displaying a playlist

Now that you've set up a playlist, it's time to play it. Here's how to run a playlist:

1. From the **Dashboard** side menu, select **Playlists**.
2. From the **Start** playlist, select the appropriate mode:

   - In Normal mode
   - In TV mode

- In TV mode (with auto fit panels)
- In Kiosk mode
- In Kiosk mode (with auto fit panels)

These modes correspond to the three view modes that are controlled by **Cycle view mode**, which can be found at the top of the dashboard. Let's look at each one to see how they differ.

Displaying playlists in normal mode

In normal mode, the left sidebar, as well as the navigation bar, row, and panel controls, are all visible. The normal dashboard controls are replaced with playlist controls.

Here is a closer look at the playlist controls:

From left to right, the controls are as follows:

- Rewind to the beginning of the playlist
- Stop the playlist from playing
- Skip forward to the next dashboard

Normal mode is useful if you don't mind the visual clutter of the left sidebar. If you do want to get rid of the sidebar, TV mode is for you.

Displaying playlists in TV mode

TV mode is similar to Normal mode in that the top *navbar*, row, and panel controls are still visible. However, the sidebar is hidden. The playlist can be enabled and disabled by typing in the *d v* shortcut.

The following screenshot shows a TV mode dashboard. Note the panel scaling and arrangement, as well as the various dashboard controls:

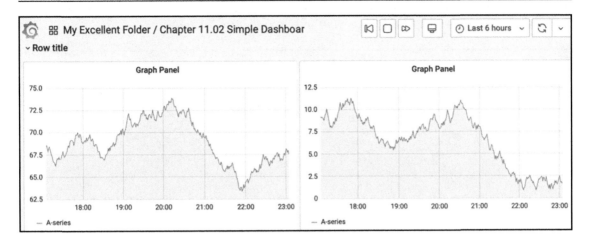

If you really want a clean display that only shows off your dashboard panels, then you want Kiosk mode. Let's take a look at Kiosk mode.

Displaying playlists in Kiosk mode

If you plan on running the playlist unattended with no visible controls, select one of the Kiosk modes. In this mode, all the controls including the side menu are hidden. Again, the playlist can be started and stopped with the *d v* keyboard shortcut.

Displaying playlists with auto fit panels

Both TV mode and Kiosk mode feature alternates that include the *auto fit* option. Autofitting causes the dashboard panels to automatically stretch or shrink to fill the entire screen space, depending on how much larger the display screen is compared to the original dashboard layout.

For example, here's a simple dashboard with two panels in **TV mode**:

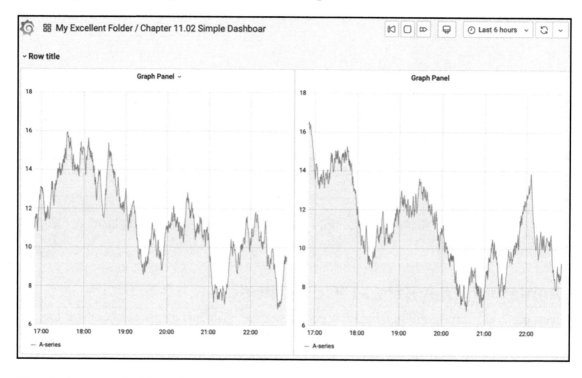

Here is the same dashboard in **TV mode** (with auto fit):

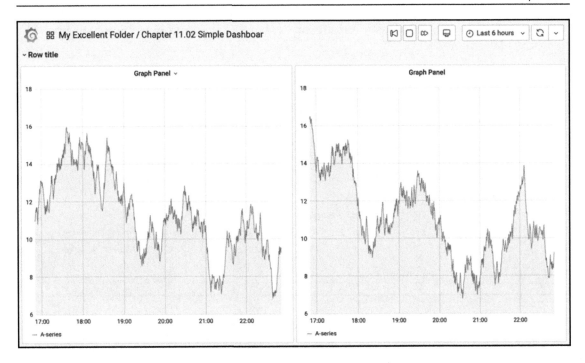

Typically, you'll want to use autofit not when you have a couple of panels you want to stretch to fit, but rather when you have a few extra panels you want Grafana to squeeze onto the screen. This can prove to be helpful when the screen size of your display is a bit different than the one you use to lay out your dashboard.

To give you an idea of how drastic autofit can be, here is the graph portion of a dashboard in Normal layout mode:

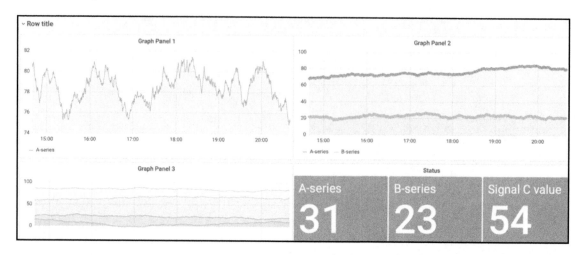

And here's the same portion of the dashboard in **Kiosk mode** (with autofit panels):

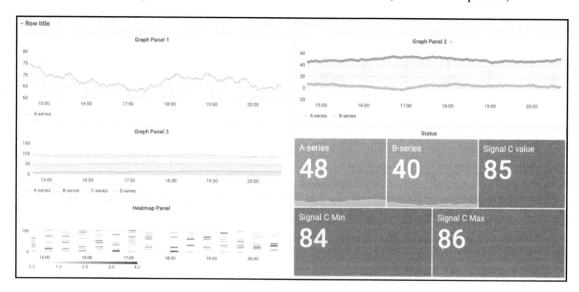

As you can see, Grafana adjusted the size of each panel in order to get all the panels to fit onscreen.

Editing a playlist

Simply clicking on a playlist in the playlists tab will open an **Edit Playlist** page, similar in structure to the **New Playlist** page. Here, you can do the following:

- Change the **Name.**
- Set the **Interval.**
- Delete dashboards by clicking the ✕ icon.
- Change the dashboard display order using the ↑↓ controls.
- Add dashboards by clicking the **+ Add to playlist** button.

That covers basic dashboard playlist features. Now, let's move on to another helpful dashboard management feature: a panel designed solely to display a catalog of dashboards!

Exploring the dashboard list panel

If you've taken a look at the **Home** dashboard, then you're already familiar with the **Dashboard List** panel. It typically displays starred dashboards (for quick reference) and a list of recently visited dashboards. It can be configured with several more options. Let's open it up and see what else we can configure it to do.

Setting dashboard list panel options

Under the **Options** section of the **Panel** tab are the following settings and descriptions:

- **Starred**: Displays starred dashboards
- **Recently viewed**: Displays recently viewed dashboards
- **Search**: Displays the results of the **Search** section
- **Show headings**: Displays the headings for each option mentioned previously
- **Max items**: Sets the maximum number of items displayed of each type

The first three are toggle switches that enable and disable the display of starred, recently viewed, and search results. The other two control whether headings are displayed and how many dashboards can be displayed at one time.

Along with **Options**, the **Search** settings are used as a search filter that allows you to specify a static list of dashboards that will always be displayed, as opposed to the Starred and Recently viewed dashboards, which are dynamically generated.

- **Search**: Searches for dashboards matching the string, partial matches included
- **Folder**: Includes all dashboards within a folder
- **Tags**: Includes all dashboards matching tags

Setting multiple search fields will return results that match all the fields. If you want to expand the search as wide as possible, be sure to set **Folder** to **All**.

If you want to get a feel for how the dashboard list panel works, either edit the one on the **Home** dashboard or just create your own!

Summary

This was a relatively easy introduction to some of the concepts involved in Grafana management. In this chapter, we looked at how to name dashboards and folders, as well as some strategies for creating folders, and also looked at starring and tagging dashboards and how they can be useful for grouping and filtering dashboards. Then, we created some dashboard playlists, a common function if you are creating dashboard presentations. Finally, we looked at how the dashboard list panel can be configured to help create catalogs of dashboards, especially by leveraging the search option and tags.

The intention here wasn't to reveal especially esoteric Grafana concepts – in fact, you may have already been working with some of the features we highlighted in this chapter. The goal was to get you to shift your thinking to a more operational viewpoint, one that must often take into account the potentially competing needs of different interested parties.

Just managing the dashboards on a moderately-sized server instance can be a challenging task, not necessarily for technical reasons, but for the inevitable social-political circumstances that arise when multiple groups must share a common resource.

It may not always be easy, but if you face these challenges head-on and engage your user community with transparency, continual improvement, and good humor, your experience will definitely be a rewarding one. Good luck!

In the same vein of handling the challenge of managing asset entities such as dashboards and folders, in the next chapter, `Chapter 12`, *Managing Permissions for Users and Teams*, we'll take on the challenge of managing actor entities such as users and teams, especially when it comes to managing simply *who accesses what*.

12
Managing Permissions for Users and Teams

In this chapter, we'll be taking a closer look at how to manage users, teams, and organizations with respect to controlling access to Grafana resources such as dashboards, folders, or data sources. During the course of this book, you've probably been logging into your site as the sole admin user, which is fine for a server limited to a local computer used almost exclusively for learning. However, it would be a completely unsuitable setup for a server supporting even a handful of users.

If you are responsible for managing your Grafana site, you'll soon be dealing with new users, and with every new user comes the inevitable question: *how much access should I allow this user?* You could set up every user with full admin permissions to do anything and everything, but what if they accidentally delete something important? What if they inadvertently create a panel that accesses a data source containing sensitive records? Conversely, if you deny all your users any permissions other than the bare essentials, what if they need to fix another user's dashboard and you're not available?

It would be beyond the scope of this book to offer a complete checklist of all the possible scenarios that you must consider before endeavoring to establish a secure, healthy Grafana environment, so we'll try to do the next best thing: give you the ability to understand how users and permissions work in Grafana, as well as how they come together to give you the flexibility to adapt your configuration to suit your specific needs.

In this chapter, we'll look at how to add users to a Grafana site, as well as how to manage the permissions for our users. Once we've addressed the fundamentals for user permissions, we'll learn how grouping users into teams can be a useful strategy for managing permissions on a larger scale. Finally, we'll look at how to partition a Grafana site into organizations that each have independent users, data sources, and dashboards, making it possible to offer the security benefits of isolation without the need to maintain multiple servers.

In this chapter, we will cover the following topics:

- Understanding key permissions concepts
- Adding users
- Setting permissions
- Establishing teams
- Administering users and organizations

Let's get started!

Technical requirements

The tutorial code, dashboards, and other helpful files for this chapter can be found in the book's GitHub repository at `https://github.com/PacktPublishing/Learn-Grafana-7.0/tree/master/Chapter12`.

Understanding key permissions concepts

Before we can delve into the specifics of adding users or setting their permissions, we need to cover some fundamental security concepts that are built into Grafana. Once you understand the terminology, it will be easier to piece together how these concepts interact to produce a coherent framework for governing user access.

Organizations

You may not have been aware of it, but for the entire time we've been learning about Grafana, we've been working inside an entity Grafana refers to as an *Organization*. Much like our universe is a single entity unto itself, this default organization, or org for short, can have its own teams, data sources, dashboards, dashboard folders, and so on. These types of resources cannot be accessed from or shared with any organization. Grafana lets you create as many organizations as you want, and while each one is completely independent of the others, users can be members of more than one organization.

Users

Obviously, anyone needing access to a Grafana site must also have some kind of account. Within Grafana, these accounts are called **Users**. In `Chapter 13`, *Authentication with External Services*, we'll look at a number of user authentication mechanisms, but for now, we'll be using regular password logins. A user can belong to multiple organizations and once logged in, can easily switch between them.

Roles

In order to determine what a user can do within a given organization, each user is assigned a role. Grafana provides three typical user roles and one special role. The typical user roles are called **Viewer**, **Editor**, and **Admin**:

- **Viewer role**: This is basically a *read-only* role in that it can't do anything except see dashboards and folders, but it can't edit them.
- **Editor role**: This can only create and edit dashboards, alerts, and folders.
- **Admin role**: This can do everything within an organization, including adding and modifying users, teams, data sources, and plugins.

The special role is called **Super Admin** and it has ultimate power over the entire site, including the ability to administer both users (including other Super Admins) and organizations.

Teams

In order to make it easier to manage the permissions for larger groups of users, Grafana includes a grouping of users called a **Team**. Within an organization, users can be assigned to teams, which may have their own permission settings. Depending on how those permissions are set, membership in a Team can even elevate the access level for a user above its defined organizational role.

With these concepts in mind, let's learn how to add new users to a Grafana site.

Adding users

While it might seem perfectly reasonable to use and manage a simple Grafana tutorial server with a single admin user, it would be impractical, if not irresponsible, to try to do the same for a Grafana site with more than even a couple of people. With that in mind, you should go ahead and establish independent user accounts for anyone that plans to access your site. It will also be your responsibility to add and delete those user accounts, set their roles, and establish what those users will be able to access within those roles.

 Initially, you probably logged in with the default `admin` user, which is installed with every Grafana instance. That user has full administrative privileges and, unless you changed it, an insecure password. This is not at all secure, so before you even add a single user, be sure to reset the password to one of your own choosing.

Adding users – by invitation only

Out of the box, Grafana only provides a single mechanism for adding users: via an administrative invitation. This is generally for good security reasons, especially if your site happens to be exposed to the internet. Generally, it's better to be in the position of controlling who can request access to your site when you must proactively reach out to prospective users. Grafana makes it easy to create those accounts and send off the invitations. It also tracks all invitations so that you can send out reminders or even retract them.

In order to invite a new user, you will need to have an account with an Admin organization role. Log in and go to **Configuration→Users**. You will be presented with a listing of all user accounts within your particular organization. To invite a new user, simply click **Invite** and submit the form (as shown in the following screenshot). You can set either a username (for a local user) or an email address. The name is optional but helpful in order to keep track of who your users are. You can choose from one of three roles, that is, **Viewer**, **Editor**, or **Admin**, but it is often safer to start with the most restrictive role: **Viewer**.

By toggling the **Send invite email** switch, you can send an email invitation, provided you entered a valid email address. If you plan to send email invites, you will need to configure SMTP on your Grafana server in order to send emails. Refer to Chapter 9, *Grafana Alerting*, for more information on how to set up SMTP with `docker-compose.yml` environment variables.

Here is a typical invitation:

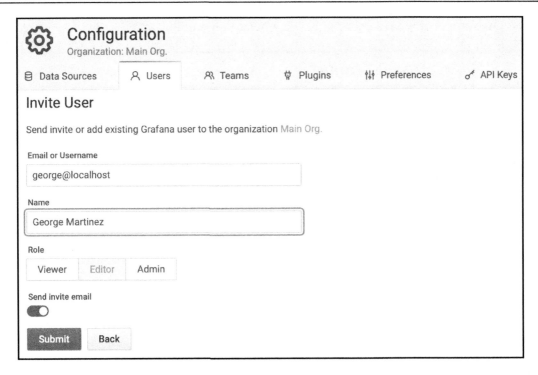

Once you've set up a new user invitation, you can see all your invited users in the **Pending Invites** tab. If you want to manually share an invitation link via another method such as a text message or Slack, click **Copy Invite** to place the URL on the clipboard for pasting:

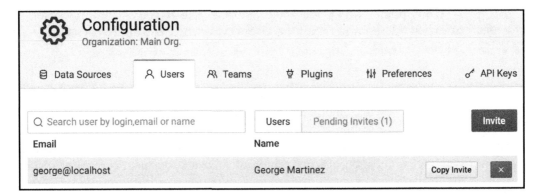

This is an example of what a user might see when following the link:

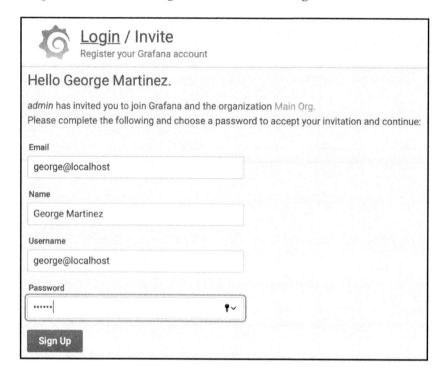

All they need to do is add a password and click **Sign Up** and they're in!

If, at any point, you decide you want to revoke an active or invited user, just click the red ✕ in either the **Users** tab or the **Pending Invites** tab, respectively.

Adding users – serve yourself

If you are in a situation where you don't necessarily need to be manually adding users to your site and you have relative confidence that you can trust your user community, you can modify your Grafana server configuration to allow users to add themselves. Bearing in mind that you may not want to make this change without consulting your IT security team first, here's how to do it.

First, you will need to modify the `users` configuration setting for `allow_sign_up` from the default `false` to `true`. If you were editing the configuration file for your Grafana server, it would look like this:

```
[users]
allow_sign_up = true
```

Since we are using Docker Compose to set our configuration, we'll use an environment variable instead. As discussed previously in Chapter 9, *Grafana Alerting*, any setting in the configuration file can be mapped to a corresponding environment variable in this way:

```
GF_<SectionName>_<KeyName>
```

The variable must be in all caps as well. In this case, the environment variable is `GF_USERS_ALLOW_SIGN_UP`. This is what our `docker-compose.yml` file looks like:

```
version: "3"

services:
  grafana:
    image: "grafana/grafana:${TAG-latest}"
    ports:
      - "3000:3000"
    environment:
      GF_USERS_ALLOW_SIGN_UP: "true"
    volumes:
      - "${PWD-.}/grafana:/var/lib/grafana"
```

Shut down your Grafana service (if one is running) and then start it back up:

```
% docker-compose down
Stopping ch12_grafana_1 ... done
Removing ch12_grafana_1 ... done
Removing network ch12_default

% docker-compose up -d
Creating network "ch12_default" with the default driver
Creating ch12_grafana_1 ... done
```

When you open the landing page for Grafana, you should see a subtle difference. There is now a **New to Grafana?** prompt and a **Sign Up** button:

Clicking the **Sign Up** button presents the user with a form they need to submit before they can be granted access. By default, all new users are set to the **Viewer** role, which is the role with the most restrictive settings. That default can be changed by altering the `auto_assign_org_role` user configuration setting.

Now that we've added users, we'll need to manage what level of access they have to Grafana. You probably want every user to be able to create and edit dashboards, but maybe you don't want them to also be able to delete them by mistake. That's where permissions come in.

Setting permissions

It's one thing to assign a role to each user for the purpose of restricting access to aspects of a Grafana site, but it would be severely limiting not to also have the ability to determine what parts of the site are accessible. Happily, Grafana allows users with Admin privileges to specify access levels for dashboards and folders.

Setting organization roles

First off, let's simply set the user's organization role. It's a straightforward process, and one that you probably followed when you first invited a user:

1. Go to **Configuration→Users.**
2. Set a **Role** for the user in the dropdown.

Here's what the **Users** tab page might look like with a handful of users:

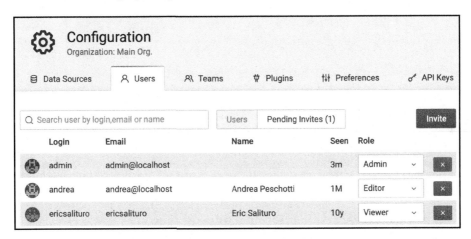

Once we've set the role for the user, we can either allow the default roles to be applied to folders or choose whether we want to add specific roles to the folder.

Setting folder permissions

Now that we've established roles for our users, we can set the access controls for our dashboards and folders. Typically, the default permissions for a folder directly map into the roles, as we described previously:

- Admin role can **Admin** the folder
- Editor role can **Edit** the folder
- Viewer role can **View** the folder

Here's what those typical folder permissions look like:

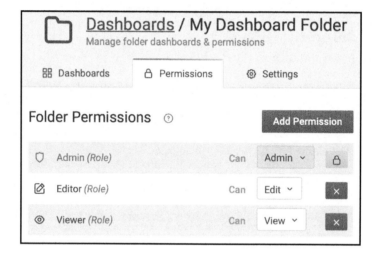

You can either modify the permissions for those roles or set additional permissions. It's easy to alter the existing permissions for a folder:

1. From the left sidebar, select **Dashboards→Manage**.
2. Click the gear icon next to the folder you wish to set permissions for (see the following screenshot):

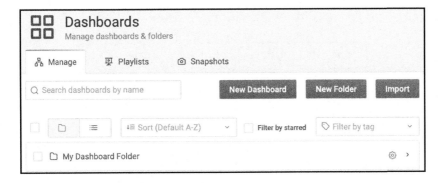

3. Go to the **Permissions** tab.
4. Select a new permission from the dropdown.

In order to add a new permission, you will need to specify whether the permission applies to a user, team, or role (for lack of a better term, let's call it a *permission target type*); the specific user, team, or role (a permission target); and the permission itself:

1. Select a folder.
2. Go to the **Permissions** tab.
3. Click **Add Permission**.
4. Select the permission target type from the drop-down.
5. Select the permission target from the drop-down.
6. Select the permission from the drop-down.
7. Click **Save.**

Permission target types can be a single user, a team (if you've created a team for your organization), or everyone with either the **Viewer** or **Editor** roles. Let's walk through a quick example for an example folder called My Dashboard Folder:

1. Select the My Dashboard Folder settings as mentioned previously.
2. Go to the **Permissions** tab.
3. Click **Add Permission**.
4. Select **User** from the drop-down.
5. Select the user **andrea** from the drop-down.
6. Select the **Admin** permission from the drop-down.
7. Click **Save.**

Here's what our example looks like while editing the user:

And that's all there is to assigning folder permissions. The workflow for dashboards is quite similar, so let's look at it now.

Setting dashboard permissions

Like folders, dashboards can also be assigned permissions, but with an additional subtlety: dashboards can inherit permissions from folders. The process of editing permissions on a dashboard is similar to how you alter the existing permissions for a folder:

1. Select a dashboard.
2. Click the **Settings** (gear) icon.
3. Go to the **Permissions** tab.
4. Select a permission from the dropdown.

Again, in order to add a new permission, you will need to specify the permission target type, the permission target, and the permission, as follows:

1. Select the dashboard settings as mentioned previously.
2. Go to the **Permissions** tab.
3. Click **Add Permission**.
4. Select the permission target type from the dropdown.

5. Select the permission target from the dropdown.
6. Select the permission from the dropdown.
7. Click **Save.**

Permission target types can be a single user, a team (if you've created a team for your organization), or everyone with either the **Viewer** or **Editor** roles. Let's walk through a quick example for a hypothetical dashboard called `My Dashboard`:

1. Select `My Dashboard`.
2. Click the **Settings** (gear) icon.
3. Go to the **Permissions** tab.
4. Click **Add Permission**.
5. Select **User** from the dropdown.
6. Select the user **esalituro** from the dropdown.
7. Select the **Admin** permission from the dropdown.
8. Click **Save**.

Here's what our example looks like:

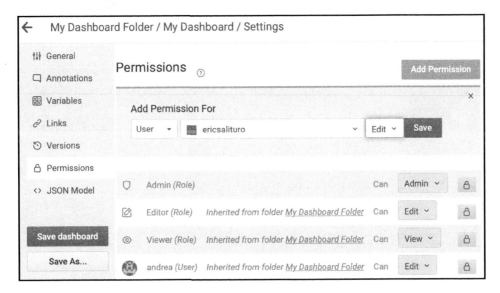

With that, we've covered setting up permissions for users, but doing so for a number of users can quickly become tedious. Because of that, Grafana has another role level that can encompass a team of users. Next, we'll look at how to set up a team, as well as how to assign permissions at the team level.

Establishing teams

Teams form the next level of a hierarchy of roles. While every user is assigned a permission level (Viewer, Editor, or Admin), you can also assign each user to a team, which can then have its own permission settings. The first thing we'll need to do is add a team.

Setting up a team

Setting up a team and adding users requires a user with an organization role of Admin. To create a team, follow these steps:

1. Go to **Configuration→Teams** from the left sidebar.
2. Click **New team**.
3. Enter the **Name** of the team and an optional **Email.**
4. Click **Create**, as shown in the following screenshot:

Once you've created a team, you can add users as members of the team, as follows:

1. Go to **Configuration→Teams** from the left sidebar.
2. Select the team you wish to add members to.
3. Click **Add member**.
4. Select a member from the dropdown menu.
5. Click **Add to team**.

The following screenshot shows what adding a team member might look like:

Now that we've added a team, we'll learn about how to set various preferences for the team, including its email address, home dashboard, and UI theme.

Team members

From the **Team** page, go to the **Members** tab to manage the team's members:

- If you need to delete a team member, simply click the red ✗ icon next to the user's entry on the team's page.
- If you need to delete a team, click the red ✗ icon next to the team entry on the **Teams** page.

Team settings

From the **Team** page, go to the **Settings** tab to change the team settings. Here is what you should know:

- Under **Team Settings**, you can rename the team and change its email address.
- Under **Preferences**, you can set the **UI Theme**, **Home Dashboard**, and **Timezone** settings.
- Changing these settings will override the organization preferences.

Permission rules

By now, you may feel that the myriad combinations of organization roles and teams, not to mention dashboard and folder permissions, are so complex that planning or troubleshooting access control issues could become intractably difficult. Nothing could be further from the truth! Grafana determines access control with some simple rules. First, permissions are defined in four ways:

- Organization role
- Team membership
- Direct permission assignment on dashboards, folders, and data sources
- Super Admin enabled

When multiple permissions are defined, the highest permission setting prevails, according to two rules:

- The organization admin role cannot be overruled.
- Lower specific permissions can be overruled by higher general permissions.

What this means practically is that setting users to low permissions (Viewer, for example) has no effect if the organizations' permission for a dashboard is higher (Admin, for example). If you need to strictly control access to a particular resource, make sure to remove any general permission settings for the resource. The best way to learn the implications of these rules is to experiment with different combinations of settings firsthand. Give it a try!

Administering users and organizations

There are two significant tasks that can only be performed by a user with the Super Admin role: management of users and management of organizations. When you logged into your brand new Grafana site as admin, you were logging in as a Super Admin, and as a Super Admin, you have the ability to create users and organizations. Managing users and organizations is accomplished through a special **Server Admin** view, which can only be accessed by Super Admins from the left sidebar.

First, let's look at how to create new users. Previously, we discussed the idea that the only way to add new user accounts is to invite someone or (with a configuration change) allow users to add themselves. Those restrictions only applied to organizations and organizational Admins. As it turns out, there is yet another way – if you're a Super Admin.

Managing users

If you have a number of users to add to your site and you need to assign them to different organizations, it might be more efficient to simply add them manually. You can add users and assign them passwords from the **Server Admin** view, all without the need to go through the process of sending out invites and waiting for the response. Here's how to create a new user:

1. From the left sidebar, select **Server Admin→Users**.
2. Click **New user**.
3. Fill in at least the **Name** and the **Password** details, as indicated by the asterisks (*). The other settings can be set by the user after they've logged in.

Once you've created a user, this is what the **User information** settings on the **Users** tab typically look like:

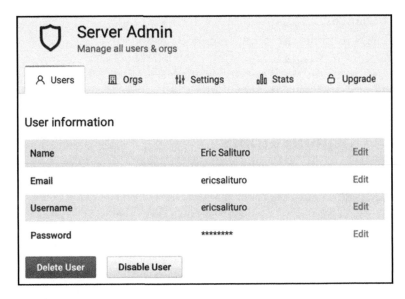

Now, let's look at how to modify a user:

1. From the left sidebar, select **Server Admin→Users.**
2. Select a user.

Now, we'll look at disabling or deleting a user.

Disabling or deleting a user

First, we'll look at how we manage the user account. Under **User information**, we can disable or delete the account, as follows:

- To delete the user, select **Delete User**.
- If you only want to block the user without deleting, select **Disable User**.

Now, let's look at elevating a user to Super Admin.

Elevating a user to Super Admin

You might be wondering how to go about giving another user the Super Admin role. You can only do this if you're a Super Admin yourself. We can elevate a user to Super Admin under **Permissions/Grafana Admin**, as follows:

1. Select **Change.**
2. Select **YES** from the dropdown menu.
3. Finally, select **Change**.

Next, we'll learn how to set user organizations.

Setting user organizations

As a Super Admin user, you can control organizational membership at a global level, which means you can add, remove, and set the role of the user for any organization. To add a user to an organization, follow these steps:

1. Select **Add user to organisation**.
2. Select an **Organisation** from the dropdown.
3. Select a **Role** from the dropdown.
4. Click **Add to organization.**

To change the user's organization role, follow these steps:

1. Select **Change role**.
2. Select the role from the dropdown.
3. Click **Save**.

To remove a user from an organization, follow these steps:

1. Select **Remove from organisation**. A user must still be a member of at least one organization.
2. Click **Confirm removal**.

You can get a lot of user account management accomplished from this one page. On the other hand, you can easily affect a lot of users, so be careful when assigning Super Admin permissions.

Organization admin and Super Admin roles

It might seem a little head-spinning to try to keep track of the differences between an Admin operating at the organization level and a Super Admin acting at the Server Admin level. What if you set the organization role of the only Admin user to Editor? Can you lock yourself out of an organization or completely out of Grafana, for that matter?

Fortunately, Grafana has some safeties in place to keep you from getting stuck. While organization Admins can set Admin permissions, Super Admins can set both Organization Admins and Super Admins.

Super Admins can, of course, downgrade a role, but not in such a way as to reduce the number of Super Admins to zero. Any such attempt will trigger an error message. That way, you, as a Super Admin, can't inadvertently lock yourself out of your ability to administer your site.

Likewise, each organization must also have at least one user at the Admin level. Any attempt to eliminate all Admins in an organization will also trigger an error. This is to prevent the only Admin from locking themselves out of the organization.

Managing organizations

The other major task performed by Super Admins is managing organizations. But why might you want to set up more than one organization in the first place? While it isn't necessary to establish multiple organizations on a single Grafana site, there are cases where you may want to establish independent Grafana sites, each with its own data sources, dashboards, and more, but you don't want to spin up multiple servers.

For example, you may have restrictions on who can access proprietary or sensitive information, and you don't want the members of one organization accessing the data sources of another. You may have particular accounting constraints that determine which plugins a particular organization has access to.

While it is simple enough to spin up another Grafana instance in this case, it is much easier, from a management perspective, to have a single deployment that's partitioned into multiple organizations. This way, you can provision data sources and plugins more easily, and the Grafana UI makes it easy to quickly switch from one organization to another. You can easily assign users to multiple organizations and grant them roles specific to the organizations they are members of.

Creating a new organization

We'll start out by creating a new organization. You will need to be logged in as a user with the Super Admin role:

1. From the left sidebar, go to the **Server Admin→Orgs** tab.
2. Select **+ New org**.
3. Fill in **Org. name.**
4. Select **Create**.

That's all there is to it! You will be automatically switched into the new organization, where you can then set the preferences for the organization.

To delete an organization, simply click the red ✕ icon next to the organization. This is an irreversible operation, so heed the scary-looking dialog box that pops up for confirmation.

Renaming and setting the organization preferences

To rename and set the organization preferences, follow these steps:

1. To rename the organization, select **Configuration→Preferences** from the left sidebar.
2. Change **Organization name.**
3. Click **Save**.
4. Under **Preferences**, you can set the **UI Theme**, **Home Dashboard**, and **Timezone** settings.
5. Click **Save**.

The **Home Dashboard** dropdown menu will be filled in with any of the organization's starred dashboards.

Switching between organizations

To switch to a different organization, follow these steps:

1. Go to your user menu at the bottom of the left sidebar.
2. At the top of the pop-up menu, the current organization will be displayed. Select it to switch it.
3. Click **Switch to** to change the current organization.

The following screenshot should help you locate the menu:

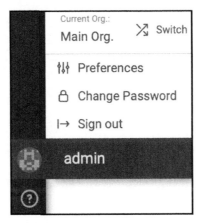

Don't worry if you don't find a good use case for establishing organizations. According to Grafana Labs, only 1% of their installed base uses organizations and, as such, they are considering de-emphasis of organizations in the future.

Now, let's summarize what we have learned in this chapter.

Summary

We covered a lot of ground in this chapter. First, we took a closer look at users, teams, and organizations and saw how roles can be mapped to permissions for dashboards, folders, and data sources. Then, we learned how organization admins can manage both users and teams. Finally, we examined how the Super Admin role can create new users and organizations.

Don't worry if it's difficult to visualize all the possibilities afforded by the Grafana permission model. It may be that, for now, you have no need to establish multiple organizations, to specify permissions on specific dashboards or folders, or even to assemble users into teams. However, as your site grows in complexity, you may find that access control issues present themselves, and you may want to come back to this chapter. Concepts that seem a little abstract right now may have concrete relevance in the future.

Throughout the course of this book, we've been using a simple password-based authentication scheme for our Grafana server, but there are a number of powerful external authentication systems available. In the next chapter, we'll take a look at a few of them. These systems are important for integrating your Grafana authentication with that of a larger organization so that users have a seamless experience, regardless of whether they are logging into their email, chats, conferences, or even Grafana.

13
Authentication with External Services

In the previous chapter, when delving into the management of users and teams, we briefly examined the options for adding and authenticating users. We also looked at how Grafana can group user memberships into teams, allowing more granular control over permissions to resources such as dashboards, panels, and data sources. Now, out of the box, Grafana provides a very straightforward authentication scheme based on authenticating against a user/password pair. New users can either be created under this scheme or they can add themselves (with a minor configuration change). Grafana provides more than a couple of variations on this mechanism, with varying levels of complexity and security.

However, the use of these methodologies is not considered ideal. In many corporate environments, user access must be strictly tracked and integrated with numerous systems, including administration and the IT department. Authentication models must provide robust security against any potential threat; they may need to scale to hundreds if not thousands of users. Under these circumstances, Grafana's native authentication would be inadequate to the task, and depending on the corporate environment, may not pass the required security reviews.

A solution to these issues can be found in a dedicated external service capable of storing users and their credentials and supporting state-of-art protocols for authenticating them. These **authentication services** work to offload most of the drudgery of maintaining user access lists, groups, authentication tokens, and so on. They tend to provide some or all of the following important features:

- **Single Sign-On (SSO)**: Authenticates the user once to access many platforms
- Universal directory services: Tracks users, groups, credentials, and contact info
- Adaptive multi-factor authentication: Verifies login with a personal confirmation
- User life cycle management: Initiates, suspends, and terminates user accounts

In the following sections, we'll first look at how Grafana can integrate with the locally deployed OpenLDAP directory service. As an alternative, we will look at three external authentication services that provide authentication through the OAuth 2 standard. We'll start with GitHub, where many software-driven organizations and individuals may already have accounts. We'll follow that with a look at Google, which many enterprises will have access to through their G Suite application stack. Finally, we will wrap things up with the Okta dedicated authentication service provider.

The following topics will be covered in this chapter:

- Authenticating with OpenLDAP
- Authenticating with GitHub
- Authenticating with Google
- Authenticating with Okta

Technical requirements

The tutorial code, dashboards, and other helpful files for this chapter can be found in the book's GitHub repository at `https://github.com/PacktPublishing/Learn-Grafana-7.0/tree/master/Chapter13`.

Authenticating with OpenLDAP

Let's start off with one of the more venerable authentication schemes available today: **Lightweight Directory Access Protocol (LDAP)**. LDAP was originally developed in the early 1990s. While it is often used to store user information for authentication purposes, it also can serve all kinds of directory information, including user groups, hostnames, network addresses, and even office addresses and phone numbers.

In this section, we'll set up a simple directory using the OpenLDAP implementation and configure Grafana to bind to the OpenLDAP server to look up users and teams. This process can be a little bit complicated, but we'll go through it step by step. It is beyond the scope of this book to go through the details of setting up and maintaining a production LDAP directory, but I will endeavor to explain things in some detail as we go along. If you are at all looking to integrate your Grafana server with an existing LDAP installation, this should give you a feel for what is involved.

The process of setting up an LDAP authentication server requires the following steps to be taken:

1. Download and install an OpenLDAP server.
2. Configure Grafana to bind to the LDAP server.
3. Test to confirm whether Grafana can connect to LDAP.
4. Add a user to the LDAP directory.
5. Perform an LDAP lookup from within Grafana.

We'll get started by downloading and configuring an open source LDAP server called **OpenLDAP**.

Setting up an OpenLDAP server

We will use Docker Compose to download an image of the OpenLDAP implementation of LDAP, which is available from `osixia`. Information about how to work with this Docker image can be found on GitHub at `https://github.com/osixia/docker-openldap`. Our Docker Compose file will ultimately contain two services: one for LDAP and the other for Grafana. The full `docker-compose.yml` file is available on this book's GitHub site in the `Chapter13` directory.

Here's the first part of the LDAP service:

```
ldap:
    image: osixia/openldap
```

Here, we're just downloading the image from `osixia`. Once we have downloaded the image, we'll need to open port `389`. If you enable support for TLS connections, you'll need to open port `636`. For demonstration purposes, we'll connect to our LDAP server over an unsecured connection:

```
ports:
    - 389:389
```

By default, the `osixia` Docker image has a predefined organization and domain, but we'd like to override that with our own. We do that with a couple of environment variables here:

```
environment:
    LDAP_ORGANISATION: "My Grafana Company"
    LDAP_DOMAIN: "grafana.org"
```

Finally, we need to create volumes in order to serve two purposes—if we want to persist our LDAP directory database and so that we can access the container's internal filesystem to add our own files. We'll need this capability later when we add a user.

Once we've created `docker-compose.yml`, we can go ahead and launch it in order to get the LDAP server up and running:

```
% docker-compose up -d ldap
Starting ch13_ldap_1 ... done
```

To confirm whether we have a running installation, we'll carry out a simple query:

```
docker-compose exec ldap \
    ldapsearch -x -w admin \
      -H ldap://localhost \
      -b dc=grafana,dc=org -D "cn=admin,dc=grafana,dc=org"
```

That's a pretty gnarly looking command, but it's not too bad if we break it down:

- The first line, `docker-compose exec ldap`, indicates that we're going to run a command inside the `ldap` container.
- The next line is the `ldapsearch` command. The `-x` option indicates that we want to use simple authentication by using `-w` as the option and `admin` as the password.
- You might be able to guess that `-H ldap://localhost` is the option for passing the server address (called `ldapuri`)—in this case, for opening a connection to an `ldap` server on `localhost`.
- The `-b dc=grafana,dc=org` option indicates the search base for our query, a kind of *root* in our LDAP search hierarchy. We are searching the domain or `dc` for `grafana.org`, which we specified in our `LDAP_DOMAIN` environment variable when we configured our service.
- Lastly, `-D "cn=admin,dc=grafana,dc=org"` specifies our search term, called a **distinguished name**. Think of it as encoding the `admin@grafana.org` login name, built by combining the common name (`cn`) and the two domain names (`dc`).

If your server is running and was configured correctly, you should get results that look something like this:

```
# extended LDIF
#
# LDAPv3
# base <dc=grafana,dc=org> with scope subtree
# filter: (objectclass=*)
# requesting: ALL
#

# grafana.org
dn: dc=grafana,dc=org
objectClass: top
objectClass: dcObject
objectClass: organization
o: My Grafana Company
dc: grafana

# admin, grafana.org
dn: cn=admin,dc=grafana,dc=org
objectClass: simpleSecurityObject
objectClass: organizationalRole
cn: admin
description: LDAP administrator
userPassword:: e1NTSEF9WUp1ZnFyQVpmM3JyU1NpeDV5b3ZjWUhKbUs5QTJlcDU=

# search result
search: 2
result: 0 Success

# numResponses: 3
# numEntries: 2
```

You should see two entries—one matching an organization of grafana.org and the other an admin user, called simpleSecurityObject, within the same organization. With this done successfully, let's go ahead and set up our Grafana server.

Configuring Grafana to use LDAP

For our Grafana server, we'll use the same Docker Compose service we've used throughout this book, but with one small change. As with the LDAP service, we will create an additional volume mapping to a local directory so that we can install a file in the container's filesystem. In the case of Grafana, we'll be installing a couple of configuration files that are necessary to enable proper LDAP support on our server.

Let's walk through our Grafana Docker Compose service. The first few lines are pretty much identical to a typical service:

```
grafana:
  image: grafana/grafana:latest
  ports:
    - 3000:3000
```

Following those lines is our first big change. We're going to tell Grafana to look for a configuration file in `/etc/grafana/grafana.ini`:

```
environment:
  GF_PATHS_CONFIG: "/etc/grafana/grafana.ini"
```

In order to access the file outside the container, we'll need to create a volume mapping. We create two—the usual one for persisting our Grafana data and one for the `config` file:

```
volumes:
  - $PWD/grafana/data:/var/lib/grafana
  - $PWD/grafana/etc:/etc/grafana
```

Finally, we'll make the `ldap` service a dependency for our `grafana` service:

```
depends_on:
  - ldap
```

Now that we've set up our service, we'll need to add two configuration files. The first file is called `grafana.ini`, which is used to override the default configuration, much like how we used environment variables in previous chapters. We could do the same in this case, but since we will be installing an additional file, we might as well go ahead and use the `grafana.ini` file. Our `grafana.ini` file is based on an example provided by Grafana and looks like this:

```
[auth.ldap]
# Set to `true` to enable LDAP integration (default: `false`)
enabled = true

# Path to the LDAP specific configuration file (default:
```

```
`/etc/grafana/ldap.toml`)
config_file = /etc/grafana/ldap.toml

# Allow sign up should almost always be true (default) to allow new Grafana
users to be created (if ldap authentication is ok). If set to
# false only pre-existing Grafana users will be able to login (if ldap
authentication is ok).
allow_sign_up = true
```

It's pretty straightforward and, with all the comments, self-explanatory. From what we see in this file, we need to install a second file in /etc/grafana called ldap.toml. This file will describe how Grafana will communicate with the LDAP server.

Our ldap.toml file also comes from the Grafana documentation, albeit with a couple of changes so that we can use it in the Docker container context. Here's an excerpt of the file (the full file can be found in the ch13 folder in this book's GitHub repository at https://github.com/PacktPublishing/Learn-Grafana-7.0/tree/master/Chapter13/grafana/etc/ldap.toml):

```
[[servers]]
# Ldap server host (specify multiple hosts space separated)
host = "ldap"
```

Pretty much the only change we've made is to set host = "ldap" so that our Grafana server can talk to the ldap server container. You should create an etc directory in your current directory and copy the files there (if they aren't already), then launch your grafana service:

```
% docker-compose up -d grafana
Creating network "ch13_default" with the default driver
Creating ch13_ldap_1 ... done
Creating ch13_grafana_1 ... done
```

Since the ldap service is a dependency for the grafana service, it will also launch (if it isn't already running). Let's check out our Grafana server to confirm that it can connect to our LDAP server.

Testing the Grafana configuration

From a browser, log in as a Grafana admin and navigate to the new icon available under the **Server Admin** left-side menu called **LDAP**. If Grafana was successful in binding to your LDAP server, you should see a page showing the successful connection to port 389 of your LDAP server:

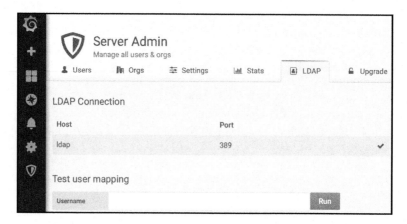

If you want to test user mapping, try searching for admin. Once we've confirmed a user lookup, we can proceed with adding users to our LDAP database.

Adding a user to OpenLDAP

In order to make our server truly useful for authentication, we'll need to add user accounts. Before we proceed, however, we need to take note of something. When we add a user to LDAP, we need to make sure the entry fields we add to the directory will be understood by Grafana. That is, when Grafana does an LDAP lookup for a user, it knows what fields in the response to look for to satisfy itself. We can find this list at the bottom of our ldap.toml file:

```
# Specify names of the ldap attributes your ldap uses
[servers.attributes]
name = "givenName"
surname = "sn"
username = "cn"
member_of = "memberOf"
email = "mail"
```

This is a list of Grafana user fields and their corresponding entries in an LDAP entry. Armed with this information, we can set up a user, making sure we include the appropriate fields. We use the ldif format for the file, which will be named new-user.ldif. Here's the file I've created for a user:

```
dn: cn=myuser,dc=grafana,dc=org
changetype: add
givenName: My
sn: User
cn: myuser
uid: cn
uidNumber: 14583102
gidNumber: 14564100
homeDirectory: /home/myuser
objectClass: top
objectClass: posixAccount
objectClass: inetOrgPerson
userPassword: {SHA}kd/Z3bQZiv/FwZTNjObTOP3kcOI=
mail: myuser@grafana.org
```

As you can see, I've included the name, surname, username, and email, and tagged these properties with the appropriate field names. The SHA-encoded user password I created using an LDAP command-line tool—slappasswd—is provided with the OpenLDAP installation in the container:

```
% docker-compose exec ldap \
    slappasswd -h {SHA} -s mypassword
{SHA}kd/Z3bQZiv/FwZTNjObTOP3kcOI=
```

Next, we'll copy this file into a directory visible to the container (inside slapd.d, for example):

```
mkdir -p slapd.d/assets/test
cp ldif/new-user.ldif slapd.d/assets/test
```

Finally, we run the ldapadd command to inform our LDAP server of the new user:

```
docker-compose exec ldap \
   ldapadd -x -w admin \
     -H ldap://localhost \
     -D "cn=admin,dc=grafana,dc=org" \
     -f /etc/ldap/slapd.d/assets/test/new-user.ldif
```

Let's break this command down:

- In our first line, we are invoking a command inside our `ldap` service container.
- In the second line, we invoke the `ldapsearch` command, which we will simply authenticate (`-x`) with the password (`-w`), `admin`.
- In the next line, we will indicate the URI for the LDAP server with the `-H` option.
- We use the `-D` option to pass the bind account name (`admin@grafana.org`).
- Following these boilerplate options is the option (`-f`) for the path to the LDIF file (as seen from inside the container). Remember that in `docker-compose.yml`, we volume-mapped our local `slapd.d` directory to `/etc/ldap/slapd.d` inside the container.

Here are the results from running the command:

```
% docker-compose exec ldap \
    ldapadd -x -w admin \
      -H ldap://localhost \
      -D "cn=admin,dc=grafana,dc=org" \
      -f /etc/ldap/slapd.d/assets/test/new-user.ldif
adding new entry "cn=myuser,dc=grafana,dc=org"
```

Looking up a user in Grafana

Now that we have a user in our LDAP, let's confirm that Grafana sees the user.

Go to **Server Admin | LDAP** and enter our new user in **Test user mapping**. You should see the following results:

Note how the Grafana fields are filled in from the corresponding fields in our LDAP entry.

There you have it! Try logging in to your Grafana server with our new user account to confirm that Grafana is authenticating against the username and password stored in LDAP.

Authenticating with GitHub

From our local LDAP authentication, we move on to three examples that all use the OAuth 2 authentication standard. It is beyond the scope of this book to go into detail about the OAuth 2 standard, but suffice to say it represents one of the most popular industry standards for application authentication. In order to use OAuth 2 to provide Grafana authentication, rather than running our own lookup service, we will leverage external providers. We will look at three different popular services, each providing similar setup techniques but serving slightly different audiences:

- We'll first look at Grafana authentication via GitHub, a common site for organizations working in the software space.
- Next, we'll look at authentication via Google, a provider common with many enterprises that depend on Google for office applications, such as Gmail and the G Suite of tools.
- Finally, we'll look at authentication with Okta, a full-service provider that is well-known for providing SSO solutions.

In each case, we'll go through the typical workflow for registering the Grafana application in order to secure a known key, then configuring Grafana to use the key to perform the necessary trusted authentication after a user has logged in to a provider account.

Without going into the gory details, the process for each is fairly straightforward and consistent:

1. Register both Grafana's login page URL and a special redirect URL for the provider to send properly authenticated users.
2. Return a client ID and a client secret, which are basically Grafana's username and password with the provider.
3. Configure Grafana with the appropriate provider information, including the client ID and secret.
4. Restart Grafana to pick up the new configuration.

Note: the instructions presented here are valid at the time of writing, but may be subject to change.

First up, GitHub. We'll need to create an authorized OAuth 2 application for Grafana to talk to. In each of the following examples, we'll assume you are registering on behalf of a Grafana server at `http://localhost:3000`. Obviously, for a production server, you'll want to use an actual host and domain name; for our purposes, it will suffice to work with our local server. Follow these steps:

1. Log in to GitHub under the account that will be responsible for the application.
2. Navigate to **Settings** | **Developer Settings**.
3. Select **OAuth Apps**. You'll be presented with the following screen:

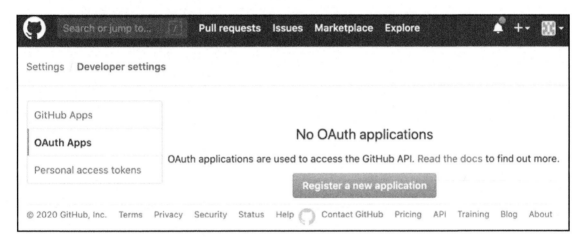

4. Click on **Register a new application**.

5. Fill in the following fields and click on **Register application**:

- **Application name**: Grafana
- **Homepage URL**: http://localhost:3000
- **Authorization callback URL**: http://localhost:3000/login/github

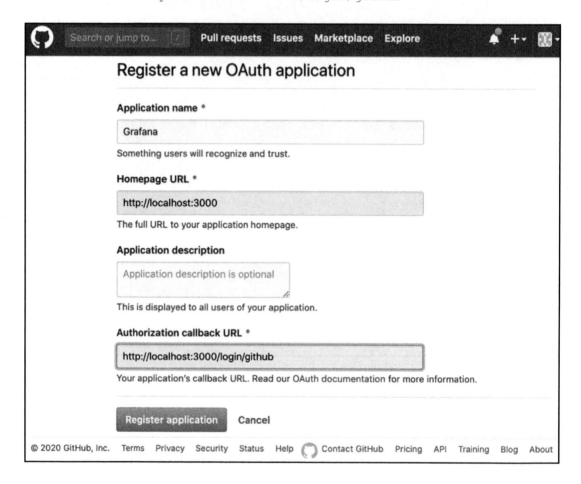

6. Copy the client ID and client secret for the Grafana configuration. You'll find them on the application page:

7. Now, add the following lines to your `grafana.ini` file:

```
[auth.github]
enabled = true
allow_sign_up = true
client_id = CLIENT_ID
client_secret = CLIENT_SECRET
scopes = user:email,read:org
auth_url = https://github.com/login/oauth/authorize
token_url = https://github.com/login/oauth/access_token
api_url = https://api.github.com/user
team_ids =
allowed_organizations =
```

Of course, you'll want to fill in your own `CLIENT_ID` and `CLIENT_SECRET`. After completing your edits of the `grafana.ini` file, restart your Grafana server. When you open `http://localhost:3000`, you should see the Grafana login page with the option for a GitHub sign-in.

Authenticating with Google

Moving on from GitHub, let's take a look at Google OAuth 2. Google has a much more elaborate system, but if your Grafana users are part of your G Suite account, this is a good way to provide them with access. After some initial steps involving the configuration of an authentication consent page, getting a client ID and client secret is simple:

1. Go to `https://console.developers.google.com/apis/credentials`:

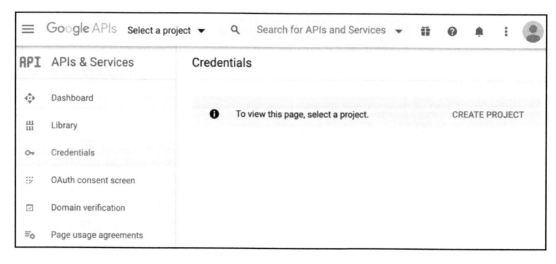

2. Create a project if you don't already have one. For our example, we'll call it
   `grafana`. Once you've created the project, you'll be returned to the **Credentials**
   page:

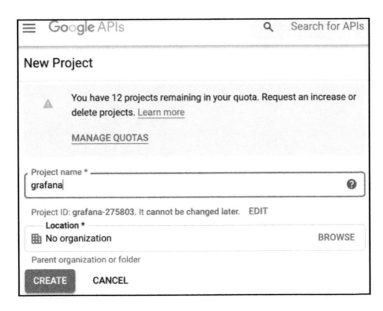

3. Select **+ Create Credentials | OAuth client ID**:

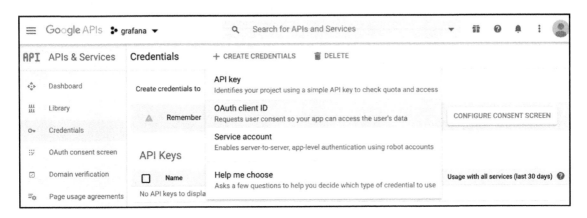

4. You'll be required to fill out an OAuth consent page. However, since this is an
   internal application, you only need to fill out the following minimal information:

   - Application type: **Internal**
   - **Authorized name**: `Grafana`

- **Support email**: `<email address>`

API	APIs & Services	OAuth consent screen

Dashboard

Library

Credentials

OAuth consent screen

Domain verification

Page usage agreements

Before your users authenticate, this consent screen will allow them to choose whether they want to grant access to their private data, as well as give them a link to your terms of service and privacy policy. This page configures the consent screen for all applications in this project.

Application type

○ **Public**
Any Google Account can grant access to the scopes required by this app.
Learn more about scopes

◉ **Internal**
Only users with a Google Account in your organization can grant access to the scopes requested by this app.

Application name ⓘ
The name of the app asking for consent

> Grafana

Application logo ⓘ
An image on the consent screen that will help users recognize your app

Local file for upload	Browse

Support email ⓘ
Shown on the consent screen for user support

esalituro@learngrafana.net	▼

5. After saving the consent screen configuration, you can finally do what you came for—create an OAuth client ID. Fill in the following information and click **Create**:

- **Application type**: Web application
- **Name**: `Grafana`
- **Authorized JavaScript origins**: `http://localhost:3000`

- **Authorized redirect URIs**: `http://localhost:3000/login/google`

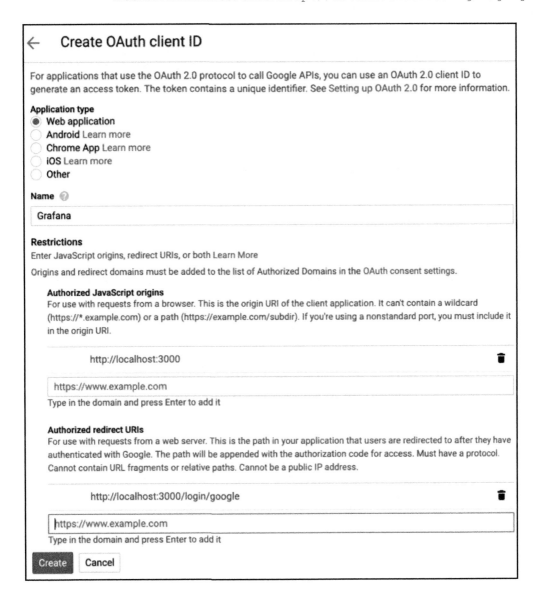

6. You should now have an OAuth ID created with a client ID and a client secret. You'll need those for the Grafana configuration:

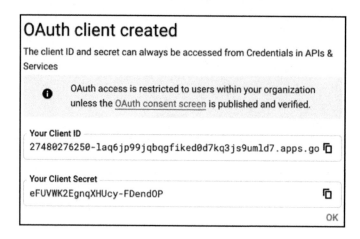

Next, we'll set up the configuration on the Grafana side. Edit `grafana.ini` and add the following lines:

```
[auth.google]
enabled = true
client_id = YOUR_CLIENT_ID
client_secret = YOUR_CLIENT_SECRET
scopes = https://www.googleapis.com/auth/userinfo.profile
https://www.googleapis.com/auth/userinfo.email
auth_url = https://accounts.google.com/o/oauth2/auth
token_url = https://accounts.google.com/o/oauth2/token
allowed_domains =
allow_sign_up = true
```

Fill in your own client ID (`YOUR_CLIENT_ID`) and client secret (`YOUR_CLIENT_SECRET`). If you want new users to be able to self-register with Google OAuth, make sure `allow_sign_up` is set to `true`. Restart your Grafana server and you should now have a Google sign-in on your Grafana startup screen.

Authenticating with Okta

Okta is a well-known authentication provider for the enterprise and is newly supported in Grafana 7. The process is very similar to Google, but only requires the registration of your application with Okta in order to generate the client ID and secret. You'll need to sign up for a developer account in order to generate the appropriate secrets. Once you've logged in to your developer account, follow these instructions:

1. Select **Developer Console** | **Applications** | **Add Application**.
2. Select **Web** and **Next**:

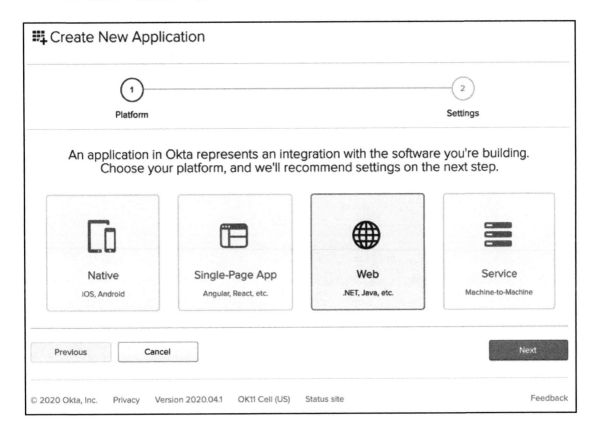

3. On the **Application Settings** page, fill in the following fields and click **Done**:

- **Name**: Grafana
- **Base URIs**: http://localhost:3000
- **Login Redirect URIs**: http://localhost:3000/login/okta

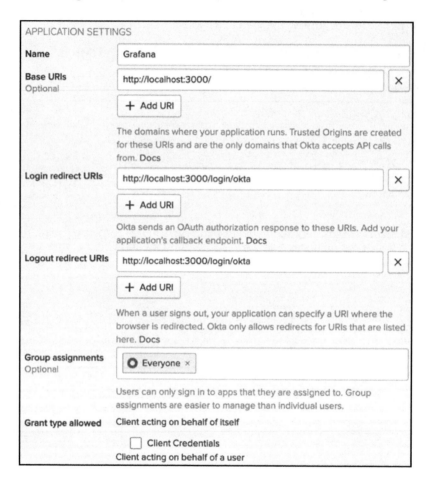

4. On the next page, under the **General Settings** tab, you'll find a **Client Credentials** box with both the **Client ID** and **Client secret** fields. Copy them for the next step:

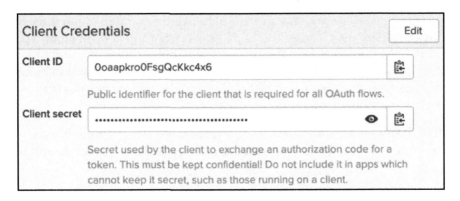

5. Add the following configuration lines to your `grafana.ini` file:

```
[auth.okta]
name = Okta
enabled = true
allow_sign_up = true
client_id = CLIENT_ID
client_secret = CLIENT_SECRET
scopes = openid profile email groups
auth_url = https://<tenant-id>.okta.com/oauth2/v1/authorize
token_url = https://<tenant-id>.okta.com/oauth2/v1/token
api_url = https://<tenant-id>.okta.com/oauth2/v1/userinfo
allowed_domains =
allowed_groups =
role_attribute_path =
```

You'll need to add your client ID (`CLIENT_ID`) and client secret (`CLIENT_SECRET`) and tenant ID (your developer login host). Restart your Grafana service and you should have the Okta sign-on available from the Grafana login screen. That completes our tour of three popular OAuth2 providers. Well done!

Summary

We certainly covered a lot of ground in this chapter. We learned about how to install and configure an OpenLDAP server and integrate it with Grafana to provide authentication lookup. Then, we walked through the process of registering Grafana with three different OAuth 2 providers: GitHub, Google, and Okta. If you want full control of all aspects of user lookup for authentication, then LDAP is certainly a viable solution. If you'd rather have authentication handled securely by a third-party provider, especially if it integrates with other user management systems in your organization, then an external OAuth provider is probably a better solution.

Yet, after all of this, we have only touched on a few of the ever-growing number of authentication options available for Grafana, so consult the Grafana documentation for more details.

In this chapter, we took a small step in integrating Grafana authentication with external cloud services. In the next (and final) chapter, Chapter 14, *Cloud Monitoring*, we will make a giant leap into the cloud. We will configure Grafana data sources to monitor cloud services, such as Amazon CloudWatch and Google Stackdriver. We'll tackle the process of setting up your cloud account to work with Grafana, even installing data sources and dashboards that are specially designed to query Amazon AWS metrics and logging. If you have any services running in the cloud, you should check it out!

14
Cloud Monitoring

In this final chapter of *Learn Grafana 7*, we'll take a brief look at Grafana's cloud integration capabilities. Grafana treats cloud monitoring as just another data source, so adding monitoring features to your cloud deployments is not much more than filling in a few fields in a data source configuration. The majority of the work lies on the provider side as you will need to spend some time on cloud console pages registering applications and generating authentication credentials.

Once you have completed the walkthroughs for each cloud provider, you should have a good idea of how to navigate parts of a cloud services management console. You will be able to create the policies, service accounts, and credentials necessary to link Grafana with cloud providers. Armed with these credentials, you should have no trouble configuring future cloud monitoring data sources.

Then, once you have access to a vast variety of cloud monitoring data resources and you start to put monitor dashboards together, you will start gaining insights into how your cloud services are performing. Over time, you may even want to establish Grafana alerts, similar to the ones we studied in Chapter 9, *Grafana Alerting*.

Space doesn't allow for tutorials on various cloud technologies, nor does it allow for a survey of all providers in the industry. We will, however, review offerings from the largest cloud providers, that is, Amazon, Microsoft, and Google.

 Note: The workflows and user experiences depicted in this chapter were accurate at the time of writing, but the cloud space is fast-moving and ever-changing, so things may look a little different by the time you get your hands on this book. Check with Grafana and your cloud provider for the most current information.

We'll assume that, prior to proceeding with this chapter, you have already established accounts with one or more of these cloud service providers and that you also have the requisite administrator permissions to provision resources and manage user accounts, application registries, and access roles.

 You should be careful when activating and using any cloud service as you may incur potentially substantial charges over time. Take care to monitor your use of these Grafana cloud data sources and disable and/or delete any unneeded cloud resources.

The following topics will be covered in this chapter:

- Configuring an AWS CloudWatch data source
- Configuring a Microsoft Azure Monitor data source
- Configuring a Google Stackdriver data source

With this in mind, let's get started with one of the first big cloud players: **Amazon Web Services (AWS)**.

Configuring an AWS CloudWatch data source

This section assumes that you have an AWS account with administrative privileges. You'll also need to be logged into the AWS Management Console in order to work through these steps. The process is relatively simple:

1. Create a policy to grant access to CloudWatch.
2. Create a user and attach the policy to the user.
3. Capture the user credentials.
4. Configure an AWS data source with the user credentials.

Now, let's look at each of these steps in more detail.

Creating the policy

The first step toward creating a policy to grant our data source access to CloudWatch is using AWS and its **Identity and Access Management (IAM)** service. To get to the service, simply type IAM into the **Find Services** box on the **Management Console** page:

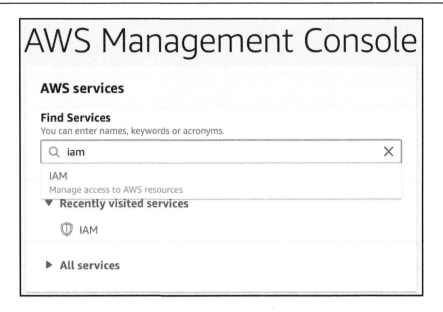

We will be creating a policy that allows Grafana to use the AWS CloudWatch API to get metrics data. Grafana has helpfully supplied a basic set of policies to start us off. Here's the JSON version of the policy:

```json
{
    "Version": "2012-10-17",
    "Statement": [
        {
            "Sid": "AllowReadingMetricsFromCloudWatch",
            "Effect": "Allow",
            "Action": [
                "cloudwatch:DescribeAlarmsForMetric",
                "cloudwatch:DescribeAlarmHistory",
                "cloudwatch:DescribeAlarms",
                "cloudwatch:ListMetrics",
                "cloudwatch:GetMetricStatistics",
                "cloudwatch:GetMetricData"
            ],
            "Resource": "*"
        },
        {
            "Sid": "AllowReadingTagsInstancesRegionsFromEC2",
            "Effect": "Allow",
            "Action": [
                "ec2:DescribeTags",
                "ec2:DescribeInstances",
                "ec2:DescribeRegions"],
```

```
    "Resource": "*"
  },
  {
    "Sid": "AllowReadingResourcesForTags",
    "Effect": "Allow",
    "Action": "tag:GetResources",
    "Resource": "*"
  }
 ]
}
```

To create the policy, follow these steps:

1. Select **Policies** from the left-hand menu and click **Create Policy:**

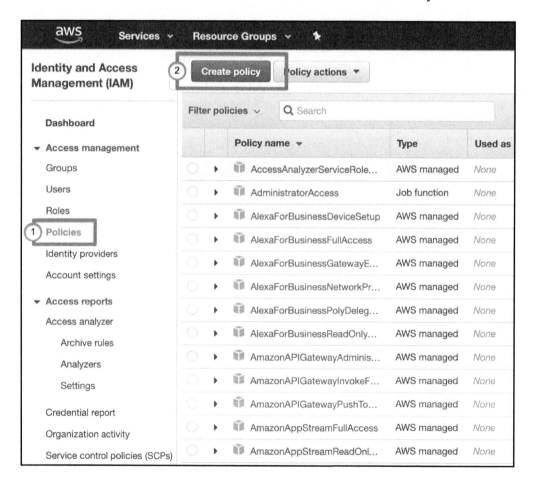

2. On the **Create Policy** page, select the **JSON** tab and replace the contents of the text box with the preceding JSON blob of code.

3. Click **Review Policy**. If the JSON text was entered correctly, you should now see three services affected by the policy: **CloudWatch**, **EC2**, and **Resource Group Tagging**. Go ahead and name your policy something descriptive, such as **GrafanaCloudWatch.**

4. Click **Create Policy** to confirm the policy's creation. You should now see a banner confirming the policy's creation.

Creating the user

Now that you've created a policy, you will need to assign the policy to a user. We'll create a specific user for this policy, named `grafana`:

1. From the IAM service page, select **Users** from the left-hand side menu and click **Add user**.

2. On the **Add user** page set the following details and click **Next: Permissions** to continue:

  - **Set user details/User name**: `grafana`
  - **Select AWS access type/Access type**: **Programmatic access**:

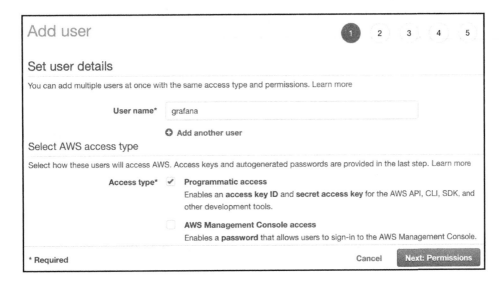

3. Select **Attach existing policies directly.**

4. Type grafana into the search box to find the **GrafanaCloudWatch** policy and check it. Click **Next: Tags** to continue.

5. Optionally, add tags and then click **Next: Review** to continue.

6. Confirm the following and then click **Create user** to proceed:

   - **User details**:
     - **User name**: grafana
     - **AWS access type: Programmatic access** – with an access key
     - **Permissions boundary: Permissions boundary is not set**
   - **Permissions summary**:
     - **Managed Policy: GrafanaCloudWatch**

7. Once you have created a user, download the .csv file to capture the user's Secrets. You'll need those for the next section, where we'll create the actual data source.

If you missed the part where we downloaded the credentials .csv file, don't worry. You can always generate a new one (illustrated as follows):

1. From the **Identity and Access Management (IAM)** left-hand menu, select **Users**.

2. Click on the **grafana** user to load the **Summary** page.

3. Select the **Security Credentials** tab.

4. Click **Create access key** to generate a new credential.

5. Click **Download .csv** to save the credentials file:

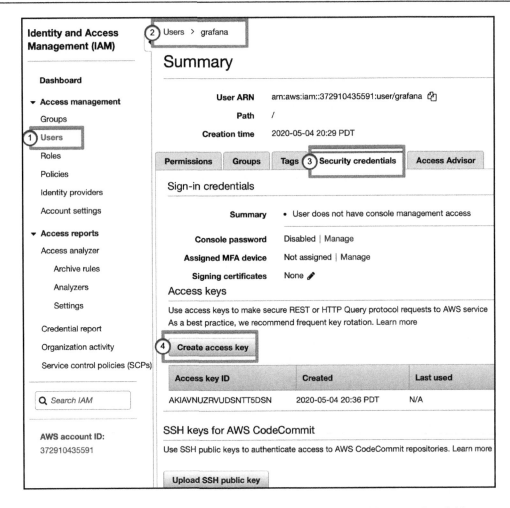

Now that you have a CSV file containing the necessary credentials, you should have everything you need to configure our CloudWatch data source.

Configure the new data source

Once you have configured AWS with a user (`grafana`) with the proper policy (`GrafanaCloudWatch`), you'll need to set up a CloudWatch data source within Grafana in order to gather metrics via the CloudWatch API:

1. From the left-hand menu, select **Configuration** | **data sources**.
2. Click **Add data source** and select **CloudWatch**.

3. You have a couple of options regarding how to configure the data source with the credentials for the Grafana user:

- Launch Grafana with the `AWS_ACCESS_KEY_ID` and `AWS_SECRET_ACCESS_KEY` environment variables.
- Load a credentials file located in `~/.aws/credentials`.
- Hard-code the credentials into the data source itself.

In this case, we are going with the third option. In a production setting, you probably want to manage the user credentials so that you can rotate them on a regular basis, without having to reconfigure the data source all the time. However, we are going with the easy path for now, so we'll just fill in the fields from our CSV file.

4. Fill in the fields as follows (see the following screenshot):

- **Auth Provider**: **Access & secret key**
- **Access Key ID**: (from the `.csv` file)
- **Secret access key**: (from the `.csv` file):

For the **Default** region, you'll want to check what region you've specified for CloudWatch. Go to the **CloudWatch** service from the Management Console and check the pull-down menu at the top right, between the **User** and **Support** menus. It should indicate a geographic region when you select the menu. The bold selection indicates your default region. In our case, we have the following:

- Default region: **us-east-2**

5. Click **Save & Test**. If everything worked as planned, you should see a green **Data source is working** indicator.

From here, you can start monitoring CloudWatch services by creating a dashboard panel and selecting your CloudWatch data source in the query.

To get you started, the data source configuration page includes a **Dashboards** tab (as depicted in the previous screenshot), where you can download sample dashboards for monitoring several Amazon AWS popular services, including the following:

- Amazon EC2
- Amazon EBS
- AWS Lambda
- Amazon RDS
- CloudWatch Logs

Each dashboard you download contains panels specifically tailored to monitor the service in question. To get started, simply select your data source from the **Data source** template variable dropdown. Try them out!

Now, let's move on and look at our next cloud provider: Microsoft and its Azure cloud service.

Configuring a Microsoft Azure Monitor data source

The next stop in our tour of the big cloud providers takes us to Microsoft Azure. The Azure Monitor data source supports four different services:

- Azure Monitor
- Azure Log Analytics

- Application Insights
- Application Insights Analytics

Fortunately, you can configure Azure to allow the data source to access all four services.

As you may recall from Chapter 13, *Authentication with External Services*, in order to generate OAuth2 Client IDs and Secrets, we needed to register our Grafana server as an *application* with the cloud service. The process is very similar for Microsoft Azure:

1. Copy the Tenant ID from Active Directory.
2. Register our Grafana application and copy the Client ID and Secret.
3. Associate the application with a Subscription ID.
4. Generate an API key for Applications Insights.
5. Create and configure the Azure Monitor data source.

Start by creating or signing into your Microsoft Azure account. We'll start from the Azure portal.

Registering the Grafana application

The first task is to register a new application so that we'll be able to generate the Application Client ID and Secret. Follow these steps:

1. The first thing you will notice is the **Tenant ID** for the Default Directory. Go ahead and copy and save it. You can even paste it into the Azure Monitor data source if you want to skip ahead.
2. From the left-hand menu, select **App Registrations** and click **+ New Registration.**
3. Fill in the following details (see the following screenshot):

   - **Name:** grafana.
   - Select **Accounts in this organizational directory only (Default Directory only - Single tenant).**
   - **Redirect URI: Web** | http://localhost:3000. Click **Register** to complete the registration process:

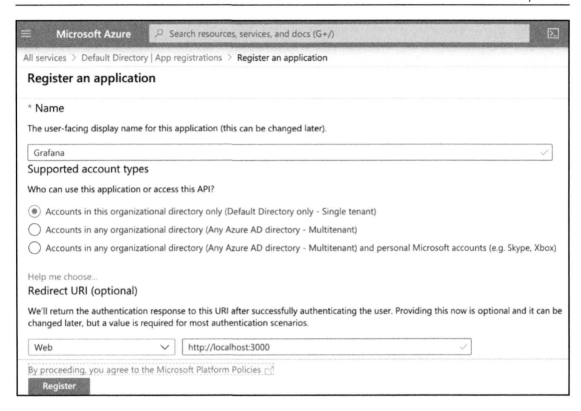

The Redirect URI is the link back to the application after authentication. Unlike the examples in `Chapter 13`, *Authentication with External Services*, we aren't authenticating a user of Grafana; here, we are authenticating Grafana as an application with Azure.

Setting the application role

Once we have an application, we'll need to set the role for it. This will dictate what level of access the data source can have. We'll set our permissions at the subscription level as that's the easiest way to do things. Follow these steps:

1. Go to the Azure portal and search for **Subscriptions.**
2. Click on the appropriate subscription. In my case, it's **Azure Subscription 1.**
3. Select **IAM Access control**. There's our old friend *Identity* and *Access Management*!

4. In the **Add a Role Assignment** box, click **Add** and fill out the following detail (see the following screenshot):

- **Role**: **Reader.**
- **Assign access to**: **Azure AD user, group, or service principal**.
- **Select**: Type `grafana` into the search box and select the **grafana** icon that appears.
- **Save** to confirm the role assignment:

In case you haven't already captured the Tenant ID and Client ID, you can find them by going back to **Active Directory** and selecting **App registrations**. Clicking on your registered Grafana application should reveal them. We only need to generate our **Application Secret** and then we're almost done!

Generating application Secrets

In much the same way as we did in `Chapter 13`, *Authentication with External Services*, we're going to generate an Application Client Secret. Follow these steps:

1. Check that you're still on your application summary under **Application registrations**.
2. From the left-hand menu, select **Certificates and secrets**. Under **Client secrets**, click **+ New client secret**.

3. Fill out the form as follows and click **Add** (see the following screenshot):

- **Description**: Grafana Client Secret
- **Expires**: **In 1 year**:

4. Click the copy icon next to the value for the generated key and paste it somewhere. You should now have enough information to begin configuring your Azure Monitor data source.

Configuring the Azure Monitor data source

Return to Grafana and from the left-hand menu, select **Configuration** | **Data Sources**. Add the Azure Monitor Data Source and configure it as follows:

- **Azure Cloud**: **Azure.**
- **Directory (tenant) ID**: enter the Tenant_ID.

- **Application (client) ID**: enter the `Application_ID`.
- Click **Load subscriptions** and select the appropriate subscription from the menu.

At this point, you should be able to click **Save & test** and get an indication of which services the data source was able to contact:

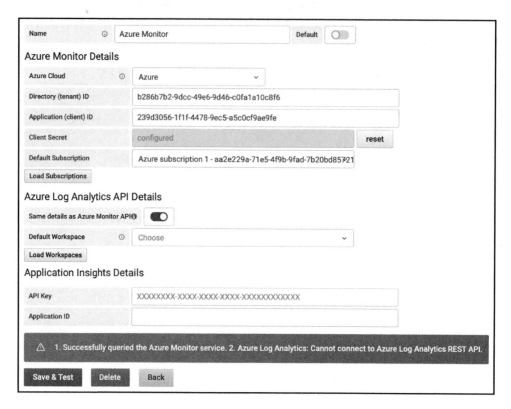

Configuring Azure Log Analytics

If you don't have a Log Analytics workspace, you'll need to create one. This process is relatively straightforward but does involve provisioning resources, which may cause you to be billed accordingly. Follow these steps:

1. From the Azure portal, search for or select **Log Analytics Workspaces.**
2. Click **+ Add** to add a new workspace.

3. Fill out the following details and click **Review + Create** (see the following screenshot):

- Project details:
    - **Subscription**: **Select a subscription from the drop-down menu**
    - **Resource group**: **Create new or select from the drop-down menu**
- Instance details:
    - **Name**: **Create a name for the provisioned instance**
    - **Region**: **Select a region from the drop-down**

4. Click **Create** to finish:

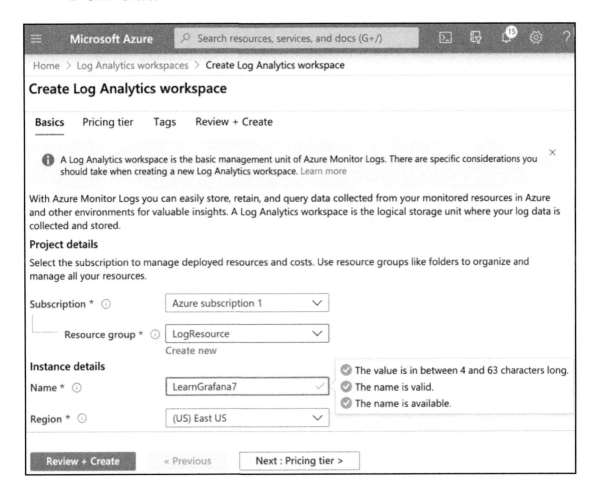

You should now be able to return to your Azure Monitor data source and complete the configuration for Azure Log Analytics API Details:

1. Same details as Azure Monitor API: **on**.
2. Load **Workspaces** and select an option from the drop-down.
3. Click **Save & Test**.

Generating the API key for Application Insights Details

The last step in our epic Azure Monitor data source configuration will be to generate the API key for Application Insights Details. Like we did for the Log Analytics workspace, we'll need to create an Application Insights resource:

1. From the Azure portal, search for or select **Applications Insights**.
2. Click **+ Add** to add a new Application Insight.
3. Fill out the following details and click **Review + Create** (see the following screenshot):

   - Project details:
     - **Subscription: Select a subscription from the drop-down menu**
     - **Resource group: Create new or select from the drop-down menu**
   - Instance details:
     - **Name: Create a name for the provisioned instance**
     - **Region: Select a region from the drop-down:**

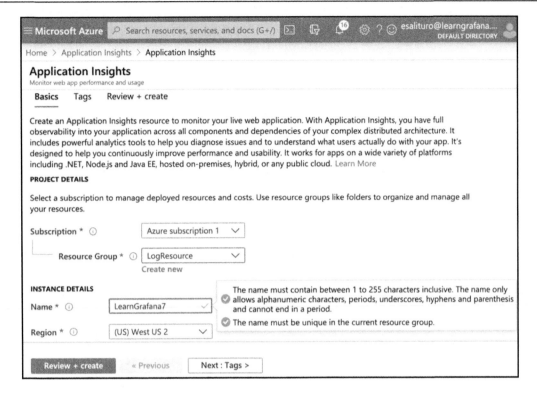

4. **Create** to finish.
5. Go to the new resource. Under **Configure**, select **API access.**
6. Copy the Application ID, as you'll need that for the Application ID in the data source.
7. Click **+ Create API key** and fill in the following details:

   - **Description**: Learn Grafana
   - **Read Telemetry**

8. Click **Generate key** and copy the API key that appears.

Return to the Azure Monitor data source and fill in the following details for the Application Insights Details:

- **API Key**: API key
- **Application ID**: Application Insights resource Application ID

Finally, click **Save & Test**. Your data source should now have access to all the available Microsoft Azure services. Well done!

Configuring a Google Stackdriver data source

Our last stop on our tour of cloud providers is with another cloud heavyweight: Google Cloud Platform and its Stackdriver (now called Google Operations) logging service. We'll go through the procedure to connect the Google Stackdriver data source. The process for connecting a local data source with Stackdriver involves only a few steps:

1. Enable the relevant monitoring APIs.
2. Create a service account with appropriate permissions.
3. Generate a JWT token.
4. Load the JWT token into the Google Stackdriver data source configuration.

To get started, log into your Google Cloud Console and select the appropriate project. It is in this project that we'll define our service account. This will be the only one our data source can access. You will need to create a separate data source for each GCP project you want to monitor.

Enabling Google Cloud APIs

After selecting your project, use the left-hand menu to navigate to **APIs & Services**. Then, follow these steps:

1. Select **+ Enable APIs and Services**.
2. Use the search box to locate **Stackdriver Monitoring API** and then select it.
3. **Enable** the API.
4. Go back to the **APIs & Services** dashboard and, again, select **+ Enable APIs and Services**.
5. This time, search for **Cloud Resource Manager API** and select it.
6. **Enable** the API.

Once you have enabled the APIs, you should be able to create a service account with the necessary permissions to access them.

Creating a Google Service Account

Go back to the **APIs & Services** dashboard and navigate to **Credentials**. Follow these steps:

1. Click **+ Create Credentials** and select **Service Account** from the drop-down menu.
2. Fill out the following fields (fill them in at your discretion) and click **Create** (see the following screenshot):

   - **Service account name**: Grafana Data Source
   - **Service account description**: Service account for Grafana Stackdriver data source:

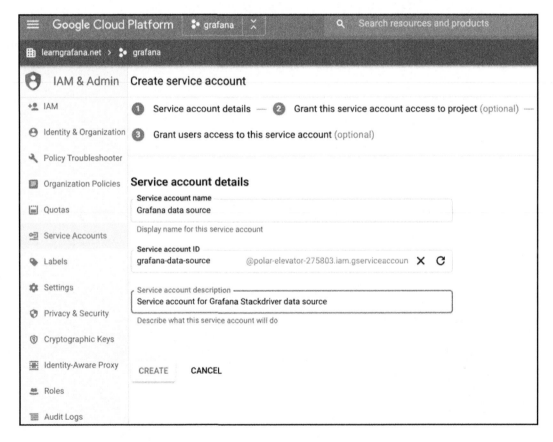

3. Now, add the **Monitoring Viewer** role, using the search box to locate it, and then click **Continue**.

4. Go ahead and click **Create Key**. If you miss this step, you can always create one later by accessing the Service Account.
5. Leave **JSON** selected and click **Create**. You'll get a confirmation popup with the name of the JWT key file.
6. Click **Done** to finish.

Configuring a Google Stackdriver data source

Now that you have the necessary JWT credentials, there's really not much more involved. Back in Grafana, go to **Configuration | Data Sources** and follow these steps:

1. Click **Add data source** and select **Stackdriver**.
2. Set **Authentication/ Authentication Type** to **Google JWT File**.
3. Select **Upload Service Account key file** or **Or paste Service Account key JSON**.
4. If the key was parsed correctly, you should see the contents of **Project**, **Client Email**, and **Token URI**.
5. Click **Save & Test** to confirm you have a valid connection to Google Cloud:

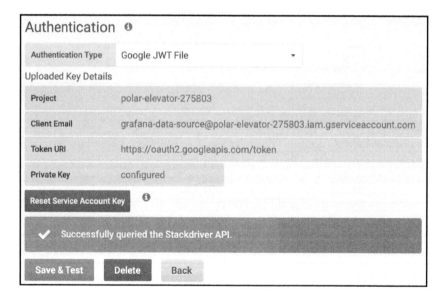

And we're done!

Summary

In this chapter, we covered Grafana integrations for three of the world's biggest cloud providers. Grafana currently provides built-in data sources for Amazon CloudWatch, Azure Log Monitor and Application Insights, and Google Stackdriver. While each service can have its own interfaces of varying complexity, the procedures are remarkably similar. They consist mainly of registering an application (or application service account), assigning a role to enable or restrict the application permissions, and generating a Client ID and Secret. Once you have the Secrets, it's only a matter of plugging them into the data source.

Not only have we reached the end of this chapter, but we've reached the end of this book! I hope you found the previous chapters as informative and enjoyable to read as it was for me to write them. By the time you read this, this book will only mark the beginning of the journey for Grafana 7. Over the course of the next few weeks and months of its release cycle, Grafana 7 will undoubtedly experience a number of feature releases beyond the initial rollout, and will only continue to grow in terms of its versatility. May your understanding grow as well. Good luck!

Other Books You May Enjoy

If you enjoyed this book, you may be interested in these other books by Packt:

Hands-On Infrastructure Monitoring with Prometheus
Joel Bastos, Pedro Araújo

ISBN: 978-1-78961-234-9

Learn how to clean your data and ready it for analysis

- Grasp monitoring fundamentals and implement them using Prometheus
- Discover how to extract metrics from common infrastructure services
- Find out how to take full advantage of PromQL
- Design a highly available, resilient, and scalable Prometheus stack
- Explore the power of Kubernetes Prometheus Operator
- Understand concepts such as federation and cross-shard aggregation
- Unlock seamless global views and long-term retention in cloud-native apps with Thanos

Learning Kibana 7 - Second Edition
Anurag Srivastava, Bahaaldine Azarmi

ISBN: 978-1-83855-036-3

- Explore the data-driven architecture of the Elastic Stack
- Install and set up Kibana 7 and other Elastic Stack components
- Use Beats and Logstash to get input from different data sources
- Create different visualizations using Kibana
- Build enterprise-grade Elastic dashboards from scratch
- Use Timelion to play with time-series data
- Install and configure APM servers and APM agents
- Work with Dev Tools, Spaces, Graph, and other important tools

Leave a review - let other readers know what you think

Please share your thoughts on this book with others by leaving a review on the site that you bought it from. If you purchased the book from Amazon, please leave us an honest review on this book's Amazon page. This is vital so that other potential readers can see and use your unbiased opinion to make purchasing decisions, we can understand what our customers think about our products, and our authors can see your feedback on the title that they have worked with Packt to create. It will only take a few minutes of your time, but is valuable to other potential customers, our authors, and Packt. Thank you!

Index

Printed in Great Britain
by Amazon

84585837R00235